soviet-american debate

1987 annual

David L. Bender, *Publisher*
Bruno Leone, *Executive Editor*
M. Teresa O'Neill, *Senior Editor*
Bonnie Szumski, *Senior Editor*
Janelle Rohr, *Senior Editor*
Lynn Hall, *Editor*
Susan Bursell, *Editor*
Julie S. Bach, *Editor*
Neal Bernards, *Editor*
Thomas Modl, *Editor*
Karin Swisher, *Editorial Assistant*

greenhaven press, inc.

577 Shoreview Park Road
St. Paul, MN 55126

contents

"[Afghanistan] is a military effort that Moscow could comfortably maintain for a long time."

The USSR Is Prolonging the War in Afghanistan

Alexander R. Alexiev

In late December 1986, the war in Afghanistan entered its eighth year. This not only brings it close to being twice as long as the "Great Patriotic War," as the Soviets call World War II, but also makes it the longest counterinsurgency war in Soviet history. None of the other anti-Soviet guerrilla wars Moscow has had to fight over the years has lasted more than eight years. The Basmachi rebellion in Central Asia (1919-1926), the first large-scale challenge to Bolshevik rule in the Muslim world, was defeated after more than seven years of bitter fighting, as were the resistance wars of the Western Ukrainian (1944-1950) and Baltic (1945-1952) peoples. Is the Afghan resistance also in danger of succumbing to relentless Soviet pressure this year or in the near future? The answer to the first part of this question is an unequivocal no. Speculation about the longer term longevity of the remarkable Afghan defiance to Soviet power, however, is a much trickier business, contingent as it is on a number of different factors not always easy to define. Nonetheless, some telling insights into the prospects for a Soviet victory or, conversely, a continuing stalemate favoring the resistance, could be derived from a close look at the evolution of Soviet strategy in Afghanistan.

It is perhaps useful to first define the term strategy as the Soviets understand it in the context of Afghanistan. Western analysts and pundits more often than not confuse Soviet strategy for winning the conflict with military behavior and objectives alone, thus giving a one-dimensional and often misleading interpretation of the reality of the conflict. To the Soviets, on the other hand, the military dimension of the conflict is just one part, and perhaps not the most important one, of a combined strategy for achieving a solution on Soviet

terms that also includes key political and economic dimensions. An understanding of the specific objectives and instrumentalities of these separate, if interrelated, dimensions of the strategy is essential for a better grasp of the struggle for Afghanistan.

Soviet Military Objectives

While Soviet political and military leaders may have initially believed that they could achieve a quick and effective solution by purely military means, this illusion must have surely dissipated after a year in Afghanistan at the latest. Since then, aware that the war cannot be won by military means alone, Moscow has conducted its military effort as just one of the elements of its overall strategy.

Soviet military operations have thus often pursued and contributed to key political desiderata. Major military objectives have included:
- Securing control of the major cities and transportation arteries in order to facilitate the consolidation of the Communist regime among the urban population, deemed more amenable than the Afghan peasantry;
- Preventing the establishment of liberated territories that would allow greater political institutionalization of the resistance;
- Terrorizing the civilian population into withdrawing support from the resistance or else leaving the country; and
- Gradually choking off mujahideen supply routes.

The tactics used to accomplish these objectives have evolved over time and have generally improved, in some cases significantly. Among the more traditional tactics used have been the establishment of large secure perimeters, often extensively mined, around the cities and alongside the major highways and periodic combined arms sweeps in resistance-held areas. Using these methods and their overwhelming superiority in firepower, the Soviets have been largely successful in securing the

Alexander R. Alexiev, "The Soviet Strategy in Afghanistan," *Global Affairs,* Winter 1987. Reprinted with permission.

three largest cities in the country—Kabul, Jalalabad and Mazar-e Sharif. They have so far failed, however, to control two other large provincial centers—Kandahar and Herat, where the mujahideen continue to mount a vigorous challenge. The Soviets have also been unable to assure the security of the road network where the resistance continues to exact a heavy toll.

Counterinsurgency Tactics

One area of unquestionable improvement in Soviet performance has been counterinsurgency tactics. This has become particularly noticeable in the past year and a half and has coincided roughly with the great intensification of the Soviet military effort following Mikhail Gorbachev's coming to power. Utilizing commando-type units, such as airborne, special assault, and independent reconnaissance forces, the Soviets have become increasingly adept at operations behind enemy lines, night ambushes, and surprise attacks. Given the uncontested Soviet dominance in the air and incomparably greater mobility, these operations have the potential of seriously disrupting resistance logistics and raising the costs of the war.

"The Soviets have become increasingly adept at operations behind enemy lines, night ambushes, and surprise attacks."

While the Soviets have improved combat tactics in many areas, they have continued to use methods of warfare that stand in contravention to internationally accepted norms of military behavior. Though there is little recent evidence of the use of chemical warfare, the Soviets have continued their policy of deliberate destruction of villages, indiscriminate carpet bombing, execution of civilian hostages, and use of booby-trapped toy bombs. Captured mujahideen are summarily executed as a rule. Such policies should be of more than passing interest to the West since they graphically demonstrate that the Soviet Union is not likely to abide by international treaties and conventions it has signed, if military objectives in a conflict dictate otherwise.

To what extent Soviet military strategy has been successful is not quite clear. Despite better performance, there is little evidence that the resistance could be defeated militarily in the immediate future. Yet, in combination with the other elements of the Soviet strategy, the military dimension looms as an ever more formidable threat seemingly with momentum on its side. Moreover, it is a military effort that Moscow could comfortably maintain for a long time. Contrary to the prevalent journalistic cliche, Afghanistan is not a Soviet

"Vietnam." The Soviet military effort presently requires some 3 percent of military manpower and less than 3 percent of military expenditures, compared with 25 and 20 percent respectively for the United States at the height of the Vietnam War.

Moscow's Political Strategy

The Soviet political warfare effort has been a key element of Moscow's strategy in Afghanistan from the very beginning, as in all other counterinsurgency campaigns in Soviet history. Realizing that the consolidation and popular acceptance of a subservient Afghan client regime is a long-term prospect under present circumstances, the Soviets have concentrated on their primary intermediate objective of transforming their war in Afghanistan into an Afghan civil war. To do that they have pursued two distinct avenues. Having built a functional and moderately reliable party apparatus, directly controlled by them at all levels, the Soviets have embarked on a sustained effort to train and indoctrinate a large body of military and political cadres, to whom the regime's administration could be reliably handed over in the future. More than 10,000 military and intelligence operatives alone were reported to have been trained in the Soviet Union and Eastern Europe by late 1985. A telling indication of Soviet long-term plans for Afghanistan is the practice of sending thousands of Afghan pre-school children for ten years or more of schooling in the Soviet Union. There are currently more Afghan students being trained at Soviet universities than in Afghanistan itself, even though Afghan curricula have also been completely Sovietized.

One area in which these Soviet efforts appear to be paying off is the regime's internal security and intelligence network. By all accounts, the Afghan state security organization Khad, set up on the muster of the KGB and directly controlled by it, is both effective and fairly reliable. With some 30,000 members it rivals the army in size and transcends it in importance and utility for the Soviets.

Next to building a loyal future cadre for the regime, the Soviets and their Kabul clients have embarked on a concerted effort designed to coopt or bribe elements of the politically relevant non-Communist elites and provide a modicum of legitimacy to the regime. This strategy has become particularly pronounced since Gorbachev's coming to power and has been expressed in calls for the "broadening of the democratic base of the Afghan revolution." In practical terms, such "broadening" has involved conciliatory gestures towards Islamic leaders, private entrepreneurs and prominent non-Communist professionals and a toning down of the harsh Marxist rhetoric characteristic of the regime. As part of this campaign, early in 1986 the Soviets replaced the ineffective and extremely unpopular Babrak Karmal with Mohammed Najibullah, the ruthless but politically astute former head of Khad. The new government has appointed a number of non-Communists to important positions as window dressing and has intensified its courting of non-party elites, so far with indifferent success.

Discouraging Afghan Nationalism

On a different level of the same policy, the Soviets have sought to coopt individual tribal chieftains and other rural notables, while at the same time pursuing policies designed to prevent the emergence of Afghan nationalism and encourage traditional ethnic and tribal tensions and rivalries. The usual approach is to offer a given tribe or clan money, weapons, and wide-ranging autonomy in return for setting up a tribal militia and denying the mujahideen passage through their territory. In this respect, the Soviets have been able to score some conspicuous successes. For instance, a key supply route to the northern half of the country through the Nuristan valley has been closed off to the resistance for almost a year because of a local chieftain's collusion with the Soviets. Moreover, this year the Soviets have been able to coopt even some tribal elements on the Pakistani side of the border, endangering vital mujahideen infiltration points in the process. In at least one case Pakistani authorities were forced to use tank units to subdue such elements. While such cooptation successes are often ephemeral, they do present a growing threat to the long-term viability of the resistance. In many areas of the country government outposts are presently more reliably manned by tribal militias than by the army itself.

The political dimension of the Soviet strategy for victory in Afghanistan also has an important external dimension. It has been expressed in two major policies. The first one has aimed to remove the Afghanistan issue from the international political agenda and public opinion to the maximum extent possible, while the second has sought to influence, cajole, or intimidate Pakistan into curtailing support for the resistance and eventually denying it the sanctuaries on Pakistani territory that are vital for its operations. The Soviets have been especially adept at the former through a combination of propaganda professing Soviet alleged willingness to reach a negotiated solution and implicit warnings to the West that raising the Afghan issue would undermine progress on arms control. . . .

Prospects for the Resistance

Faced with this determined Soviet strategy, the resistance has nevertheless endured, with mounting difficulties. On the positive side, there has been a noticeable professionalization of the mujahideen, many of whom have been in the field for several years. The guerrilla force is further characterized by growing guerrilla numbers of full-time mujahideen,

as opposed to the early years of the war. There has also been a marked improvement, especially quantitatively, in the resistance arsenal. In the past two years, the mujahideen have started obtaining some long-range weapons such as the Chinese-made 107mm multiple rocket launcher, which though not particularly accurate, has provided a boost psychologically.

"The Soviets . . . have continued to use methods of warfare that stand in contravention to internationally accepted norms of military behavior."

There are, however, some serious problems that, if not ameliorated, could lead to the gradual unraveling of the resistance in the next two to three years. On the operational side, the most glaring weakness, after seven years of fighting and high doses of Western verbal support, continues to be the virtual lack of effective anti-air weapons. Despite an occasional SAM-7, the main air defense means the mujahideen possess is an antiquated 12.7mm Soviet-designed machine gun that is useless against the deadly and heavily armored Soviet helicopter gunships. The lack of effective anti-air weapons precludes any lasting resistance gains, while the availability of modern Western anti-air weapons and well-trained crews is virtually guaranteed to dramatically raise the cost to the invaders and provide operational breathing room for the guerrillas on the ground. There have been persistent reports in the media about the ostensible delivery of U.S.-made Stinger heat-seeking missiles. Should this be the case, in more than token numbers, we could expect a much-needed boost in resistance capabilities. Given the record thus far, however, one must remain skeptical until more solid evidence is provided. [In 1984] similar noise was made about the delivery of a Swiss anti-air gun said to be ideal for Afghan conditions. Little has been heard of it since.

The Need for Better Weapons

Nor are anti-air weapons the only area in which resistance supporters have failed to provide it with truly effective tools of the trade. For instance, since the beginning of the war, the primary long-range weapon available to the mujahideen has been the Russian 82mm mortar, which is of World War II vintage. It is not particularly accurate and has a range of only three kilometers. Knowing this, the Soviets have surrounded their bases with mined, free-fire security belts three to five kilometers deep. Mujahideen mortar effectiveness against Soviet installations has understandably been negligible. Yet there are a number of excellent and highly portable Western mortars that have ranges of five to six kilometers. None have ever been supplied. The situation is not much better with respect to a number of simple items that could significantly improve performance. One of the major causes of casualties among the resistance presently is the wide use of anti-personnel mines by the Soviets. This problem could easily be ameliorated if the mujahideen were supplied with easy-to-use and inexpensive hand-held metal detectors. This has yet to be done. Also in short supply are range finders, maps, night-vision devices and even boots and sleeping bags. One cannot avoid the impression that aid to the resistance is provided in a haphazard way, without serious thought being given to helping it achieve its maximum potential. Apart from problems in the operational dimension, the Afghans' struggle has increasingly been pushed off the international agenda and relegated to the status of a half-forgotten side show. Here, despite astute Soviet propaganda, the West must take a major share of the blame. There has been no effort, for instance, to seriously discuss the outrageous Soviet behavior in Afghanistan within the framework of East-West arms control and security negotiations, let alone make progress in these issues contingent upon genuine progress toward a peaceful and equitable solution of the conflict. Further, the West has never seriously considered steps to delegitimate the Kabul regime in international forums and enhance the visibility and legitimacy of the resistance alliance. In fact, most Western countries, including the United States, still maintain diplomatic relations with the Afghan puppet regime, thus implicitly providing a modicum of legitimacy to what is easily the least legitimate regime in the world today.

> "The Soviets have embarked on a sustained effort to train and indoctrinate a large body of military and political cadres, to whom the regime's administration could be reliably handed over in the future."

Should present trends continue, the prospects of the resistance would appear bleak in the long term. There is nothing preordained about such an outcome though. A determined Western effort to assist the mujahideen in raising the cost to the Soviets to the maximum possible level could change this outlook. To do that, the West must aid the mujahideen to achieve their full military potential, while, at the same time, undertaking a concerted effort to increase the political cost to Moscow, both

internationally and domestically. Contrary to conventional wisdom, the Kremlin is not immune to pain or oblivious to cost/benefit ratios. The tragedy of the Afghan people has been that, despite their indomitable courage, they have not been able to afflict more than marginal pain on the aggressors, while paying themselves a price of nearly genocidal proportions. It should not be forgotten that the Soviet war on the Afghan people, which to date has resulted in a million killed and five million exiled from a pre-war population of 15 million, already qualifies as one of the more brutal wars in this less than benign century.

The West's Role

Finally, a case could be made that Western determination to assist the Afghans in mounting a more effective resistance, even if ultimately unsuccessful, would have demonstrated to Moscow the political will to resist Soviet expansionism and undoubtedly would be taken into consideration in Soviet decisions on future adventures. Conversely, failure to do so could only reinforce Soviet perceptions of Western weakness and inability to stand up to even the more blatant encroachments and will serve to encourage further aggressive behavior.

Alexander R. Alexiev is senior analyst for Soviet affairs at the Rand Corporation, an independent, nonprofit organization engaged in scientific research and analysis.

*"If hostilities . . . continue, it is only
because outside forces, notably the
USA, do not want to establish peace."*

viewpoint**127**

The US Is Prolonging
the War in Afghanistan

Phillip Bonosky

I last visited Afghanistan in 1980. Six years later the situation can be summed up in this way: (1) The Democratic Republic of Afghanistan has successfully defeated a sustained counterrevolutionary attempt, backed by the U.S. and other imperialist powers, to overthrow it by "force and violence." (2) On the basis of its actual control of the country, the DRA can claim that the war has, for all logical purposes, ended and all that remains is for the imperialist side to concede this fact. (3) If hostilities nevertheless continue, it is only because outside forces, notably the USA, do not want to establish peace because of what are, in Reagan's eyes, important strategic reasons.

As a CIA source told the *Wall Street Journal* (April 9, 1984),

> The professionals say that [the Moslem rebels] aren't going to win. The most we can do is give them incremental increases in aid, and raise the costs to the Soviets.

On July 28, 1986, Mikhail Gorbachev announced that the Soviets would *unilaterally* withdraw six regiments of the Soviet army from Afghanistan, preliminary to withdrawing *all* of them if a political agreement can be reached. Peace-minded people who may have been baffled by how to understand the Afghan situation, with its specific complicating features (the presence of Soviet troops) should now see it precisely for what it is. It is not a case of Soviet invasion and occupation, followed by a stubborn refusal to leave the country, keeping it oppressed and exploited (the way imperialism does). It is an imperialist ploy to keep the pot boiling, part of a policy of maintaining a constant threat against the USSR, and also India—and beyond India all Southeast Asia.

Thus the resistance of the Afghan patriots to counterrevolution is an important contribution to the security of that area and to the peace of the world.

US Arrogance

Reagan's answer to Gorbachev's declaration that Soviet troops would return to Soviet soil was typically arrogant, the same insolence with which he greeted Gorbachev's continuation of a moratorium on Soviet nuclear tests. Reagan torpedoed the "proximity talks" that had been going on in Geneva between Pakistan and Afghanistan through the office of UN representative Diego Cordovez. These talks had been in process since 1980, and had reached a certain measure of agreement on key questions, including the withdrawal of Soviet troops. Even before scuttling these talks, Reagan had signalled his intentions by publicizing a meeting he held with Afghan counterrevolutionary leaders, pledging money and arms to them, and hinting that, at an appropriate moment, he would recognize them as the leaders of the "genuine" Afghan government.

These acts make all talk about wanting peace in Afghanistan so much hot air. The lips move, but they are out of synch with the action. The fact is that Reagan *does not want to permit* the Soviet Union to withdraw its troops from Afghanistan. The propaganda plums to be gained from their presence are too valuable. Only on the Afghanistan question does the U.S. find itself in the majority at the UN. While posing as a champion of "peace and democracy," the Reagan Administration makes sure that a situation does not develop which will permit peace and democracy.

Meanwhile, there is a crescendo of the grossest kind of propaganda against the Soviets and Afghans. It observes no limits or proprieties.

In 1985, acting through its Commission on Human Rights, the UN appointed Felix Ercora to head an "investigation" of human rights in Afghanistan. After

Phillip Bonosky, "Afghanistan Revisited," *Political Affairs*, September 1986. Reprinted with permission.

two visits to Pakistan, where he "interviewed Afghan refugees," Ercora came back with a report, duly issued by the UN, which found that the Afghan government violated human rights.

Unpublicized was the fact that this same Felix Ercora, an Austrian national, had voluntarily joined Hitler's forces early in his career. And this was no wayward impulse. He continued his pro-Nazi activities after the defeat of the Third Reich as a member of the "Organization of Germans from the Sudenland." His "investigation" of "human rights" in Afghanistan is a mockery of every word in the assignment—"investigation" and "human rights."

"The fact is that Reagan does not want to permit the Soviet Union to withdraw its troops from Afghanistan."

Not to be outdone, Helsinki Watch also came in with a report, predictably mimicking Ercora's. Helsinki Watch is the brainchild of Robert L. Bernstein, who has reduced the once prestigious Random House publisher to a conduit for anti-Soviet propaganda carried on in refined, hypocritical style.

All this—and much more—is reported in the mass press, which never raises embarrassing questions as to sources and aims of anti-Afghan propaganda. Toward the noble end of anti-Sovietism all lies are truth enough. With this formula Hitler led millions to their graves.

Afghan Reality

What is the Afghan reality? Is there any fire where there is so much smoke? How much truth is there in the allegation that the Soviets are "invaders," that they came into Afghanistan against the wishes of the people, who oppose their presence and run for their lives to the safety of Pakistan? What is the reality of the military situation? Can the Afghan situation be settled independently of a general political settlement—a new detente—between the USSR and the USA? Is it true, as the *New York Times* claims, that

> Even by this century's standards, the occupation has been notable for its violence. A devastated land remains unpacified, the party remains divided and the puppets in Kabul remain universally despised. (May 6, 1986.)

Is it true, as this same editorial claims, that the situation in Afghanistan, which "has been all but formally annexed" [to the USSR], remains hopeless—that "the Soviet hope of quickly raising a loyal Afghan army was dashed long ago"?

In another editorial it accepted the former Nazi Ercora's "report" at face value, and in its parson's prose opined:

Equally devastating has been the world's judgement of Soviet barbarities in Afghanistan. In its first inquiry into the crimes of a Communist country, a UN commission [Ercora's, they mean—P.B.] confirmed the use of toy-bombs to cripple children and savage tactics to slaughter and starve civilians. . . . This dirty war has so far cost 500,000 lives and driven three million Afghans into exile. Even so, most of the country refuses to lie subdued. If the Soviet Union's war bleeds on, it will say nothing new about the behemoth that launched it. But it will tell a good deal about the stature of the Soviet leader who inherited it. (Ibid.)

So, cheers for Gorbachev's withdrawal of Soviet troops as a step toward ending the war?

Don't hold your breath. . . .

Refuting American Slanders

Refutations of these slanders were forthcoming from authoritative sources, including general secretary of the People's Democratic Party of Afghanistan Najib, in answers to questions I asked during the week I spent in Kabul in July [1986].

To begin with the most crucial—where does the war stand? Who's winning, who's losing?

Answers came from Brigadier General Abdul Hao Ulome. Gorbachev had just made his announcement that the Soviets would take out six regiments, and the natural question was: How would this unilateral action affect the military situation? Could the Afghan army handle it alone if the entire Soviet army finally departed?

Yes, was his answer. If all the Soviet soldiers left tomorrow, the present Afghan army could easily take care of the motley group of *dushman* (bandits)—on condition that American and other foreign support to them is ended:

> Our [Afghan] army is today much bigger than it was in 1980 [put then at 80,000 by bourgeois sources, which claimed that it was later cut in half by desertions.—P.B.]. On the other hand, the quoted number of Soviet troops—120,000 to 140,000—is wrong; there are far fewer Soviet troops than that.

He added that the present Afghan army is a disciplined, organized and effective fighting force, highly motivated, a true people's army. The Afghan army carries on the main burden of the war—a point which Najib also stressed—with the Soviet troops acting mainly as backup. The Soviet presence discourages those who dream of sending a professional army across the border into the country. Relations between Soviet and Afghan army personnel are good, the general went on: the Afghans learn from the Soviets, who remain visitors in a country which they came to help.

In addition to the regular army, the general pointed out, Afghanistan today is truly an armed nation. There are, at present, some 120,000 civil defense units, which include armed workers who protect their factories and armed peasants who stand guard over their fields, irrigation systems and crops. To these forces must be added the militia and the police. Women take an active role in the country's defense and so do the youth.

A development which has tilted the balance to the government side, he pointed out, is the decision of the tribes on the Pakistan-Afghan border to move from passive resistance to the counterrevolution to active resistance. This past year, a High Jirgah (council) of Nationalities and Tribes of the Frontier Area was held in Kabul, with 3,700 representatives. A decision was made to mount an offensive against the incursions of the *dushman* forces. Sharp clashes with regular Pakistan army units have taken place. In December, the Pakistan army invaded the "gray area" between the two countries, and attacked the Afridi and Shinwari Pushtoon tribes, which had begun to harass counterrevolutionary bands passing through their territory into Afghanistan proper. This army was badly battered. Some of its Pushtoon soldiers refused to fire on their brother Pushtoon tribesmen, and the army had to be withdrawn. More and more instances of "rebels" joining the government side are recorded as life in the so-called refugee camps becomes ever more intolerable.

A small item in the *Times* in May 1986 noted:

> Although there is widespread sympathy for the Afghan refugees who have fled to Pakistan, there is also concern that they compete with Pakistanis for jobs. Recently, there have also been concerns that the refugees are engaged in smuggling, drug manufacturing and other illicit activities.

Unnamed among these illicit activities is black marketeering and the buying and selling of girls (as young as 12) for prostitution. Bitter gun battles between rival factions have intensified, expressed also by repeated bombings. Actually, most Pakistanis would like to see an end to the camps and the war.

Internal security has tightened considerably since I was last in Kabul. Today visitors to public places, including parks, are frisked by guards. Then it was possible for counterrevolutionaries to slip in and out of the city almost at will, plant their bombs, or pour their poisons in the drinking water of school children, and skip off again to Peshawar in Pakistan to report to their CIA instructors. Supplied with Stinger missiles, they would fire rockets at random at populated areas, killing men, women and children, destroying buildings, schools, mosques, planes, etc. Bombs were planted in shopping centers, movies, trolley buses. In September 1984, a bomb exploded in Kabul International Airport, killing 11 and injuring 22. Others wreaked property damage amounting to an estimated 45 billion afghani.

False Charges

General Abdul Hao Ulem contemptuously dismissed the charge that the Soviet and Afghan government forces booby-trapped children's toys, a charge made by, among others, Jeane Kirkpatrick when she was Reagan's mouthpiece at the UN.

Children's toys were indeed booby-trapped—by the counterrevolutionaries, for whom terror is the only weapon. "We are a humane army," the general said simply. *The fact* is that all over Afghanistan, hospitals staffed with Soviet doctors have tried to put together children blown apart, not only by booby-trapped toys, but by bombs aimed at their schools by the Mujahadin.

"While posing as a champion of 'peace and democracy,' the Reagan Administration makes sure that a situation does not develop which will permit peace and democracy."

The hills around Kabul show the jagged profiles of guns aimed at the distant mountains, and from time to time you can hear a *boom* from them, a continuing reminder of what awaits counterrevolutionaries. Helicopters send out flares as they patrol the hills to head off and detonate heat-seeking Stinger missiles which, as Andrew Cockburn writes, have proven disappointingly ineffective:

> Recent reports from Afghanistan show that out of as many as 18 Stingers fired at enemy warplanes, not one has downed its target. (*New York Times*, July 22, 1986.)

(Actually *one* did, but more about this, later.) . . .

The general secretary of the People's Democratic Party of Afghanistan, Najibullah, or Najib as he is more often called, lacked 15 days to his 40th birthday when I interviewed him. Like many other Afghan revolutionaries, he was born into a civil servant's family. Like many, too, he is an Oushtoon (an exception: Sultan Ali Keshtman, a Hazara). In 1964 Najib graduated from the Habibia Lyceum, and in 1975 he graduated from the Medical Faculty of Kabul University. But he never practiced medicine. By 1975 he was already 10 years a member of the Party, and his revolutionary activities had earned him two jail sentences.

At the 18th plenary session of the PDPA Central Committee in 1986, he was elected—on Babrak Karmal's motion—general secretary of the PDPA, replacing Karmal in that office.

General Secretary Najib

Najib denies that his election implies either basic disagreement with Karmal's policies or a basic shift in the Party's orientation. When he assumed his position in May, his major criticism of the past focused on "lack of energetic action." He went on to say, "We have a well thought out and balanced strategy but are weak when it comes to putting it into practice. Many good ideas and plans are drowned in verbiage and remain on paper." Vigor is the key to his style. He places great emphasis on the need to accelerate all social processes and to insist on efficiency, honesty and dependability.

Najib quickly answered questions I had brought. The main question was whether an end to hostilities could be expected from negotiations then going on in Geneva. (Soon to be abruptly stopped by Reagan.) Gorbachev had announced that some Soviet troops would be unilaterally withdrawn from Afghanistan. Najib pointed out that this confirmed the position always held by the two countries—that as soon as the situation warranted, Soviet troops would be withdrawn. He underlined the fraternal assistance the Soviets had rendered them in their hour of need. It was an instance of international solidarity, he pointed out.

"If all the Soviet soldiers left tomorrow, the present Afghan army could easily take care of the motley group of dushman (bandits)—on condition that American and other foreign support to them is ended."

Najib stated that the only differences in the Geneva negotiations were over details of the proposals for Soviet troop withdrawals. Other sources report that the Americans (through the Pakistani negotiator) wanted an immediate withdrawal, while the Soviets called for a phased withdrawal, testing whether their leaving the scene would encourage new, hostile incursions into Afghanistan by Pakistani army units.

Najib denied that the change in general secretary had any bearing on the negotiations. He dismissed the suggestion that any settlement could be reached at the price of significantly modifying the revolutionary essence of Afghanistan.

Najib repeated what others had already made clear. The Afghan army could wage the war on its own if imperialist backing was removed from the counterrevolutionary bands. As for the Soviet "limited military contingent," in principle the Soviets were committed to full withdrawal, beginning with the return of the six regiments.

He pointed out that despite the war, social progress had not stopped. Some

> 335,000 peasant families have so far received title to land free of charge.... From March 21, 1981, to March 20, 1986, state and cooperative sectors of the national economy have grown 47 per cent. Industrial production has grown by 25 per cent. So far more than 1.5 million people have learned to read and write. Women of our country not only participate in production, administration and culture but also,

shoulder to shoulder with men, work and struggle in the armed defense of the homeland and revolution. There has been a considerable change in the orientation of the tribes in our country toward the defense of our revolution. The local elections establish grounds for the realization of true democracy. The people of Afghanistan chose their way once and forever with the victory of the glorious April Revolution.

Probably no single episode characterizes the Reagan Administration's rogue-elephant role in the world today than the fate of Charles Thornton.

Charles Thornton

Ostensibly a reporter for the *Arizona Republican*, Thornton was recruited by one Dr. Robert Simon, ostensibly of the University of California. Actually, as Thornton tells in his diary (recovered after his death), "He works for the CIA." That was at the end of 1985.

If you wanted to go illegally to Afghanistan, Dr. Simon was the man to know. His specialty was (and is) recruiting "volunteer medical teams" to go to the assistance of wounded Mujahadin. Oddly enough, instead of carrying medicine, the "doctors" carried guns. Their aim was not to heal but to kill. Dr. Simon had already sent about 200 such "teams" on just such strange missions of mercy. Tied in with the French outfit "Doctors Without Borders," Dr. Simon knew all the ropes.

Thornton, with Dr. Judd Jensen and John Moughan (a male nurse), both Americans, and Peter Schluster, a photographer for an Arizona paper, slipped illegally across the Pakistan-Afghan border early in September 1985. They were equipped with West German passports (which you don't pick up at the local grocery) and, led by an Afghan counterrevolutionary, Malanga by name, they spent 17 days "behind the lines" near Kandahar.

They had chosen the right kind of leader in Malanga, for when the village of Kaare-Nainje, where he used to hold sway, was liberated, Afghan government forces found two wells stuffed with human heads. This 29-year-old "holy warrior" expressed his religious fervor by beheading his victims and stuffing their heads in wells. He would have been delighted to give Dan Rather a sample of his technique if Rather had been there then, instead of in early 1980, when Rather had to content himself with having the local heroes stone peasants for the benefit of his CBS cameras.

Did Thornton and his "humanitarians" witness an exhibition of Malanga's skills? Afghan sources say they did. On Sept. 4, 1985, an Afghan airliner was brought down as it left Kandahar. Among the dead were seven women and six children. Afghan sources claim that the Stinger missile that shot down the civilian plane had been brought by Thornton and his friends, who actually filmed the firing and the crash of the plane.

To his diary at least, Thornton confided his real aims and opinions. Early in his trip he wrote in his diary that it was not medicine he intended to bring to the "rebels" but guns. On September 11, for instance, he told his diary (which he never expected to fall into the wrong hands): "At times I sort of shudder when I think of the people around me whom we call our friends."

Well he might have shuddered—if he called Malanga a "friend"! Next day he was writing:

> The longer I live among the mujahid rebels, the greater is my belief that they'll never succeed. Time is not on their side. Villagers are becoming increasingly disillusioned with their methods, which bring nothing but bombs and violence. When the children of these peasants grow up and finish school, it will be the end of the mujahid fighters.

Earlier, September 7, he had recorded the opinion of Karl Freigang, a West German posing as a representative of the German-Afghan Committee:

> Freigang believes that the ringleaders are mercenary and their mullahs corrupt. He refers to them as bandits, says victory for them is out of the question, and ridicules their statement as to the extent of territory under their control. . . . Mujahid rebels have degenerated into gangs of marauding rabble.

Thornton paid with his life to learn that. One of the "gangs of marauding rebels," led by a local gangster by the name of Nabib, a rival for Malanga's turf, ambushed the party near Shahwalikot, in Kandahar province, and two Americans, including Thornton, were killed.

"Anyone who pretends for a moment . . . that there is a 'democratic' stake in Reagan's Afghan policy, are not only deceiving themselves but are luring others . . . to their deaths."

This isn't the end of this grisly tale. It seems that Thornton's body disappeared from the scene. In due course Dr. Simon got a message from a "religious lunatic" who claimed he had Thornton's body and was holding it until Dr. Simon forked over the dollars he had promised this "lunatic"—to build a clinic.

Dr. Simon eventually washed his hands of the whole affair, complaining that Habibullah Akhund had "inaccurately represented his authority, had zero control over the area and lied to us about the mujahadeen under their control." And, he added somewhat huffily: "We have no intention of meeting his demand. We intend to ignore it entirely." (*New York Times*, April 12, 1986.)

Thus ended this glorious episode, so typical of the entire squalid business.

Anyone who pretends for a moment, as Helsinki Watch cynics maintain in the face of all the facts, that there is a "democratic" stake in Reagan's Afghan policy, are not only deceiving themselves but are luring others like Thornton to their deaths. They are as guilty of the barbarous crimes committed in Afghanistan as are the cutthroats on the scene.

What, then, of the future? The Reagan Administration has made it clear that it does not intend to reach any settlement. A spokesman for the President even went so far as to say that in the coming summit, if ever it transpires, the American side does not intend to focus on arms control—which it dismisses as a "single issue"—but instead intends to stymie the meeting on discussion of "regional issues," especially Afghanistan.

Reagan has declared,

> We want to talk about arms control but not exclusively because we want to talk about regional issues. We mean, what is the Soviet Union doing in Afghanistan if they are such peace lovers? What are they doing in Afghanistan and when are they going to get out? (*New York Times*, August 21, 1986.)

This from a man who had just announced that he was going to train contra cutthroats to take over Nicaragua! . . .

Afghan Goals

The Afghan government and Party today look forward to (1) sealing their borders to counterrevolutionary bands; (2) extending the Revolution's popular base to include all classes of Afghans except the out-and-out criminals; (3) widening grassroots democracy so that every village in the country elects its own representatives; (4) speeding up industrialization and accelerating solution of the question of land and water; (5) making further efforts to solve the national question by persuading all Afghan tribes to participate in social life.

Even as things now stand, Afghanistan is in control of its internal life and is able to conduct its foreign policy—as a nonaligned nation—on a just and democratic basis. As its army grows more powerful and skilled, it becomes more of a reliable shield protecting the gains of the revolution. If a political agreement ending the war can be reached, it will be sufficient to meet all of Afghanistan's security requirements.

What is required of American public opinion is to take a new look at Afghanistan and, with Thornton in mind, draw the necessary conclusions. The last two lines in my book on Afghanistan still hold true: "Afghanistan *is* Nicaragua. The peace of one is the peace of the other."

Phillip Bonosky is the author of Washington's Secret War Against Afghanistan.

The USSR Is Attempting To Dominate Southwest Asia

Elie Krakowski

The Soviet invasion of Afghanistan in December 1979 was a vivid demonstration of how the Soviets now see themselves, how they see the outside world, and what they believe they can do to it. The invasion was Moscow's first *direct* use of force outside the Soviet bloc since World War II. For the first time since that war, Soviet forces invaded an independent, non-aligned, Third World state. The applicability of the "Brezhnev doctrine," by which Moscow had arrogated unto itself the right to intervene militarily in a "socialist" state, was apparently being extended beyond the Soviet bloc. The Soviet invasion thus marked the beginning of a new phase in Soviet foreign policy. . . .

We will argue that the tactics of the Soviets—in particular their building up of northern Afghanistan even as they destroy the southern parts—suggest a far-seeing strategy for dominating all of Southwest Asia. This would involve the incorporation (whether through annexation or otherwise) of the northern provinces of Afghanistan, the political destruction of Pakistan, and the creation of subservient rump-states between India and the newly-drawn border of the Soviet Union. . . .

Beyond Afghanistan

It remains to look at what Soviet policy in Afghanistan and the region has actually been since the invasion. To what degree is it an attempt merely to consolidate their control over Afghanistan? To what degree does it represent preparation to go beyond Afghanistan toward the possible dismemberment of Pakistan?

In the seven years since the invasion, Soviet policy has undergone some modifications and adjustment, but it has remained unchanged in its essence. Except for the period immediately following the invasion,

when Moscow thought it would be able to crush the resistance swiftly, the basis of Soviet strategy has been a long-term, relatively limited commitment designed to minimize costs and casualties. The Soviet approach has had two basic components: to outlast the resistance and to keep international attention to a minimum.

The second component in Moscow's strategy should not be underestimated. Minimizing international attention to Afghanistan has been crucial to the successful pursuit of Soviet objectives. Outside attention to the war translates into active material and moral support for the resistance; and while the importance of material support is obvious, the value of less tangible kinds of support can be immense. Because the guerrilla character of the war, almost by definition, diminishes the importance of the purely military aspect, the psychological component plays a role that is perhaps equally significant.

Accordingly, the Soviets have attempted outright intimidation of independent journalists. This has included a threat, made publicly by the Soviet ambassador to Pakistan in 1984, to kill journalists venturing into Afghanistan. And they have made good on that threat; reporters have been chased and kidnapped and killed. The Soviets have also bombed clinics and hospitals—even when clearly marked with a red cross—in order to dissuade French and other voluntary medical and humanitarian organizations from operating inside Afghanistan, reporting their observations, and thus generating interest in the war among their compatriots and the world at large.

Soviet Deception

Moscow has used negotiations to the same end. The so-called "proximity talks" between Pakistan and the Soviet puppet regime in Kabul, held under United Nations auspices in Geneva since 1983, have

Elie Krakowski, "Afghanistan & Beyond: The Strategy of Dismemberment," *The National Interest,* Spring 1987. Reprinted with permission.

been encouraged by the Soviet Union as a means of deceiving the West into thinking that a solution is attainable through negotiations alone. The objective is to make the outside world believe that some "minor" concessions on its part would resolve the problem, and that the West can therefore forget Afghanistan and return to business as usual. Underlying such an approach is a keen Soviet understanding that once democracies lose interest, "recommitting" themselves becomes a difficult, if not an impossible, proposition.

As for the military dimension of the struggle, the wearing down of the resistance has been pursued via a strategy of terror, which includes indiscriminate killing, chasing the population out of the country or at least into the cities where they can be better controlled, and co-opting the people. While the co-optation has not, on the whole, been very successful, the other methods have been more effective: Afghanistan's pre-war population has been reduced by fully one-third. There are some 4.5 to 5 million refugees in Pakistan and Iran (3.5 to 4 million of them in Pakistan alone, the world's largest refugee population). There are an additional 2 million internal refugees, most of whom have fled to Kabul and several other cities. And, although figures on Afghanistan have never been precise, it is possible that as much as 9 percent of the total pre-invasion population has been killed. The military effort has not been designed to seize and hold ground; instead, the Soviets have carried out periodic sweeps intended to keep the resistance off balance and to wear it out. This has entailed keeping Soviet forces in the major cities and a number of garrisons.

To use Mao's comparison of guerrillas supported by the population to fish swimming in water, the Soviet approach in Afghanistan has been gradually to empty the water out of the bowl, thereby killing the fish. Whereas at the beginning of the war the resistance could rely on the local population to provide it with food, the situation has now been reversed; in a number of areas, the population—if indeed it still remains—expects the resistance to provide it with the means of sustenance. (Depopulation, while in some respects a clearly disastrous development, does make it possible for the resistance to worry less about Soviet retaliation against the civilian population. With appropriate logistical improvements, the resistance could operate in areas heretofore avoided.)

Growing Strength of the Resistance

Despite the continuing pressure brought to bear on it, the resistance, far from becoming demoralized, has become increasingly effective. It has been able to inflict high losses on the Soviets in both material and men. The Afghan puppet army on which the Soviets initially attempted to rely has, despite some improvements, remained largely incompetent and

unreliable. The decision to rely on Soviet special forces (including *spetznaz*) as the key to Soviet counterinsurgency strategy, reflected in the large increase of such forces in Afghanistan since 1985, is no doubt a response to the growing resistance capabilities.

"Moscow has . . . been paying careful attention to the underlying bases of long-term control."

Moscow has also been paying careful attention to the underlying bases of long-term control. Early in the war, Soviet authorities in Afghanistan began to reshape the Afghan educational system along Soviet lines. The Afghan curriculum now strongly resembles that of the USSR. In order to increase divisions among Afghans along ethnic lines, thus facilitating control, the Soviets have introduced the use of local languages in the schools, replacing the Dari *lingua franca*. Russian has replaced all other foreign languages in the curriculum and has become requisite for advancement in Afghan society, as it is for non-Russian nationalities in the USSR. In part because of the Afghan public's resistance to these educational changes, Soviet authorities have undertaken what can only be described as extensive kidnappings of young children, forcibly sending them to the Soviet Union for "education" for periods of "at least ten years." According to resistance and other sources, between 1980 and 1985 more than 50,000 Afghans were sent to the Soviet Union for training. Of these, almost 24,000 were young people, and the majority of those—20,000—were children between the ages of four and eight. In addition to indoctrinating the Afghans, Moscow has been building up KHAD, the Afghan equivalent of the KGB. These measures reflect the single-minded Soviet devotion to the building of cadres who will ultimately—or so the Soviets hope—take over on behalf of their masters.

North and South

Although clearly seeking the pacification and control of Afghanistan in its entirety, Moscow has applied a differentiated, regional approach to the incorporation of Afghanistan within the Soviet empire. The north is viewed as distinct from the south and southwest, and different policies are applied to the two parts of the country.

This distinction had already been established in Tsarist times when the Hindu Kush was described by Tsarist officials as the "natural" boundary between the Russian and British empires. This view, then mere wishful thinking, now governs Soviet expansion. Topography, ethnicity, and natural resources all favor such a distinction. The northern region of Afghanistan is contiguous to Soviet territory and readily accessible; it is also flatter than the terrain further south and therefore easier to pacify. A large portion of the people in the north are of the same ethnic stock as the people in contiguous areas of Soviet Central Asia—Tajiks, Turkomans, and Uzbeks. This is not the case south of Hindu Kush, where the majority is ethnically linked to the Pushtuns of Pakistan. Moreover, most of Afghanistan's natural resources are found in the northern part of the country.

A strategy designed to restore Soviet control at the pre-invasion level, or even one intended to consolidate a more direct kind of Soviet power over the entire country, would aim at developing resources south of the Hindu Kush as well as north of it. Such a strategy would also seek to apply a more or less evenhanded approach to the key cities of the country. Instead, Moscow has sought both to exploit and to build up the northern region while wreaking havoc, destruction, and desolation on the rest of the country.

In the north, Moscow has promoted the development of the Amu Darya (Oxus) river separating the Soviet Union from Afghanistan. Gas and electricity projects have been undertaken. Two dams have been built for irrigation purposes in the Kunduz and Herat areas, and several others are planned. The economic effort has also included the exploitation of natural resources and the construction of factories. These economic policies have gone hand in hand with actions aimed at the retention of the population. That this has been a matter of policy is evident from a number of indicators: Moscow has sought to "buy" the ethnic groups of the north by playing up to their strong sense of ethnic pride and encouraging the use of their mother tongues, heretofore given less prominence. Moscow constantly emphasizes the common traditions, culture, and languages shared by the northern ethnic groups and their "brethren" in Soviet Central Asia. There have been a significant number of exchanges of delegations—especially cultural—with Soviet Central Asia, particularly in the last two or three years. Soviet media in both Russian and Central Asian languages have frequently emphasized the high degree of "well-being" and "achievement" attained by the same ethnic groups "under Soviet sovereignty."

Less Military Force in the North

Soviet military operations in the north have for the most part been small-scale—in contrast to the sweeps in other areas—and have relied more heavily on KHAD and the regime's militias than on Soviet troops. In contrast to other areas, where villages are attacked seemingly at random in terror operations, in the north the Soviets appear to attack only *mujahedin*

positions and those villages and cities which actively support the resistance. The ratio of police/militia to regular Afghan forces in the northern zone differs markedly from that in the rest of the country. In the north, there are only two Afghan army divisions, each with a limited strength of 3,000; the police forces, on the other hand, number about 30,000, and the Mohafiz (the locally raised militia—literally, "Protection") number 12,000 to 13,000, organized into eleven guards brigades. Whereas the army represents the Kabul regime, the guards brigades are equated with local control—and it appears that they are meant to provide the northern zone with a separate force.

"Moscow has sought to destroy not only opposition to its rule but the very existence of the population and its means of subsistence."

Sayyed Nassim Shah, the Afghan who has headed the northern zone since 1983, reportedly spent sixteen years in Tashkent and Moscow for training before he was brought back to Afghanistan in 1982 and made a member of the Central Committee of the PDPA [People's Democratic Party of Afghanistan]. As far as is known, no other Afghan official in any other part of the country has been given this kind of prominence. His unique position is further highlighted by the fact that at the November 1985 Afghan Communist party plenum, he was the only official singled out by name and praised by Babrak Karmal for "effective leadership" in the pacification of the north. Another barometer of Soviet intentions is the changing fortunes of the Setem-i-Milli, an organization that has long sought the separation of northern Afghanistan from the rest of the country. Under the king and later under Daoud, the Setem-i-Milli demanded only regional autonomy within the Afghan state; now it is calling for complete separation from "Pushtun domination." Moreover, a number of members of Setem-i-Milli appear to be in the upper echelons of the northern zone Communist administrative structure.

Destroying the Population

Soviet policy in the northern zone takes on even greater significance when it is compared with policies in the rest of the country and with actions directed across the border at Pakistan since 1985. In the rest of the country, Moscow has sought to destroy not only opposition to its rule but the very existence of the population and its means of subsistence. Such major cities as Herat in the west and Kandahar in the south have been subjected to attacks and heavy bombardment that have reduced significant portions of these cities to rubble. In 1985, a Swedish observer who visited Herat described it as looking like Hiroshima. In early 1986, a resistance commander in Kandahar told a German doctor that the pre-war population of 250,000 had been reduced to about 35,000. Irrigation networks, crops, and villages have been destroyed, and the land depopulated and turned to desert.

"Soviet strategy in the region [is] . . . the insuring of favorable conditions for the further expansion of Moscow's influence in South Asia as a whole."

These patterns suggest that in the north, Moscow is creating a gradual accretion to its Central Asian empire, while through the systematic devastation of the other major areas it is insuring that a weak vacuum will exist in the rest of the country. Rumors of Soviet plans to annex the north while creating a pseudo-state under the Kabul regime in the south were widespread as early as 1979, under the Taraki-Amin regime and months before the invasion. In 1980, the Soviets secretly annexed the Wakhan salient in northeastern Afghanistan, in the guise of "clarification of existing borders," thus giving the USSR a direct border with Pakistan. Wakhan and possibly parts of Takhar are reportedly administered directly, as Soviet territory, from Dushanbe.

Since 1985, the Soviets have significantly increased the level and intensity of their operations. The continuation of military operations during the winter months (already begun the year before) became more pronounced in 1985. Efforts to interdict resistance supply routes became less haphazard, much more frequent, and more intense in both ferocity and firepower. Military operations began to involve the frequent use of special forces (*spetznaz* and others). Indeed, 1985 saw a significant increase in the numbers of Soviet special-purpose forces in Afghanistan. Small-scale operations and night ambushes, often involving thirty to fifty men, increased significantly. Accompanying these shifts, there has been a greater emphasis on the training and use of Afghan communist commando forces; these, backed up by heavy Soviet air support and firepower, have been used with increasing frequency. . . .

Further Expansion

Soviet strategy in the region has moved from being essentially concerned with the consolidation of Soviet power in Afghanistan itself (as was the case at the time of the invasion) to the insuring of favorable conditions for the further expansion of Moscow's

influence in South Asia as a whole. Soviet strategy can be seen as consisting of two distinct but related steps: The first is the eventual absorption of the northern half of Afghanistan, whether through formal annexation or less formal means; the second is the creation of small, dependent buffer states between India and the Soviet empire.

Under such a scheme, Afghanistan as such would disappear—or, to use the Soviet lexicon, it would finally "reflect the national aspirations of the peoples" of the area. The Uzbeks, Tajiks, and others in the north would be "reunited" with their "brothers" in the Soviet Union, while the Pushtuns and Baluchis on both sides of the border would be united in their own states, "free" from the "domination of the imperialists." Since most of the Pushtuns and Baluchis are in Pakistan, the establishment of such "national entities" as "Pushtunistan" and "Independent Baluchistan" cannot be accomplished without the end of the Pakistani state.

It seems probable that the Soviets do not attach equal significance to each of these objectives, or to the steps involved in attaining them, at least not at this point. The absorption of northern Afghanistan should be seen as a core objective, while the creation of new, weak, and smaller buffer states (entailing the dismemberment of Pakistan) constitutes—for now—a secondary, less proximate objective.

Soviet Objectives

Moscow's distinctly different policies regarding northern Afghanistan and the rest of the country make little sense outside of the larger Soviet design outlined above. The systematic destruction of cities, the depopulation of a belt of territory around the north, the exclusive development of resources in the north, the pronouncements by Karmal—these policies do not fit in well with a supposed Soviet intention to control all of Afghanistan but to go no further. These policies do, however, make a great deal of sense if the goal is the creation of weak buffer states from the Hindu Kush south to the Indian Ocean—states that would be almost entirely dependent on Moscow not only for development but for their very existence. The irredentist pressures being generated within the Pushtun communities in both Afghanistan and Pakistan would further heighten Pushtun dependency upon Moscow for the realization of these irredentist goals. (The Soviet government has been on record since at least 1955 as supporting Afghan demands for a plebiscite through which the Baluchis and Pushtuns of Pakistan would determine their political future, including the option of "rejoining" Afghanistan.)

The gradual approach followed by Moscow raises some interesting questions. Why should it not, for instance, attempt to incorporate all of Afghanistan?

Why take a differentiated approach that builds the north and kills the south? Why not go about securing wider Soviet objectives in an even more open and blunt manner? The Soviet Union, conscious of charges that it seeks to establish a land route to the Persian Gulf and aware that there may well be significant opposition to moves in that direction, is attempting to arrive at this result without arousing firm opposition. Moscow is aware that even India would resent having the Soviet Union itself as a neighbor, and that too abrupt and direct an approach might jeopardize the relationship with New Delhi that the Soviets have established over a period of many years and at significant cost. (The argument advanced by some that Moscow and New Delhi might conspire to divide up Pakistan and launch coordinated military operations toward that end does not have much to support it. If such temptations ever existed on the Indian side, they must have dated to the period before the Soviet invasion of Afghanistan.)

"*The Soviet leadership is . . . laying the groundwork for the establishment of several smaller states . . . that would be under total Soviet influence.*"

The Soviet leadership is therefore laying the groundwork for the establishment of several smaller states that would appear to be the creation not of outside forces but of indigenous political aspirations—states that would be under total Soviet influence, while providing India and the rest of the world with the illusion of buffers between the Soviet empire, the Indian subcontinent, and the Indian Ocean.

Trends in Soviet Policy

It is important to realize that the above analysis is meant to point to trends in Soviet policy and intentions. It is not meant to be taken as a description of a predetermined, inevitable future. There are a number of factors militating against the success of such a Soviet approach. To begin with, Soviet success with regard to Afghanistan is far from assured. Continued improvements in resistance armaments, training, and capabilities can go a long way toward frustrating Soviet designs inside Afghanistan and even force a Soviet withdrawal. So can greater international media and diplomatic attention. In Pakistan, it is far from clear that Soviet efforts at subversion and at winning over the Pushtuns and the Baluchis to the Soviet way of seeing things can make significant headway. From all appearances, the majority of Pushtun and Baluchi see their future as being tied to Pakistan rather than

to a Communist Afghan puppet. And, while Soviet attempts to buy off some of the tribal chiefs in Pakistani border areas are a nuisance, they do not materially change a way of doing business there that has traditionally proven inconclusive for those engaging in it. In the final analysis, however, whether or not the Soviets succeed in subverting the region will depend, in large part, upon how determined the other interested parties are in their resistance to Soviet designs. Karl Marx's observation regarding nineteenth-century Russian imperialism applies equally well, if not better, to twentieth-century Soviet imperialism: "The Russian bear is certainly capable of anything, so long as he knows the other animals he has to deal with to be capable of nothing."

Elie Krakowski is head of the office of regional defense in the international security affairs division of the Defense Department.

"The USSR sent a limited contingent of its troops to Afghanistan in order to help it protect its borders from foreign invasion."

viewpoint 129

The USSR Is Helping the Afghan People

Eugenia Juanarena

Each nation makes a revolution in keeping with its established views, its way of life, customs and circumstances. Revolutions have always encountered great difficulties. The past is reluctant to leave the stage, it fights to the end and resorts to every possible means to regain what has been lost. People who were born and lived under an old regime preserve the baneful prejudices of the past even if they wish to change the existing social order and take part in the revolution.

A genuine revolution is carried out by a nation led by persons who are inspired and selfless but who are also human; they come from the midst of the people and have their flaws and weaknesses. Our "original mother", the glorified Great French Revolution of 1789-1794, could not do without the guillotine, and Robespierre himself, as many others, paid with his life for his revolutionary ardour. No revolution has been free from mistakes. But who would dare cast the first stone? Only those who have not risked joining revolutionaries in order to put an end to the unjust order of things.

The Afghan people jubilantly received the news of the fall of Prince Daud's regime and the programme of revolutionary reforms. The Afghan revolution was also a "revolution of carnations". Tanks and rifles were decorated with flowers. People in towns and in the countryside danced and celebrated when they heard about the first decrees, the reduction of debts to the usurers, the seven-hour working day and the cut in prices of essential goods.

Difficulties in the Revolution

But serious difficulties came very soon. The party, which had functioned since its foundation underground or semilegally, lacked trained personnel. The working class was not numerous and had little experience in class struggle. The best party members had gone off to fight the bandit gangs which came from across the border, bringing terror and death, burning down villages, destroying schools, torturing teachers and doctors.

There were differing opinions within the party ranks as to the ways of developing the revolution. Some thought it necessary to act without haste, without forcing the religious and illiterate people to profess ideas that were too advanced for them. Others, carried away by the first successes, rejected stage-by-stage development and wanted to achieve a socialist revolution at once.

Strange and Terrible Developments

The former, sensible view seemed too conservative to some young party members who much preferred the latter. Their leading representative was Hafizullah Amin, a mathematics teacher trained in the United States and an energetic and ambitious man. Guided by his desire to seize power he posed as Taraki's fervent supporter. His leadership ability and the extremist ideas he preached enabled Amin to reach the highest ranks of party leadership very quickly. After the revolution he began gradually removing those who hindered his attainment of complete power. In the summer of 1978 Amin already managed to debar from leadership a considerable group of party workers loyal to the revolutionary cause. In March 1979 he secured his appointment as prime minister. In September of the same year Amin, supported by his adherents and numerous relatives, ordered Noor Mohammad Taraki to be arrested. Then Amin announced that Taraki was ill and soon had him killed. Next he seized the posts of General Secretary of the PDPA [People's Democratic Party of Afghanistan] Central Committee and Chairman of the Revolutionary Council.

Meanwhile the revolution continued to move along. Life did not stand still, and thousands of

Eugenia Juanarena, *Afghanistan Chooses a New Road.* Moscow: Novosti Press Agency, 1986.

problems had to be settled without delay. Party members worked day and night fulfilling their assignments, but they also began to think about the causes of such strange and terrible developments.

It does not much matter whether Amin was an agent of some secret service who had deliberately penetrated the ranks of the People's Democratic Party or was goaded by his own ambition and lust for power. What matters is that his policy and his actions played into the hands of the revolution's enemies. . . .

"[The People's Democratic Party of Afghanistan] took the difficult decision to . . . ask the Soviet Union for assistance in protecting the country's borders from external invasion."

The revolution was in grave danger. Amin's activities aroused great anxiety and indignation among party members and all patriots. It was no longer possible to put up with crimes perpetrated in the name of the party and revolution. That was not what party members had risked their lives for, fighting many years for the realization of their splendid dream of social justice and progress in their country. It was not for that that party members had spent years of their lives in prisons or in hiding. They had not gone through all that for a conceited satrap to destroy everything so lovingly created under such harsh conditions. But the party kept its head and did not lose its nerve. It calmly proceeded to take steps to ensure that its beloved Afghanistan would not be plunged back into medieval darkness, would not fall into the rapacious clutches of the United States the way Thailand, Taiwan, South Korea and the Philippines had, would not become another Chile under Pinochet. It was necessary to save the April revolution. Fortunately its leaders were still at liberty.

Asking the Soviet Union for Help

At one of their secret meetings they took the difficult decision to throw down Amin and ask the Soviet Union for assistance in protecting the country's borders from external invasion.

On December 27, 1979 almost all military units went over to the side of the people. Only Amin's personal guards remained loyal to him and tried to protect him, but they were promptly swept away. This was the end of Amin's power, of his black rule.

A new Revolutionary Council of the DRA and the republic's new government headed by Babrak Karmal were formed on December 28, the day following the overthrow of Amin's anti-popular regime. The ministers of the new government were both PDPA members and non-party persons. Many ministers had just been released from prisons or come out of hiding.

The events of December 27-28, 1979 marked the onset of a new stage of the April revolution which enhanced the popular, progressive nature of the national-democratic revolution and furnished new, more favourable conditions for its development and expansion.

On December 29, 1979 the chairman of the Revolutionary Council made a speech over Radio Kabul. *Le Monde* in this connection wrote that he announced to the people in the name of Allah the merciful the fall of Hafizullah Amin, paid tribute to President Taraki who had died for the cause of the revolution and said that henceforth state power belonged to the people of Afghanistan, that the new government included representatives of all the democratic and progressive forces in the country under PDPA guidance and stated that all political prisoners would be freed and that employment would be ensured for all.

Radio Kabul said that the Revolutionary Council "will respect the rights of all nationalities and ethnic groups of Afghanistan and will ensure genuine respect and guarantees for the sacred religion of Islam and the clergy", "will pursue a peaceful foreign policy, a policy of positive and active neutrality" and "in the international arena the DRA will act together with the forces of peace for the freedom of nations, against the forces of war, reaction and imperialism, it will be a loyal and active member of the United Nations and a true friend and ally to the working people of the Muslim World".

Sending Soviet Troops

During 1979 the Afghan government, acting in accordance with the provisions of the Treaty of Friendship, Goodneighbourliness and Cooperation Between the USSR and the DRA, concluded on December 5, 1978, and also with Article 51 of the UN Charter, repeatedly approached the Soviet Union with requests for units of the Soviet Army to be sent to the DRA. In response to these repeated requests a limited contingent of Soviet troops was sent to Afghanistan to help repel the external armed intervention.

Afghan newspapers have published juridical documents that demonstrate the basis for the actions of the government which asked for assistance and of the Soviet government which provided it.

Article 4 of the Soviet-Afghan treaty reads:

"The high contracting parties acting in the spirit of traditions of friendship and goodneighbourliness, and also of the United Nations Charter, shall consult each other and take appropriate measures with the consent of both parties, in order to ensure the security, independence and territorial integrity of both countries. The high contracting parties shall continue to promote their cooperation in the military sphere in order to strengthen their defensive capability".

The appearance of the first Soviet tank on Afghan territory marked the collapse of the United States' hopes for imposing its domination on that country. The US ambassador in Kabul informed the State Department that Afghanistan could be considered "lost for the free world".

A History of Revolution

It was not the first time that Afghanistan had tried to do away with an unjust regime. But all the previous attempts ended in failure and were followed by endless troubles.

Throughout the 19th century any possibility of liberation caused bloody and devastating wars; British troops and their hired helpers launched punitive raids, destroying everything in their way; the British crown bribed the feudal chiefs of the Pashtoon tribes living in an area which now borders Pakistan to incite their men to rebellion, and the rebels sieged towns, burned villages, robbed and exterminated the population. Recalcitrant amirs were dethroned, banished or exiled to India. British newspapers of the time accused such Afghan rulers of infringing upon British property and interests in India since they endangered security and peace in the region. Amirs who sought to liberate their country were insulted by the Western press.

"During 1979 the Afghan government . . . repeatedly approached the Soviet Union with requests for units of the Soviet Army to be sent to the DRA [Democratic Republic of Afghanistan]."

This sad fate was also shared by the innovator amir Amanullah Khan who attempted to scramble out of the trap laid by Britain with the support of the feudal reactionaries. The British not only set certain tribes against others and all the tribes together against the brave amir; they also barbarously raided Afghan territory. Amanullah Khan was overthrown, the country was launched back into poverty and backwardness, and the rule of injustice and cruelty was restored.

Nor did imperialist pressure on Afghanistan cease after the Second World War when the Americans took advantage of Britain's weakened positions and came here fully determined to conquer the Asian markets. Each time Afghanistan disobeyed, refused to join the CENTO and SEATO military pacts, the US government retaliated with blockade, boycott and the time-honoured practice of rousing the frontier tribes to rebellion through the time-tested expedient of bribery and clamour that "Islam is in danger". The Western press was generous in supplying a broad range of epithets to commentaries on the subject: "Afghanistan is in Russian hands" and "The free world's interests are in danger". As they would in any other country, the Americans, like their predecessors, relied on extreme reactionary elements which were always at hand, and they spared no dollars in oiling the wheels of aggression.

Help from Russia

Afghanistan was led by a revolutionary party, the People's Democratic Party of Afghanistan whose members intended neither to transfer their country to the hands of reactionaries, obscurantists and the Americans nor to allow Afghanistan to become like Pinochet-ruled Chile. So when the country was attacked, when the United States and Pakistan launched an undeclared war against it, began to provide feed, train and arm unfortunate victims of ignorance and poverty and support their frenzied leaders, the fascist-like aristocrats descendents of those who had always opposed any attempt to win liberation, then the party took resolute steps. The legitimate bases for those measures were the treaty with the USSR signed in December 1978 and the UN Charter.

The Soviet Union was aware that in fulfilling the request for military assistance it would provide a pretext for stepping up a campaign of hostility and slander. But it also understood well what it meant to fight back single-handedly. As soon as the Great October Socialist Revolution was carried out in 1917 Soviet Russia was flooded with the troops of more than ten foreign states, and Western countries, "humane" as they were, armed and supported internal counterrevolution. During the Second World War the USSR also had to fight the Nazi aggressor single-handedly until the second front was opened in June 1944.

So the Soviet Union could not stand by and watch indifferently the ruthless bleeding of its neighbour and friend, a country which had performed a revolution, a country with common interests and common enemies, a country which was in mortal danger and which asked for help. The USSR sent a limited contingent of its troops to Afghanistan in order to help it protect its borders from foreign invasion. This was an act of international solidarity and, I would say, of soul-stirring nobility.

Foreign Discord

This immediately set off an unheard-of cacophony of slander whose initiators were in striking discord. The reports of the media were most controversial. The French weekly *L'Express* related that the Soviet troops consisted of Uzbek and Turkmenian soldiers whose language and ethnic features made them indistinguishable from Afghans "whose national feelings will thus not be hurt". The West German weekly *Der Spiegel* categorically stated that "there were no soldiers from the southern border republics among the Soviet troops, since Moscow feared the rise of fraternal sentiments between Muslims on both sides of the iron curtain." *Le Monde* discovered that "Soviet soldiers evidently participate in street-fighting in Kabul" and that "profound silence reigns in the capital's streets patrolled by Soviet military services". At the same time the UPI correspondent reported from Kabul that "the Western journalists have discovered little evidence of Soviet military presence." It was also claimed that the Afghan troops and police had been disarmed by the Soviet units, while BBC and then the Voice of America reported that fierce fighting was going on between Soviet and Afghan troops.

"Afghan newspapers have published juridical documents that demonstrate the basis for the actions of the government which asked for assistance and of the Soviet government which provided it."

The United States promptly announced its sanctions against the Soviet Union. Neither the warnings of certain economists nor the farmers' protests against the embargo on the sale of grain to the USSR could induce the US government to call off the repressive measures even though the Pentagon and the State Department knew that propaganda, embargo and bans would not help them make the Soviet Union leave Afghanistan and allow the United States to suppress the revolution.

In his article "Washington: Useless Blackmail" Fodé Amadou referred to such influential newspapers as the *Wall Street Journal*, *The Washington Post* and the *International Herald Tribune* which in late 1979 and early 1980 felt it was absurd to believe that Moscow could be made to compromise by refusal of credits which it could do without. The article quoted the following dialogue at the US National Security Council:

"State Secretary Cyrus Vance asked President Carter:

"'Wouldn't it be wise to quell the passions so that the US government would not have to take measures that would have to be cancelled one day or which would be regretted?'"

"Zbigniew Brzezinski retorted sharply:

"'May I remind you that Franklin Roosevelt once said: "We must be prepared for any sacrifices to protect the honour and dignity of the United States."'

"Vance objected:

"'But 1941 [Pearl Harbor] is not 1980: there was no threat of a nuclear war then, and I do not see what honour and dignity of the United States is in danger in Kabul. Probably in Teheran, but in Kabul?'"

US Intervention

Why then was it necessary to launch an unprecedented campaign against Afghanistan and apply sanctions against the Soviet Union? One should not fail to take into account the 1980 presidential elections in the United States, the shah's fall in Iran, and the desire to ease the economic crisis through the sale of arms. But at the heart of it all was the fact that the United States, like Britain before the First World War, took upon itself the mission of suppressing revolutionary and liberation movements, of rallying and supporting all counterrevolutionaries.

The US television company ABC reported on July 18, 1981 that the CIA coordinated and organized the supply of weapons to the "resistance movement" in Afghanistan with the help of some of the region's countries.

"The decision to supply arms", *The Washington Post* wrote on February 15, 1980, " . . . is a significant step beyond the aid the United States was providing Afghan insurgents *prior to the Soviet invasion*".

"The Administration may decide to supply some if not all of Pakistan's military needs to be used for the Pakistani forces or for clandestine transfer to Moslem rebels in Afghanistan" (*The New York Times*, January 14, 1980).

"Seven Pakistan-army divisions have been deployed along the border with Afghanistan . . ." (*The Daily Telegraph*, January 19, 1980).

The Western press, radio and television, which had more than enough correspondents in Kabul, continuously fed the public with cock-and-bull stories about thousands of Soviet soldiers killed, destroyed tanks, the mutiny of the Afghan army, and so on.

On January 17, 1980, the Revolutionary Council of Afghanistan announced the explusion from the country of three US journalists. *The Daily Telegraph* correspondent wrote on January 23 that the departure of the American journalists was followed by a considerable decrease of stories about armed clashes and bloody incidents, stories which grew out of information obtained from diplomatic sources. The British correspondent wrote that he had not met a single person who had seen with his own eyes a dead body, an armed fight or a military helicopter in action. The shops were open, people were queuing up for cinema tickets, and life in Kabul would look normal were it not for the curfew. . . . The American embassy in Kabul was constantly spreading false reports about the rebels' victories, which made one doubt the credibility of information coming from the United States.

Unfortunately, newly independent countries have been forced to concentrate mainly on building a strong army in order to protect themselves, to save the revolution, rather than immediately beginning the practical implementation of social, economic and cultural reforms. This was the case when revolution triumphed in Russia, Cuba, Nicaragua, Angola, Ethiopia and other countries. . . .

Counterrevolutionary Tactics

The enemies crossing the border—a mixture of religious fanatics ensnared by the former feudal lords, robbers and hired killers—avoid open encounters with army units. They lay ambushes, raid villages, mix with bazaar crowds and stab their victims in the back, and destroy public property. In short, they follow the instructions provided in the notorious manual issued by the CIA for its hired killers, the Nicaraguan counterrevolutionaries, which recommends a "selective approach to violence".

"The Soviet Union could not stand by and watch indifferently the ruthless bleeding of its neighbour and friend."

The counterrevolutionary gangs murder and torture mullahs who refuse to obey them, as well as teachers, doctors and students. Is this not reminiscent of the "Phoenix project" which the United States effected in Vietnam in order to exterminate the intelligentsia and party cadres? They kill and torture workers, peasants and also women, in defiance of the Shariat, the canonical law of Islam, which holds the murder of an innocent woman to be a mortal sin. Like in Vietnam they get paid for severed heads. They have no mercy even for children, above all those of PDPA members. They burn down or blow up schools, yes, schools first and foremost. They destroy hospitals and mosques, wreck cooperatives, market buildings and restaurants and demolish bridges, dams, roads, cinemas and historical monuments. They poison water. They force peasants and traders to pay tribute. These groups are often hostile to one another, and their quarrels sometimes turn into battles for the "right" to exact tribute from peasants; the latter, who have nothing to pay with anyway, flee in terror to the mountains or into the interior of the country, or cross the border and fall into the hands of cruel, heartless people who herd them to refugee camps in Pakistan.

According to official data published in 1984, since the revolution began counterrevolutionary gangs had destroyed 1,814 school buildings, 31 hospitals, 11 health centres, 14 per cent of the transport facilities and 14,000 kilometres of telephone lines, ruined 906 peasant cooperatives and put out of service irrigation systems and industrial enterprises. The total damage caused by the counterrevolutionary crimes already exceeds 35,000 million afghanis.

What is more, the United States supplies the counterrevolutionaries with chemical weapons left over from the Vietnam War where three kilograms of herbicides and defoliants per person had been sprayed (see data published by the Library of Congress on July 30, 1971). This heinous weapon, from which people in Vietnam are still suffering, was employed by the rebels in Herat and Ghazni in March, April and July of 1980. Fortunately the bandits were captured. Huge containers with deadly gas were displayed to foreign journalists and submitted as evidence to the United Nations. The horrible bombs carried a label with the inscription in azure blue: "Pennsylvania 15681 USA". . . .

The US Propaganda Campaign

The United States attempted to hush up the atrocious incidents by launching a violent campaign against the USSR accusing it of using napalm and chemical weapons against *dushman* gangs. Several expert commissions could not find a single credible fact to support the malicious allegation. But despite the fact that the US Defense Department was forced to admit that there was no evidence of the use of chemical weapons by the Soviet Union and that the same conclusion was made by a group of UN experts some newspapers continued and still continue to repeat such claims.

There is, generally speaking, a vast difference in the manner and essence of actions of the Left and Right forces. The Soviet Union does not seek vengeance on Germany on "an eye for an eye" principle, and the Cubans and Nicaraguans did not torture Batista's or Somoza's criminals. The Argentinians do not form "death squadrons" to settle accounts with murderers and hangmen. The Right behave differently. They committed crimes at Sabra and Shatila camps, Franco killed one million republicans, and countless Chileans have been murdered by Pinochet's butchers.

We, the Left, believe in man, in reason and justice, we value our dignity and respect that of others, we have a sacred cause, revolution, which gives birth to a wonderful personality.

Eugenia Juanarena is a Uruguayan journalist and artist who has contributed to the Marcha, Epoca, El Popular, Tiempo de Cambio, *and other Uruguayan newspapers.*

The US Is a Threat to Nicaragua

Daniel Ortega

Editor's note: The following viewpoint is excerpted from Daniel Ortega's statement to participants in an international peace march for Central America in Managua.

Approximately twenty-five to thirty questions have been asked. We always like you to ask questions, and then we make a speech to the group as a whole. We want to make a speech in which all the people play a part. In this case, it is you, the peace marchers, and us, the officials serving the Nicaraguan people. . . .

You are touring the Central American countries during the month of December, as it was done in the days when Saint Joseph and the Virgin Mary were traveling around seeking a place where they would be given shelter so that Christ could be born. No one wanted to give them shelter until they came to a humble manger where, according to history, Christ was born.

Nicaragua wants to be a humble manger for you because we really want peace, we want peace. The Nicaraguan people are struggling for peace; they are struggling for peace by shedding their blood every day. This is done because we want to be an independent nation; because we want just and respectful relations with great countries like the United States. We are facing a policy that is mistaken, selfish, arrogant, and is being adopted by U.S. leaders. We want to have a true democracy, and we are working to create it.

Every time I have spoken with U.S. journalists and they have attempted to use U.S. democracy as an example, I tell them that we do not really envy U.S. democracy. How can we envy a regime, a system like the one which prevails in the United States, which claims to be democratic and yet in the

twentieth century, in 1960, violently countered the U.S. blacks' struggle to have their civil rights recognized? This cannot be an example of democracy for Nicaragua. It is a system that has annihilated the Indian population in the United States and has exploited and discriminated against the black population. The struggle continues today. . . . This is a problem which must be solved by the U.S. people by developing their democracy, by building their democracy.

US Violations of Law

What are the United States' relations, as a democratic nation, with countries like Nicaragua? These relations cannot be described as democratic; these relations violate the U.S. Constitution's basic principles. The United States is violating international laws by claiming it has the right to attack Nicaragua. It is also violating the principles of its own constitution, which hypothetically compel the U.S. government to respect international law.

Every time the United States disregards the International Court of Justice's jurisdiction, it is acting in an irrational way, it is acting in a monstrous way, because it is imposing or trying to impose a policy of force over the policy of law and reason. Every time the U.S. Congress discusses how to attack the Nicaraguan people; every time the U.S. Congress approves $27 million to continue developing the U.S. government's terrorist policy against Nicaragua; every time the U.S. authorities state this is all right because the counter-revolutionary forces, the mercenary forces, are being attacked by the Sandinista army's helicopters; when all these criminal actions are carried out, which have already meant the death of more than 11,000 Nicaraguans, that is acting like a monster, and it is an act of genocide.

Nicaragua is a small nation, which has little more than three million inhabitants. Since we have still

Daniel Ortega, "North America's Crimes," in *The Continuing Crisis: US Policy in Central America and the Caribbean,* edited by Mark Falcoff and Robert Royal. Washington, DC: Ethics and Public Policy Center, 1987.

not had a census, we are still not sure whether we are 3.2 or 3.4 million people. Anyway, the United States is killing Nicaraguans every day, and when a policy of extermination is launched through economic and military means, and political isolation, that is called genocide, and we are defending the Nicaraguan people's right to build their democracy.

What kind of democracy are we building here in Nicaragua? A democracy that first of all has given the people the right to speak, to express themselves, to criticize, to organize themselves. A democracy that for the first time in history gave our people truly free elections, in which for the first time in Nicaragua's history seven political parties participated, including right to ultra-left parties. The parties that did not participate in these elections did not do so because they did not want to.

Now, in my opinion, this is not an East-West conflict. This is what the United States is trying to make you believe. I think it would be better to make a human chain from Managua to Washington.

The Unpayable Debt

We were also asked about the official exchange rate. You must have been changing dollars already. Well, this is a very complex problem, in which we are seeking ways to encourage the productive sector. In fact, we have an exchange rate that is favorable for the productive sector. This is part of the complexities of the international economic crisis, which is particularly affecting the Latin American countries. The debt is a terrible burden that crushes our people's possibilities for development. We fully agree with President Fidel Castro when he says that the debt is unpayable. I believe that all of Latin America is in total accord with this even if it does not say so. The debt is unpayable. Therefore it is impossible to collect.

"The United States is killing Nicaraguans every day."

The United States deals with this problem by attempting to divide Latin America. Latin America has begun to close ranks in the face of the threat against Nicaraguan sovereignty and around the foreign debt problem. These two great problems are uniting Latin America. The United States is desperately attempting to divide Latin America. It is working to isolate Nicaragua, to find the support of countries other than the Central American countries to intervene in Nicaragua. The United States uses the economic problem, the foreign debt problem, to divide Latin America. They are approaching the Latin American countries one by one to make them negotiate in accordance with the IMF's [International Monetary Fund] standards, which are good only for

strangling the Latin American people's economies.

However, we have a great deal of confidence in the Latin American peoples. The Latin American peoples have mobilized on behalf of Nicaragua because the sovereignty of Latin America is at stake. The Latin American peoples have also rallied round the foreign debt problem. Therefore, we trust that the Latin American governments will respect their peoples' will. The United States will continue to struggle—as it is doing now—to make the OAS [Organization of American States] regress to what it was in the sixties, when it was party to the move to isolate Cuba and later to the Yankee invasion of the Dominican Republic. The United States is attempting to make Latin American history turn back in time. It has not realized that history cannot be turned back in Latin America or that Latin America will win the battle for sovereignty, the battle against the foreign debt, and for peace.

A Peace-Keeping Proposal

I forgot to mention a proposal in connection with U.N. troops that would be used in peace-keeping forces in Central America. Our foreign minister has addressed this idea in general terms also. Moreover, we presented a proposal to Costa Rica to post a multilateral force at the border. Those talks began in Paris. The French government expressed its willingness to help us promote this idea. However, the United States opposed this and blocked the proposal. We know that the United States has veto power in the United Nations. Proposals like this one are difficult to implement. We must struggle to change the policy the United States is currently upholding.

We were asked what you can do for this struggle for peace. The attitude of the U.S. government and people must be changed. What are you doing? A great deal. This march for peace is really unprecedented in Central America. I had never heard of a march similar to this one in Latin America. This peace march is bringing together voices and consciences of citizens from all over the world; from New Zealand, Norway, Canada, the United States, Guatemala, Colombia, Panama, and . . . how many other countries? These are citizens of the world united in a brotherhood with the Central American peoples, and tonight with the Nicaraguan people, in the struggle for peace.

I assure you that all the Central American people welcome you joyously. I am sure that the Costa Rican people love you because they know that you want peace between Nicaragua, Costa Rica, and all Central America. We are sure that those who sow hate in Central America are few. The Central American people sow love. That is why we welcome you with love, and we will continue to struggle and fight with love, and we are sure that you will always stand beside us for the sake of peace.

Consequently, allow me to thank you for this gesture of peace on behalf of my people.

This is a democracy that was immediately attacked by the current U.S. leader. As soon as he assumed the government, President Reagan immediately launched actions against Nicaragua. These actions have resulted in the destruction of schools constructed by the revolution, the destruction of health centers built by the revolution, the destruction of centers for children, development centers built by the revolution, of cooperatives promoted by the revolution, of machinery and tractors that were given to peasants who never before had any machinery or tractors, and, the most brutal result, the loss of thousands of Nicaraguan lives—the murder of hundreds of children under twelve years of age, the murder of women, of young people. Nicaragua has been experiencing a real genocide.

A History of US Intervention

Now, what can the Nicaraguan people do in the face of this genocide? We have heard about the peaceful resistance struggle, and we admire struggles such as the ones led by Gandhi and Martin Luther King, Jr. However, we have our own historical tradition. We have our own characteristics, and when the first Yankee filibusters invaded Nicaragua in the last century, there was no place for peaceful resistance. The Nicaraguan people carried out an active resistance, and even with stones the Yankees were defeated then in Nicaragua.

Then came the U.S. army intervention at the beginning of the century, at a time when the Soviet Union did not even exist. There was the Russia of the czars. What was the pretext when U.S. troops invaded Nicaragua in 1912? There was no Soviet Union then. It could not have been the threat of the Soviet Union—what was the United States' pretext to invade Nicaragua then? The pretext of its arrogance, its colonial mentality. That was their real pretext to invade our country. The Nicaraguan people resisted the U.S. invasion actively. Then came the time of Sandino. At that time, the Soviet Union could be blamed because by then it existed. However, because the Mexican revolution was closer, it was easier to blame the Mexican revolution. There had been no Cuban revolution yet. That is why the Mexican revolution carried the blame. There was active resistance.

The Nicaraguan people have traditionally followed the line of active resistance. We must not forget that Christ, who was a true pacifist, at one time had to raise his whip to drive the thieves out of the temple. We believe that the Nicaraguan people's struggle is in line with non-violent resistance. We are seeking peace. We are defending peace. We are defending it actively. If we did not defend peace with rifles we would lose everything we have accomplished. This is

the kind of struggle the Nicaraguan people have carried out. It is within Latin American's tradition of struggle. We have followed tradition and history in defending ourselves.

We respect those who philosophically uphold and practice pacifism and non-violent resistance. And we repeat: We find that non-violent resistance and the effort we are doing through active resistance—which costs the lives and sacrifice of thousands of Nicaraguans each day—are compatible.

Attacking a Non-Aligned Nicaragua

The Nicaraguan people's struggle is complex and difficult. To harvest or grow coffee in Nicaragua implies risks, including risking one's life. Workers, teachers, and doctors risk their lives. The mercenary forces fire against teachers, doctors, and workers every day. They are attempting to destroy everything that stands for progress and life in the revolution, and, as we said, all this is the work and deed of the U.S. government, which cannot stand to see a small nation be independent and non-aligned.

"As soon as he assumed the government, President Reagan immediately launched actions against Nicaragua."

I was asked whether Nicaragua could remain a non-aligned country. Let me say this: The United States is attacking us precisely because we are non-aligned. The United States would be much more cautious about attacking us if we were part of a military bloc. However, it is easier for the United States to attack a country that is not a member of any military bloc, even though it does attempt to frame the Central America conflict within the East-West confrontation to justify its aggressiveness. This is not an East-West confrontation. This is a confrontation that is taking place within the United States. American consciences are in conflict because the U.S. government is intent on maintaining a policy of force in Central America. The United States cannot allow small countries like Nicaragua to be independent. They begin with the premise that if one is not under their power, one is against them. The United States only accepts submission. It is inconceivable for the United States that a nation as small as Nicaragua refuses to submit itself.

I say that this is a problem for the U.S. conscience because the United States has continued to feel the same as it did in the past century regarding its relations with Latin America. This means that the U.S. conscience either has not completed its evolution or has not even begun to evolve. The U.S. president reflects this poor U.S. conscience, and its deformation. Many times, U.S. congressmen have not discussed the way to reach an understanding with Nicaragua on respectful relations. They have rather discussed the best and most intelligent way to pressure Nicaragua, whether it is the Reagan way or one proposed by others. They have discussed the best way to force the Nicaraguan people to submit to them. . . .

The State of Emergency

This situation of aggression we are withstanding has compelled us to establish a state of emergency. It is true that the state of emergency is a political decision, but it also proves the respect we have for juridical issues, because it would be justifiable if we adopted other kinds of measures, but we have not done so. Instead, we have resorted to a legal document, meaning the state of emergency, to defend the revolution in a legal way. Many governments, including the U.S. government, use the state of emergency to justify their policies and economic embargo against Nicaragua.

"What was the pretext when U.S. troops invaded Nicaragua in 1912? There was no Soviet Union then."

However, the state of emergency will disappear in our country the moment the aggression disappears and we have again a normal situation. The aggression has affected the Nicaraguan society and provoked tension among the political forces in Nicaragua, and the United States has offered the military solution. This has provoked expectation among certain Nicaraguans who oppose the revolutionary process, but this is understandable.

Some Nicaraguans have a submissive attitude toward the United States and see the U.S. armed forces as a power that attacks Nicaragua. They assume that the United States will win this battle because it is a powerful nation with innumerable resources and Nicaragua is a small nation; and this creates tension within our country.

When the United States offers the armed solution, many Nicaraguans are easily attracted either because they are gullible or because they have no political experience. They are thus compromised in armed counter-revolutionary actions. This is how some Nicaraguans and Miskito Indians become involved in armed counter-revolutionary actions. Even the Somocista guards who live in Honduras became involved in the armed actions when the United States brought them weapons and paid them salaries. If the United States came to Honduras and, instead of offering weapons and salaries to the guards, offered tractors and plows to till the land in

Honduras, there would be no counter-revolutionary forces. The same thing would have happened with the Miskitos if they had been offered food, clothes, and work instead of weapons. . . .

We were also asked if the Nicaraguan government would authorize the creation of a human chain from the U.S. embassy to the Soviet embassy. Well, we have no reason to impose any restrictions on you. You are free to do whatever you want here. You are in free Nicaragua.

Daniel Ortega was elected president of Nicaragua in 1984.

"One [cannot] understand what is happening in Central America without understanding its role as a component in Soviet global strategy."

viewpoint **131**

The Soviet Union Is a Threat to Nicaragua

Robert R. Reilly

The first remark to make about the components of Soviet strategy is that they are in the service of a strategy that is global. If one does not understand this elementary and profound fact, one will see the components as isolated wholes or will not see them at all. This myopia makes it difficult to explain President Reagan's policies in respect to Central America and elsewhere, because there is a tendency within the media to focus on a subject in isolation, out of context, and, by so doing, to invite ridicule. Nicaragua—they may ask—what possible threat could Nicaragua pose to the mighty United States? Or Cuba—what kind of threat could Cuba pose? Are Cuba or Nicaragua going to attack the United States? As these questions invite ridicule, laughter, and a conclusion that the President is suffering from an excess of anti-Communism, the real dangers the West may be facing are overlooked.

In an interesting passage in his book, *Breaking with Moscow*, Arkady Shevchenko says: "One day, while we were lunching at his dacha in Vnukovo, I asked Gromyko what he saw as the greatest weakness of U.S. foreign policy toward the Soviet Union. 'They don't comprehend our final goals,' he promptly responded, 'and they mistake tactics for strategy. Besides they have too many doctrines and concepts proclaimed at different times, but the absence of a solid, coherent, and consistent policy is their biggest flaw.'"

Obviously if the United States does not comprehend the "final goals" of the Soviet Union, it will have an incoherent policy. The principal problem of U.S. foreign policy has been the lack of a consensus as to what the final goals of the Soviet Union are. In other words, the American intellectual and foreign policy community is still divided over

the meaning of Communism. And, depending on which view is regnant in a given administration, "the doctrines and concepts" guiding U.S. foreign policy change. Thus, the inconsistency which Gromyko observed.

This confusion is due to no fault on the part of the Soviet Union, which constantly reiterates its purpose. The updated draft of the Communist Party platform from Gorbachev proclaims that "the advance of humanity toward socialism and Communism . . . is inevitable," that "the international Communist movement is the vanguard of . . . all forces of the world revolutionary process," and that "the citadel of international reaction is U.S. imperialism." As clear as these statements may be, their meaning is less than clear to some people in the West.

A Metaphysical Enterprise

It is not worth discussing the components of a strategy unless one understands the principles which the strategy is designed to serve. The purpose which animates a strategy also determines its shape. Therefore, it is necessary at the beginning, to make the nature of the Soviet enterprise explicit.

The nature of the Soviet enterprise is not primarily political. Nor is it primarily military. The Soviet enterprise is essentially a metaphysical one, though it reveals itself in political and military manifestations. In many practical ways, this point can be clearly seen in respect to the situation in Nicaragua today. The complaint heard most often from the people of Nicaragua is that it is no longer possible to lead a private life. Under Somoza, as long as one was not engaged in active opposition to the regime, one could have a private existence and would not be bothered by the dictatorship. Somoza had limited ambitions, as do all authoritarian rulers. He confined his control to politics.

In Nicaragua today, this privacy is not possible.

Robert R. Reilly, "Components of Soviet Global Strategy," *The Wanderer*, June 19, 1986. Reprinted with permission.

Everything is politicized. One must actively support the revolution. One must undergo an internal transformation and become the new socialist man. No one is exempt. Not even the isolated Miskito Indians, who have been herded into concentration camps.

Why? Because the Marxist-Leninist enterprise is aimed at the fundamental transformation of reality: the construction of the city of God without God, here on earth; healing man without God; eliminating sin by locating it within classes and within social structures, the destruction of which will lead to a cleansing of earth and the dawning of a New Age.

"The Russians are imperialists, too, you know. It seems that the Soviet Union is trying to corral the United States using Nicaragua as one of the fenceposts."

This vision is pursued with no moral restraint by the cadres of Communism, because, with the removal of the transcendent, there is nothing that is morally impossible for them to do. The only source of moral restraint is in God Himself, and with God's removal, as Dostoevski said, everything is permissible. And everything is seen as permissible by Marxist-Leninists in pursuit of their terrestrial paradise, including mass executions and, of course, the elimination of human rights, which they do not believe in the existence of.

An Ersatz Religion

Communism is an ideology which addresses itself to the fundamental questions of human life which are otherwise answered by what one calls religion. It is, therefore, an ersatz religion. That is why the system of Communism outlives the person who temporarily inhabits it as its leader, Stalin, Andropov and now Gorbachev. It is a systematic attempt to control every aspect and facet of life on this earth so as to effect its fundamental and elemental change, a change as profound as that promised by Christ in the Second Coming. As long as some element of life escapes that control, Marxists have the excuse that their revolution has not succeeded because counterrevolutionary elements still exist and will exist until the Communists are able to gain control of everything. This, of course, is why by nature the Soviet enterprise is a global enterprise.

Several other concrete examples can illustrate the essential, totalitarian nature of Communism. Some say today that there are no longer true believers in Communism. Within the Soviet Union, to a large extent, this may be true. Many members of the Communist Party are members simply out of self-interest, because of the enormous privileges

members of the Communist Party enjoy, and others for the simply opportunistic purpose that they would like to be on what they mistakenly perceive to be the winning side. We can see, however, from recent experiences in Afghanistan and Central America that there are those that are still genuinely animated by Communism as a metaphysical crusade. For instance, just before the Soviets moved into Afghanistan, but after the Communist *coup d'etat,* the Communist Afghan rulers tested the reliability of the Afghan officer corps by placing the Koran on the floor and requiring the officer to step on it. If he failed to do so, the penalty was execution.

An Example from Nicaragua

A recent example from Nicaragua is a man by the name of Prudencio Baltodano. Prudencio Baltodano was a peasant and an Evangelical preacher from the Blue Fields area of Nicaragua. He was apprehended by Sandinista military forces, who informed him that they had his name on a list, that they knew he was an Evangelical preacher, and that they were now going to show him what they did to Evangelical preachers: "So, you had better pray to your God now and see if He can save you." During this time, they were at pains to tell him, "We are atheists, we don't believe in God." They tied Prudencio to a tree and cut off his ears. After a short debate as to whether they should waste a bullet on him, they slit his throat, bashed his forehead in with a rifle butt and left him for dead.

Miraculously he survived and was found by ARDE, the forces of Eden Pastora, operating in southern Nicaragua. He was taken to Costa Rica, then to Washington, where by providential chance he was discovered just before he was ready to leave because he could not pay his motel bill. The surgeon general of the United States Army made Prudencio his personal designee so that he could receive the necessary medical care. Prudencio Baltodano promised God that if he survived his ordeal he would give his personal testimony as to what was happening in Nicaragua. He made it very clear that, although he had lived to tell the tale, others were not so fortunate. . . .

Within this understanding of the metaphysical nature of the Soviet enterprise and its necessarily global strategy, it is possible to examine in their proper context the components of that strategy—in this case, as an example, Central America. Anyone who claims to understand the current situation in Central America without grasping its roots in dire poverty, huge disparities of wealth and social injustice would be a fool. But one would be equally foolish to say one could understand what is happening in Central America without understanding its role as a component in Soviet global strategy.

What is that role? Last summer in Managua,

Cardinal Obando y Bravo, certainly one of the bravest men in Central America, made the following statement: that although the Sandinista government constantly warns of the threat of "U.S. imperialism," "the Russians are imperialists, too, you know. It seems that the Soviet Union is trying to corral the United States using Nicaragua as one of the fenceposts."

A Lesson from History

The Cardinal's remark is a succinct encapsulation of Soviet strategy in the Caribbean. To understand how this strategy may work as a component in their global plan, it would be helpful to recall the role it played in the history of a recent conflict with a similarly motivated, ideological regime.

In the first eight months of 1942, a task force of Nazi submarines operating in the Caribbean and the Gulf of Mexico sank 263 allied merchant ships. The Nazi submarines were operating from ports off the coast of occupied France nearly 4,000 miles away. There were seldom more than eight submarines present at any given time due to the tremendous logistical difficulties of operating over that vast expanse.

In 1942, every country on the periphery of the Caribbean and the Gulf of Mexico was in hands friendly to the United States. In 1942, Cuba was assisting the United States in anti-submarine warfare. Yet, so huge was the devastation caused by the Nazi submarines that the British Royal Navy had to divert three escort groups from the North Atlantic to protect ship convoys in the front yard of the United States.

In the North Atlantic, in that same eight months, one million tons of shipping went down to Nazi submarines. One and a half million tons were lost in the Gulf and Caribbean, 50 percent more than in the North Atlantic. There is little doubt that had the Nazis been able to sustain this rate of damage, the ability of the United States to reinforce its few remaining allies in the world, principally Great Britain, would have been severely called into question and perhaps, ultimately, its own existence as well.

Everything that Admiral Doenitz knew, who directed that operation for the German Navy, Admiral Chernavin of the Soviet Navy knows today. Except Admiral Chernavin finds himself in a strategic position in the Caribbean and the Gulf that the Nazis would never have dreamt they could have obtained, so great are its strategic advantages.

The Grenada Factor

In order to understand those advantages, one must have some appreciation for the importance of the five principal sea lanes into and out of the Caribbean and the Gulf of Mexico, which carry close to 50 percent of U.S. exports and almost 50 percent

of U.S. imports. Those five sea lanes are: the Straits of Florida, the Yucatan Channel, the Windward Passage between Cuba and Haiti, the Mona Passage between the Dominican Republic and Puerto Rico, and then, down at the end of the eastern arc of Caribbean island states, the Straits of Trinidad, next to Grenada.

With their near acquisition of Grenada through their Cuban proxies, and a consolidating Marxist-Leninist regime in Nicaragua, the Soviets came very close to triangulating the Caribbean. With that near acquisition of Grenada, the Soviets were physically contiguous to four out of the five vital sea lanes of the United States. The captured material on Grenada revealed a series of secret treaties between Grenada and the Soviet Union, Grenada and North Korea, and Grenada and Cuba. Also discovered were five million rounds of ammunition and ground-to-air rockets, which, coupled with the behavior of the Cuban construction workers with their automatic repeating rifles, led to the clear conclusion that the Cubans were constructing something other than a tourist facility.

"With their near acquisition of Grenada through their Cuban proxies, and a consolidating Marxist-Leninist regime in Nicaragua, the Soviets came very close to triangulating the Caribbean."

(Other interesting things were learned in Grenada from the captured documents about how the Soviet Union and Eastern bloc had been transshipping war material to Nicaragua and to the FMLN in El Salvador.)

Seventy-five percent of U.S. oil comes through these five principal sea lanes. In the event of any cutoff of supplies from the Middle East, that percentage would go up as more oil would be imported from Venezuela and Mexico. Over 90 percent of certain U.S. strategic minerals come through these sea lanes: cobalt, manganese, and titanium. Fifty percent of U.S. supplies to NATO are slated to travel through these sea lanes, more specifically, 40 percent of them are scheduled to go through the Straits of Florida.

A Grave Threat to the US

What sort of threat does this proximity of the Soviet Union and its proxy forces represent to the United States? First of all, Cuba. Cuba is an island of some 10,000,000 people. It has an armed force of some 280,000, with 200 modern jet fighters, MIG 21s and 23s (recall that there are only 300 jet interceptors dedicated to the defense of the continental United States), about 950 tanks, 50 patrol boats, and three modern diesel submarines. Cuba has become very adept at projecting its forces overseas as there are some 40,000 to 50,000 Cuban troops in Africa today in Mozambique, Ethiopia, and Angola, and over 10,000 Cubans in Nicaragua. The disposition of Cuban forces has led one pundit to suggest that Cuba is now the largest country in the world, because its army is in Africa, its capital is in Moscow, and its people are in Miami.

Twenty-five percent of Cuba's GNP is annually donated by the Soviet Union or, more accurately, given for services rendered. Some military scholars have estimated that a military effort to take out Cuba would have to approximate or exceed in scale the extremely costly campaign against the island of Okinawa at the end of the Pacific war in 1945.

Next Nicaragua. The first thing one notices about Nicaragua is its proximity to the Panama Canal, through which pass 11,000 ships a year. But Nicaragua today has no naval forces of which to speak. However, it has undertaken the largest military buildup ever seen in the history of Central America.

In order to keep this buildup in perspective, one should recall that Nicaragua is a tiny country of 2.6 million people. Under the late dictator, Somoza, there was a National Guard of 10,000 men. Somoza had three old Sherman tanks. Today, the Sandinistas have an armed force of over 120,000, including militia and reserves. Their announced intention is to build an army of 250,000, which will give Nicaragua close to the highest military to civilian ratio in the world. Mexico is a country of some 75 million people, yet soon Nicaragua will have a larger armed force.

Nicaragua has 150 tanks and 200 other armored vehicles. There are 167 tanks in all of Central America. One hundred and fifty of them are in Nicaragua, the other 17 are in Guatemala. The Sandinistas have 45 fix-winged aircraft and 30 helicopters, at least a half dozen of which are the MI 24 Hind military helicopters from the Soviet Union, the same kind the Soviets are using to devastate Afghanistan and Jonas Savimbi's UNITA forces in Angola. . . .

Sandinista Strategy

What, one must ask, is this enormous Sandinista military buildup for? Why? "To defend ourselves against Yankee imperialism," is, of course, the daily chorus from Managua. But this answer is inadequate in two essential respects. One of them is simply the facts of history. The Sandinistas came to power in July of 1979 in much the same way as Castro came to power in 1959 when he arrived in Havana wearing a Rosary around his neck. The Sandinistas arrived in Managua as one part of a broad democratic coalition of nearly 20 groups against

Somoza. They were thought by many at the time to be no worse than naughty social democrats. Certainly not Marxist-Leninist.

They proved to be otherwise. Castro had counseled them. He told them specifically not to make the same mistakes that he did in 1959-1960. In 1959, Castro formed a coalition government decorated with bourgeois window dressing. But, as a true ideologue, he eliminated it. In fact, Castro's direct remark as to the fate of the democratic elements in his original coalition is as follows: "I threw them away like the bourgeois garbage they are." Now, he chided the Sandinistas, do not do this. Keep the democratic elements in your cabinet in nonessential posts, so as to deceive the West. This way, you can have your revolution and the United States will pay for it.

For the first year and a half, Castro's strategy worked. The United States gave the Sandinistas $118 million in economic aid and helped to arrange over twice that amount in international loans. The Sandinistas, however, as true Marxist-Leninist zealots, began internal repression and expelled the genuinely democratic elements from their original coalition.

"While refusing the presence of the U.S. Peace Corps, the Sandinistas welcomed in Nicaragua the Soviets, Cubans, East Germans, the PLO, and other elements of the Soviet foreign legion."

This, of course, was in direct contravention of the promise of a free and pluralistic society which the Sandinistas had made to the Organization of American States as the condition upon which the OAS and the United States recognized the Sandinista government in 1979.

The hand of friendship from the United States was out from the beginning. Daniel Ortega was in the White House with President Jimmy Carter, but it is very much to President Carter's credit that it was he who cut off the economic aid to the Sandinistas because of the overwhelming evidence at that time of their exportation of terror and subversion. President Reagan, in 1981, offered to resume the aid as an offer of fresh friendship, telling the Sandinistas that if they would only stop their covert aggression against their neighbors, further aid and the friendship of the U.S. would follow. Three months later (April 1st, 1981), President Reagan had to end the offer of aid because of the overwhelming evidence that the Sandinistas continued their behavior.

The other historical facts which refute the "U.S.

imperialism" thesis is that the Sandinistas began the military buildup immediately upon their assumption of power in July, 1979. While refusing the presence of the U.S. Peace Corps, the Sandinistas welcomed in Nicaragua the Soviets, Cubans, East Germans, the PLO, and other elements of the Soviet foreign legion. While the U.S. was delivering economic aid, the Sandinistas began construction of 40 new military bases and laying the groundwork for an enormous expansion of military personnel. Within weeks of taking over, the FSLN opened training camps in Nicaragua for the Salvadoran FMLN guerrillas (Farabundo Marti Liberation Front).

In March, 1981, the Sandinistas were already in Moscow signing a party-to-party accord between the FSLN and the Communist Party of the Soviet Union for mutual support and cooperation. All of this took place two years before the armed resistance to the Sandinistas began in the spring of 1982, making the excuse that their military increases were for defensive purposes completely implausible.

"As Humberto Ortega told the Sandinista military . . . 'Marxism-Leninism is the scientific doctrine that guides our revolution.'"

The second reason that the Sandinista explanation of their military buildup as purely defensive cannot be maintained is what the Sandinistas themselves have said.

In 1983, the Sandinista defense minister, Humberto Ortega, addressed the Nicaraguan Council of State on the necessity of using conscription to fill the ranks of the FSLN army. He said, in effect, that the military buildup in Nicaragua was not in response to an external threat but was in fulfillment of the historic mission of the FSLN party. What is the historic mission of the FSLN party?

A Marxist-Leninist Party

The Sandinistas were founded in 1961 in Tegucigalpa, Honduras, as a Marxist-Leninist party. As Humberto Ortega told the Sandinista military in a speech 20 years later: "Marxism-Leninism is the scientific doctrine that guides our revolution . . . our doctrine is that of Marxism-Leninism." Tomas Borge, one of the three original founders, is the only survivor of the early days. He currently presides as minister of the interior, which is an especially powerful post since it controls the secret police. By 1969, this minuscule party had organized itself well enough to publish a party platform.

In that party platform it had as one of its objects: "a struggle for a 'true union of the Central American peoples within one country,' beginning with support for national liberation movements in neighboring states." In other words, the original vision of the Sandinista, or FSLN party, was the incorporation of all of Central America into a Marxist-Leninist whole. Its goals were transnational from the beginning. . . .

These are the stakes, and this is why President Reagan has given such an emphasis to his policy on Central America, why he will not give up on it, and why indeed he is succeeding in obtaining the support of the American people and of the U.S. Congress for continuing economic aid (75 percent of U.S. aid to Central America is economic), but also for the continued military assistance to El Salvador, as well as the essential aid to the freedom fighters in Nicaragua.

The basis of this support is the growing public understanding of Central America's role as a component of Soviet global strategy, wherein it serves as a lever to force the bifurcation of the United States and Western Europe so as to place Western Europe in a situation where it must see its future in terms of the Soviet Union rather than of the United States. . . .

President Reagan has a clear comprehension and grasp of what Soviet global strategy is. He has made great strides in ensuring that the American people do as well, so that they, with their Western allies and Japan, can assure that the Soviet global enterprise, which is a metaphysically corrupt one, will founder upon the intellectual, spiritual, and military resolve of the West.

Robert R. Reilly is a senior advisor for public diplomacy and attached to the US embassy in Bern, Switzerland.

"The Soviets and the Sandinistas must not be permitted to crush freedom in Central America and threaten our own security on our own doorstep."

viewpoint **132**

The US Must Fight the Soviet Threat in Nicaragua

Ronald Reagan

My fellow Americans, I must speak to you about a mounting danger in Central America that threatens the security of the United States. This danger will not go away; it will grow worse, much worse, if we fail to take action now. I am speaking of Nicaragua, a Soviet ally on the American mainland only two hours flying time from our own borders. With over a billion dollars in Soviet-bloc aid, the communist government of Nicaragua has launched a campaign to subvert and topple its democratic neighbors.

Using Nicaragua as a base, the Soviets and Cubans can become the dominant power in the crucial corridor between North and South America. Established there, they will be in a position to threaten the Panama Canal, interdict our vital Caribbean sea lanes, and, ultimately, move against Mexico. Should that happen, desperate Latin peoples by the millions would begin fleeing north into the cities of the southern United States, or to wherever some hope of freedom remained. . . .

Gathered in Nicaragua already are thousands of Cuban military advisers, contingents of Soviets and East Germans and all the elements of international terror—from the PLO to Italy's Red Brigades. Why are they there? Because, as Colonel Qaddafi has publicly exulted: "Nicaragua means a great thing, it means fighting America near its borders—fighting America at its doorstep."

For our own security the United States must deny the Soviet Union a beachhead in North America. But let me make one thing plain. I am not talking about American troops. They are not needed; they have not been requested. The democratic resistance fighting in Nicaragua is only asking America for the supplies and support to save their own country from communism.

Ronald Reagan, in an address to the nation from the Oval Office on March 16, 1986.

The question the Congress of the United States will now answer is a simple one: will we give the Nicaraguan democratic resistance the means to recapture their betrayed revolution, or will we turn our backs and ignore the malignancy in Managua until it spreads and becomes a mortal threat to the entire New World?

Will we permit the Soviet Union to put a second Cuba, a second Libya, right on the doorstep of the United States?

A Mortal Threat

How can such a small country pose such a great threat? Well, it is not Nicaragua alone that threatens us but those using Nicaragua as a privileged sanctuary for their struggle against the United States.

Their first target is Nicaragua's neighbors. With an army and militia of 120,000 men, backed by more than 3,000 Cuban military advisers, Nicaragua's armed forces are the largest Central America has ever seen. The Nicaraguan military machine is more powerful than all its neighbors combined.

This map [president points to map including South America, Central America and the US] represents much of the Western hemisphere. Now let me show you the countries in Central America where weapons supplied by Nicaraguan communists have been found: Honduras, Costa Rica, El Salvador, Guatemala. Radicals from Panama to the south have been trained in Nicaragua. But the Sandinista revolutionary reach extends well beyond their immediate neighbors. In South America and the Caribbean, the Nicaraguan communists have provided support in the form of military training, safe haven, communications, false documents, safe transit and sometimes weapons to radicals from the following countries: Colombia, Ecuador, Brazil, Chile, Argentina, Uruguay, and the Dominican Republic. Even that is not all, for there was an old communist slogan that the Sandinistas have made clear they honor: The road to victory goes through Mexico.

If maps, statistics and facts aren't persuasive enough, we have the words of the Sandinistas and Soviets themselves. One of the highest-level Sandinista leaders was asked by an American magazine whether their communist revolution will—and I quote—"be exported to El Salvador, then Guatemala, then Honduras, and then Mexico?" He responded, "That is one historical prophecy of Ronald Reagan that is absolutely true."

Well, the Soviets have been no less candid. A few years ago, then Soviet Foreign Minister Gromyko noted that Central America was, quote, "boiling like a cauldron" and ripe for revolution. In a Moscow meeting in 1983, Soviet Chief of Staff, Marshal Ogarkov, declared: "Over two decades—there are Nicaragua"—I should say, "there was only Cuba in Latin America. Today there are Nicaragua, Grenada and a serious battle is going on in El Salvador."

But we don't need their quotes; the American forces who liberated Grenada captured thousands of documents that demonstrated Soviet intent to bring communist revolution home to the Western hemisphere.

"It is not Nicaragua alone that threatens us, but those using Nicaragua as a privileged sanctuary for their struggle against the United States."

So, we're clear on the intentions of the Sandinistas and those who back them. Let us be equally clear about the nature of their regime. To begin with, the Sandinistas have revoked the civil liberties of the Nicaraguan people, depriving them of any legal right to speak, to publish, to assemble or to worship freely. Independent newspapers have been shut down. There is no longer any independent labor movement in Nicaragua nor any right to strike. As AFL-CIO leader Lane Kirkland has said, "Nicaragua's headlong rush into the totalitarian camp cannot be denied but—by anyone who has eyes to see."

Civil Rights Abuses

Well, like communist governments everywhere, the Sandinistas have launched assaults against ethnic and religious groups. The capital's only synagogue was desecrated and firebombed—the entire Jewish community forced to flee Nicaragua. Protestant Bible meetings have been broken up by raids, by mob violence, by machine guns. The Catholic Church has been singled out—priests have been expelled from the country, Catholics beaten in the streets after attending Mass. The Catholic primate of Nicaragua,

Cardinal Obando y Bravo, has put the matter forthrightly. "We want to state clearly," he says, "that this government is totalitarian. We are dealing with an enemy of the Church."

Evangelical pastor Prudencio Baltodano found out he was on a Sandinista hit list when an army patrol asked his name: "You don't know what we do to the evangelical pastors. We don't believe in God," they told him. Pastor Baltodano was tied to a tree, struck in the forehead with a rifle butt, stabbed in the neck with a bayonet—finally his ears were cut off, and he was left for dead. "See if your God will save you," they mocked. Well, God did have other plans for Pastor Baltodano. He lived to tell the world his story—to tell it, among other places, right here in the White House.

I could go on about this nightmare—the black lists, the secret prisons, the Sandinista-directed mob violence. But, as if all this brutality at home were not enough, the Sandinistas are transforming their nation into a safe house, a command post for international terror.

The Sandinistas not only sponsor terror in El Salvador, Costa Rica, Guatemala and Honduras—terror that led last summer to the murder of four U.S. Marines in a cafe in San Salvador—they provide a sanctuary for terror. Italy has charged Nicaragua with harboring their worst terrorists, the Red Brigades.

The Sandinistas have even involved themselves in the international drug trade. I know every American parent concerned about the drug problem will be outraged to learn that top Nicaraguan government officials are deeply involved in drug trafficking. This picture, [president shows a picture of a Nicaraguan airfield] secretly taken at a military airfield outside Managua, shows Federico Vaughn, a top aide to one of the nine Commandantes who rule Nicaragua, loading an aircraft with illegal narcotics, bound for the United States.

No, there seems to be no crime to which the Sandinistas will not stoop—this is an outlaw regime. . . .

A Strategic Country

Through this crucial part of the Western Hemisphere passes almost half our foreign trade, more than half our imports of crude oil, and a significant portion of the military supplies we would have to send to the NATO Alliance in the event of a crisis. These are the choke points where the sea lanes could be closed.

Central America is strategic to our Western alliance, a fact always understood by foreign enemies. In World War II, only a few German U-boats, operating from bases 4,000 miles away in Germany and occupied Europe, inflicted crippling losses on U.S. shipping right off our southern coast.

Today, Warsaw Pact engineers are building a deep

water port on Nicaragua's Caribbean coast, similar to the naval base in Cuba for Soviet-built submarines. They are also constructing, outside Managua, the largest military air field in Central America—similar to those in Cuba, from which Russian Bear Bombers patrol the U.S. east coast from Maine to Florida.

How did this menace to the peace and security of our Latin neighbors, and ultimately ourselves, suddenly emerge? Let me give you a brief history.

The Nicaraguan Revolution

In 1979, the people of Nicaragua rose up and overthrew a corrupt dictatorship. At first the revolutionary leaders promised free elections and respect for human rights. But among them was an organization called the Sandinistas. Theirs was a communist organization and their support of the revolutionary goals was sheer deceit. Quickly and ruthlessly they took complete control.

Two months after the revolution, the Sandinista leadership met in secret, and, in what came to be known as the "72-hour Document," described themselves as the "vanguard" of a revolution that would sweep Central America, Latin America and finally the world. Their true enemy, they declared: The United States.

Rather than make this document public, they followed the advice of Fidel Castro, who told them to put on a facade of democracy. While Castro viewed the democratic elements in Nicaragua with contempt, he urged his Nicaraguan friends to keep some of them in their coalition, in minor posts, as window dressing to deceive the west. And that way, Castro said, you can have your revolution and the Americans will pay for it.

And we did pay for it. More aid flowed to Nicaragua from the United States in the first 18 months under the Sandinistas than from any other country. Only when the mask fell, and the face of totalitarianism became visible to the world, did the aid stop.

Confronted with this emerging threat, early in our administration I went to Congress and, with bipartisan support, managed to get help for the nations surrounding Nicaragua. Some of you may remember the inspiring scene when the people of El Salvador braved the threats and gunfire of communist guerrillas, guerrillas directed and supplied from Nicaragua, and went to the polls to vote decisively for democracy. For the communists in El Salvador it was a humiliating defeat.

The Freedom Fighters

But there was another factor the communists never counted on, a factor that now promises to give freedom a second chance—the freedom fighters of Nicaragua.

You see, when the Sandinistas betrayed the revolution, many who had fought the old Somoza dictatorship literally took to the hills, and like the French Resistance that fought the Nazis, began fighting the Soviet Bloc communists and their Nicaraguan collaborators. These few have now been joined by thousands.

With their blood and courage, the freedom fighters of Nicaragua have pinned down the Sandinista army and bought the people of Central America precious time. We Americans owe them a debt of gratitude. In helping to thwart the Sandinistas and their Soviet mentors, the resistance has contributed directly to the security of the United States.

"Ask yourselves, what in the world are Soviets, East Germans, Bulgarians, North Koreans, Cubans and terrorists from the PLO and the Red Brigades doing in our hemisphere, camped on our own doorstep?"

Since its inception in 1982, the Democratic Resistance has grown dramatically in strength. Today it numbers more than 20,000 volunteers and more come every day. But now the freedom fighters' supplies are running short, and they are virtually defenseless against the helicopter gunships Moscow has sent to Managua.

Now comes the crucial test for the Congress of the United States. Will they provide the assistance the freedom fighters need to deal with Russian tanks and gunships, or will they abandon the Democratic Resistance to its communist enemy?

Fighting the Communists

In answering that question, I hope Congress will reflect deeply upon what it is the resistance is fighting against in Nicaragua. Ask yourselves, what in the world are Soviets, East Germans, Bulgarians, North Koreans, Cubans and terrorists from the PLO and the Red Brigades doing in our hemisphere, camped on our own doorstep? Is that for peace?

Why have the Soviets invested $600 million to build Nicaragua into an armed force almost the size of Mexico's, a country 15 times as large, and 25 times as populous. Is that for peace?

Why did Nicaragua's dictator, Daniel Ortega, go to the Communist Party Congress in Havana and endorse Castro's call for the worldwide triumph of communism? Was that for peace?

Some members of Congress ask me, why not negotiate? That's a good question, and let me answer it directly. We have sought, and still seek, a negotiated peace and a democratic future in a free Nicaragua. Ten times we have met and tried to reason with the Sandinistas. Ten times we were rebuffed. Last year, we endorsed church-mediated negotiations between the regime and the resistance. The Soviets and the Sandinistas responded with a rapid arms buildup of mortars, tanks, artillery and helicopter gunships.

Clearly, the Soviet Union and the Warsaw Pact have grasped the great stakes involved, the strategic importance of Nicaragua. The Soviets have made their decision—to support the communists. Fidel Castro has made his decision—to support the communists. Arafat, Qaddafi and the Ayatollah Khomeni have made their decision—to support the communists. Now, we must make our decision. With Congress' help, we can prevent an outcome deeply injurious to the national security of the United States. If we fail, there will be no evading responsibility—history will hold us accountable. This is not some narrow partisan issue; it is a national security issue, an issue on which we must act not as Republicans, not as Democrats, but as Americans.

Preserving Freedom

Forty years ago Republicans and Democrats joined together behind the Truman Doctrine. It must be our policy, Harry Truman declared, to support peoples struggling to preserve their freedom. Under that doctrine, Congress sent aid to Greece just in time to save that country from the closing grip of a communist tyranny. We saved freedom in Greece then—and with that same bipartisan spirit we can save freedom in Nicaragua today. . . .

"Clearly, the Soviet Union and the Warsaw Pact have grasped the . . . strategic importance of Nicaragua."

You know, recently one of our most distinguished Americans, Clare Boothe Luce, had this to say. . . . "In considering this crisis," Mrs. Luce said, "my mind goes back to a similar moment in our history—back to the first years after Cuba had fallen to Fidel. One day during those years, I had lunch at the White House with a man I had known since he was a boy—John F. Kennedy. 'Mr. President,' I said, 'no matter how exalted or great a man may be, history will have time to give him no more than one sentence. George Washington—he founded our country. Abraham Lincoln—he freed the slaves and preserved the Union. Winston Churchill—he saved Europe.' 'And what, Clare,' John Kennedy said, 'did you believe—or do you believe my sentence will be?' 'Mr. President,' she answered, 'your sentence will be that you stopped the communists—or that you did not.'"

Well, tragically, John Kennedy never had the chance to decide which that would be. Now, leaders of our own time must do so. My fellow Americans, you know where I stand. The Soviets and the Sandinistas must not be permitted to crush freedom in Central America and threaten our own security on our own doorstep.

Ronald Reagan, president of the United States, firmly opposes the Sandinista government in Nicaragua and has proposed aid to the contra forces.

The Soviet Threat Is Fabricated

Council on Hemispheric Affairs

Editor's note: The following viewpoint is a response by the Council on Hemispheric Affairs (COHA) to a speech given by President Ronald Reagan. The italicized quotes contained in the article are excerpts from his speech.

"Now let me show you the countries in Central America where weapons supplied by the Nicaraguan Communists have been found: Honduras, Costa Rica, El Salvador, Guatemala. Radicals from Panama—to the south—have been trained in Nicaragua. But the Sandinista revolutionary reach extends well beyond their immediate neighbors. In South America and the Caribbean, the Nicaraguan Communists have provided support in the form of military training, safe haven, communications, false documents, safe transit and sometimes weapons to radicals from the following countries: Colombia, Ecuador, Brazil, Chile, Argentina, Uruguay and the Dominican Republic."

Although viewers of the President's speech saw most of the hemisphere turn red before their eyes on a map the President used to illustrate these charges, the administration's oft-recited claims of Nicaraguan subversion throughout the Americas remain unproven. Indeed, they have almost always been made by the White House, rather than the supposedly aggrieved nation. Of all of the nations that he cited, only one or two of them—outright U.S. allies—have supported his charges.

The Myth of a Soviet Threat

"I am speaking of Nicaragua, a Soviet ally on the American mainland only two hour's flying time from our own borders."

A report by Dr. Carl Jacobsen of the University of Miami, written in 1984 on contract to the State Department, found "ambivalence" on the part of the Soviet Union toward the Sandinistas, whose

The Council on Hemispheric Affairs, "Misleading the Public: Ten Areas of Misrepresentation in President Ronald Reagan's March 16, 1986 Speech on Aiding the Nicaraguan Contras," April 3, 1986.

revolutionary strategy they considered adventurist, and which bypassed the country's traditional communist parties. Of general Soviet regional policy, he wrote that "Moscow appears ready to concede" that Central America "is America's back yard, and that Washington has the same 'right' to intervene in Nicaragua as she has in Afghanistan." Jacobsen suggested that Moscow's principal interest in Nicaragua is the propaganda harvest, which would be particularly bountiful should Washington intervene directly. He emphasized that the Soviets were in no way prepared to come to the military defense of Nicaragua.

On several occasions the Soviets have declared that, in the final instance, defending the revolution in Nicaragua must be the Sandinistas' responsibility. Similarly, Fidel Castro has repeatedly warned Nicaraguan President Daniel Ortega that Cuba cannot and will not guarantee Nicaragua's security, just as he cautioned the late Grenadian leader Maurice Bishop that Havana could not defend that island nation.

In the March 16, [1986] issue of *The New York Times*, an unidentified State Department Soviet expert was quoted as doubting the White House prediction that Nicaragua will become another Cuba saying that, "They [the Sandinistas] have calculated that a base would precipitate a military move by the United States to eliminate it." He also noted that the Kremlin would not "risk a single soldier" to save the Sandinistas. Certainly this was the case with Chile in 1973, as well as Grenada in 1983. More to the point, the question is why would it be relevant for either the Soviet Union or, for that matter, the Sandinistas, to permit a base to be located in Nicaragua that would be entirely vulnerable to the predominance of U.S. military might in the region. As Nicaraguan Foreign Minister Miguel D'Escoto was quoted as saying on the matter of supposed Nicaraguan aggressive intent, in light of the reality of U.S.

power, "we may be stupid, but we're not suicidal."

"...the American forces who liberated Grenada captured thousands of documents that demonstrated Soviet intent to bring Communist revolution home to the Western hemisphere."

Jacobsen's analysis—that Moscow's ambitions in the region have more to do with propaganda and trouble-making than with a strategic master plan—is in fact confirmed by a careful analysis of the Grenada documents. The thousands of pages of documents the U.S. invasion forces seized primarily discuss commercial ties between the Soviet Union and Grenada—saying little about Soviet military involvement in the region. As a State Department source told COHA, "You won't find a smoking gun," or a "master plan," in the Grenada documents.

"On several occasions the Soviets have declared that ... defending the revolution in Nicaragua must be the Sandinistas' responsibility."

In his speech the President selected what his advisors thought to be the most incriminating quote from the most incriminating document in the captured collection—but even at this the Soviet statement is tame and reveals little. The notes from a March 10, 1983 Moscow meeting between George Louison, Minister of Agriculture in the Maurice Bishop government and Marshall Ogarkov from which President Reagan suggested was a direct quote of the latter's words, mainly concerned Grenada's fears of being attacked. Louison paraphrased Ogarkov in his notes as saying something to the effect that "two decades ago, there was only Cuba in Latin America, today there are Nicaragua, Grenada, and a serious battle is going on in El Salvador." At most, this assertion is merely a descriptive one, characteristic of Eastern bloc booster rhetoric of the vigorous health of "progressive" regimes, and not at all necessarily implying a sinister plot, as was the purport of the Reagan reference. The document, as is the case with all other Grenada material seized by the invading U.S. military, certainly does not show Ogarkov or the Russians taking credit for the Central American ferment, or reveal any Soviet-Cuban role in such developments.

The same can be said of the President's disingenuous alleged quote from Soviet Foreign Minister Andrei Gromyko—that "Central America was 'boiling like a cauldron' and ripe for revolution." What one could not tell during Reagan's speech, but can see from its written text, is that Gromyko only said that the region was "boiling like a cauldron"—the rest is the President's language. Again the Soviet statement merely describes events, and does not reveal any kind of Russian plan for regional revolution. But, to his television viewers, the President clearly meant them to understand that Gromyko was laying out the Soviet line of subversion by putting into his mouth the words: "ripe for revolution."

It is easy to make allegations about what a nation's intentions may be. But what is conspicuously absent from the president's proclamations is any real evidence of the Sandinistas' aggressive designs.

Backing Neutrality

"Using Nicaragua as a base, the Soviets can become the dominant power in the crucial corridor between North and South America. Established there, they will be in a position to threaten the Panama Canal, interdict our vital Caribbean sea lanes and, ultimately, move against Mexico."

As the President's televised map showed, Cuba is already in an excellent position to threaten the Caribbean sea lanes, and Havana certainly has a much more capable military than Nicaragua. The Panama Canal has been recognized as essentially indefensible ever since World War I—a lone saboteur could destroy a key lock, causing the Gatun Lake to drain. Mexico, to which the President referred more than once, is apparently undisturbed by the threat of Nicaraguan subversion. It has been a key backer of the Contadora process and is one of Nicaragua's principal trading partners.

Moreover, there is little evidence of support for the contras in countries closer to Nicaragua. A poll taken in Costa Rica on behalf of the President-elect Oscar Arias, found that only 9.5% of all Costa Ricans support contra funding, while an overwhelming majority backed neutrality. Emboldened by this result, Arias publicly opposed contra aid in February [1986], saying "it won't get a more open society in Nicaragua, you won't get a negotiation with the anti-Sandinistas." "If I were Mr. Reagan," said Arias, "I would give that money to Guatemala, El Salvador, Honduras and Costa Rica for economic aid, and not military aid for the contras."

An earlier Gallup poll, cited by the administration as showing Costa Rican support for the contras, was commissioned by the USIA [United States Information Agency] and excluded anyone with less than 7.5 years of education, or "unfamiliar" with the subject, an extraordinary procedure meant to produce predictable results. The USIA's poll was so compromised that the Gallup organization, whose Costa Rican franchise was the Center for International Development, made it a point to later say that CID was not under its jurisdiction.

"Today, Warsaw Pact engineers are building a deep-water port on Nicaragua's Caribbean coast, similar to the naval base in Cuba for Soviet-built submarines. They

are also constructing, outside Managua, the largest military airfield in Central America. . . ."

The Atlantic Coast port of Bluefields has been modernized with Bulgarian aid. This improvement helps handle Nicaragua's growing trade with Europe and is a critical element in Managua's national economic development plans. Currently Nicaragua has no navy beyond a few French-provided coast guard vessels. There are no plans to acquire submarines and Nicaragua has offered repeated guarantees to the U.S. not to permit any foreign military bases or foreign military use of Nicaraguan facilities.

Nicaragua has no foreign military bases, and has repeatedly offered to sign the Contadora treaty, which would outlaw all foreign military presence in the region. Likewise, Nicaragua has consistently offered bilateral guarantees to the United States on the matter of bases and the presence of foreign troops. . . .

The Contras

"You see, when the Sandinistas betrayed the revolution, many who had fought the old Somoza dictatorship literally took to the hills, and like the French Resistance that fought the Nazis, began fighting the Soviet bloc Communists and the Nicaraguan collaborators. These few have been joined by thousands."

Seven thousand National Guardsmen fled Nicaragua after July 1979; many ended up in Honduras, where they took to cattle-rustling, smuggling, and other cross-border brigandage. From these people the Reagan administration in early 1982 formed a 1500-man commando force, which it told Congressional intelligence oversight committees was aimed at the interdicting Sandinista arms smuggling to El Salvador. This force essentially became the Nicaraguan Democratic Force (FDN).

"The Soviet statement merely describes events, and does not reveal any kind of Russian plan for regional revolution."

A 16 July 1982 "Weekly Intelligence Summary" by the Pentagon's Defense Intelligence Agency, leaked in 1984, described the FDN's September 15th Legion as a "terrorist" organization headed by former National Guard officers. An April 1985 report by the House/Senate Arms Control and Foreign Policy Caucus demonstrated that 12 of the top 13 FDN commanders were former members of Somoza's National Guard. . . .

The tactics of the contras—something the President did not address in his speech—are also a clear indication that they cannot be considered a democratic force. They have consistently attacked

teachers, health workers, and agricultural specialists in the countryside. Last September [1985], contras from the Nicaraguan Democratic Front (FDN) kidnapped five women teachers and took them across the border to Honduras. According to one of the victims who escaped, the soldiers raped and tortured them. Also during September, a contra force attacked the town of Serrano, burning the dispensary and the school and torturing and killing two unarmed teachers. . . .

Reagan's Charades

[In] June [1985] Reagan promised Democrats who voted for "humanitarian" contra aid that he would, in return, resume bilateral talks. He reneged.

Reagan is trying the 90-day negotiation tactic again. Apparently, he hopes this time that, while the legislators recognize his intention to set such extreme demands that Managua can not possibly meet them, the negotiating ploy may be seen as a way for them to accede honorably to the President's demand and justify their vote to their constituents.

Without safeguards, a three-month delay would be no more than another conveniently-timed administration diplomatic charade such as Salvadoran President Jose Napoleon Duarte's offer to negotiate with the FMLN [National Liberation Front] if the Sandinistas will sit down with the contras. This artificial, U.S.-sponsored linkage is a non-starter, rejected out of hand by both the FMLN and Managua.

Similarly, the appointment of Philip Habib as special envoy to Central America has little to do with serious peace overtures. The selection of Habib merely capitalizes on his past image as the troubleshooter who helped get Marcos out of the Philippines. In contrast to his usual reserve in talking to the media about his diplomatic missions, such as the one to Lebanon, Habib's short tenure in Central America has transformed him into a veritable font of Reaganesque extremist quotations on the need for contra funding, and he has backed up the President's groundless assertion that Latin leaders support aid to the contras even though they oppose it publicly.

As long as the administration can continue waging its war against Nicaragua, it is clearly the United States rather than Nicaragua which lacks "the political will and flexibility" which the Caraballeda message cites as the key to overcoming the obstacles to constructive bilateral dialogue between the two countries.

The Council on Hemispheric Affairs is a research and education organization which monitors US-Latin American policy and Canadian-Latin American policy.

viewpoint 134

Angola Is a Soviet Client State

Jack Kemp

Angola is fighting its second revolutionary war in 10 years. Dr. Jonas Savimbi and his UNITA [the National Union for the Total Independence of Angola] movement helped liberate the country from Portuguese colonialism in 1975, and he is now fighting to free Angola from Soviet and Cuban-backed forces which seized the government in the vacuum left by Portugal's withdrawal. I believe it should be U.S. policy to assist Savimbi's struggle for freedom and independence in Angola.

Angola's government is propped up by 35,000 Cuban mercenaries and 1,200 Soviet and East bloc advisers and personnel. It has violated the basic human rights of its political prisoners by torture and beatings "inflicted with fists, wooden sticks, belts . . . and electric shocks" (according to an Amnesty International report), prolonged detention, and arbitrary death penalties. Trade unions are run by the government, which was cited by the International Labour Organization for practicing forced labor. Media censorship is widespread; it goes without saying that only one political party is legal in Angola, the ruling Marxist party.

UNITA Victories

After Congress prohibited U.S. assistance to the Angolan freedom fighters under the 1975 Clark Amendment, Savimbi received no help from us. The Clark Amendment forced him to turn to a government whose racial policies he abhors, as we all do—South Africa.

UNITA's morale is high and the movement has widespread support among Angolans, according to the State Department's 1984 human rights report. Using limited weapons, the freedom fighters have downed Soviet MIG aircraft and HIND helicopter gunships, capturing Russian rifles. UNITA has its

capital in the town of Jamba and a *de facto* government over a third of the country.

Early in 1985, it seemed that for the first time in history, a Soviet/Cuban-imposed despotism in Africa would be forced to share power with anti-communist forces or face the possibility of being deposed. But a late communist counter-attack has severely blunted Savimbi's drive toward independence.

Legislation offered by Sen. Claude Pepper, myself, and a bipartisan group of members of Congress would provide a modest $27 million in non-lethal humanitarian aid for UNITA's movement for independence from Soviet neo-colonialism. This is less, by some estimates, than the amount of tax revenues Chevron pays the government every two weeks for its Cabinda province oil refinery operations. As House minority leader Bob Michel wrote to Secretary of State George Shultz, "United States support for UNITA—even in such a small way—is not only a geostrategic but a moral necessity."

Opposing Soviet Colonialism

Angola's government is an outpost of white, Soviet-style colonialism on the African continent. Soviet/Cuban colonization of Angola is reactionary; it flies in the face of history. I believe anti-colonial liberation in Africa is a categorical imperative for democracies. We Americans have no right to sit on our hands while soldiers from Cuba and commanders from the USSR crush the aspirations of 5 million African blacks.

Assistance to the Angolan liberation movement falls under the Reagan doctrine, which says that the U.S. should materially help freedom fighters against Soviet-dominated governments. The doctrine has been described by proponents and opponents alike as the most significant American foreign policy movement in many years. I agree with that assessment. But since the general doctrine as well as

Jack Kemp, "The Reagan Doctrine in Angola," *Africa Report*, January/February 1986. Reprinted by permisssion of *Africa Report*. Copyright © 1986 by the African-American Institute.

its specific application to Angola are controversial, I would like to discuss some of the objections raised against both.

There are two opposing points of view regarding the Reagan doctrine. One is that it represents "interventionism." The other, correct viewpoint in my judgment is that it protects our national security interests as well as our faith in the principles of freedom.

Aid Is Practical

Critics of assistance to Jonas Savimbi claim that the proposal is just a right-wing imperative that bears no relation to the "realities" on the ground. But the original sponsor of the bill to provide assistance is a Democrat, Sen. Pepper of Florida. A recipient of 70 and 80 percent Americans for Democratic Action ratings in the 1980s, he would be quite surprised to hear that he is part of the "right-wing."

The notion that conservatives are so preoccupied with "ideology" that we disregard "practicality" turns the truth upside down. In the 1970s, if there was anything that distressed those on the left of the political spectrum, it was a foreign policy they regarded as merely pragmatic and empty of ideological content. "Pragmatic realism" in the last decade would have suggested defending governments strategically important to U.S. security interests when its internal opponents have ties to the Eastern bloc or other anti-U.S. forces.

> "The Soviets derive both economic benefits . . . and political/military advantages from their campaign to destabilize and assert control over the whole region."

But for the liberal left, ideology said that the United States must withdraw if that government's record on human rights did not meet some impeccably high standard. Thus Iran fell to the Ayatollah; thus Nicaragua fell to the Marxist Sandinistas, with tragic results for both peoples, with unhappy consequences for us, and with the elimination of all hope for civil rights and freedom of dissent in either country. That truly was the triumph of ideology over reality.

The reality on the ground in Angola is not very complicated. The Marxist-Leninist MPLA [Popular Liberation Movement of Angola] government remains in power only because of the support given by Cuban troops and Soviet weaponry. The quid pro quo is that the Soviets derive both economic benefits (by way of Chevron oil revenues) and

political/military advantages from their campaign to destabilize and assert control over the whole region.

Although assistance to anti-Marxist freedom fighters is basic to the Reagan doctrine, the State Department has been opposing support for UNITA, arguing that the United States is brokering negotiations to withdraw foreign forces. But aiding UNITA does not prevent a political settlement. On the contrary, the expense to the government of keeping its Cuban phalanx is high—estimated at between $500 and $800 million a year. In order to break the Soviet/Luanda alliance, the cost of the Soviet and Cuban presence must be increased enough to exceed the benefits and advantages. If the resistance is provided with effective help, the government's ability to hold power will be so difficult that it will be compelled to reach an accommodation with the Angolan people and forces controlling over a third of the country. There is no other way to get serious negotiations going, for the simple reason that if UNITA cannot fight, the MPLA government has no incentive to negotiate.

The key then is "effective help." Is $27 million in humanitarian assistance, as provided under the Pepper-Kemp bill, enough to do the job? Of course not. Its purpose is humanitarian. Those people and tribes that are aligned with the freedom fighters have been entirely cut off from the little social support which was provided by the state for a decade. Medicine, food, education, and training are desperately needed by these impoverished African people. Our USAID [United States Agency for International Development] programs never reach them. This modest $27 million dollar emergency assistance is intended to help correct the omission.

Covert Aid Is Needed

Covert assistance, to be sure, is also at issue, and it must be provided. The United States need not bear the entire burden, however. By supporting UNITA, we can signal to other non-communist nations, black and white, that there is now an opportunity to liberate an African nation from neo-colonialism, and hopefully some may choose to help. On the other hand, by refusing assistance we cause others within and outside of Angola to lose hope too, and refrain from any involvement.

This consideration cannot be stressed enough. The highest ranking Soviet defector, Arkady Shevchenko, who was familiar with Moscow ruling circles in the 1970s, has written that Leonid Brezhnev interpreted Congress' 1975 decision to cut off all assistance to Savimbi as a sign that the Kremlin might raise Cuban troop strength in Angola, and the U.S. would say little. And that is what Brezhnev proceeded to do. Burke's famous expression was never more apt: "All that is required for evil to triumph is for good men and women to do nothing." It is an inescapable reality of our time that the United States must lead the Free World, or the Free World will not have a leader. If the principles of individual dignity and the idea of human rights are not defended by the U.S. in a material way, they cannot be defended successfully by anyone else.

The Fight for Freedom

In Angola today, the dominant occupation is not debating club meetings where the comparative virtues of Edmund Burke and Karl Marx are discussed. Black Angolan men and women have had to take to the jungle and the bush to escape oppression and regroup their forces, taking their supplies of food and medicine, mortars and weapons from any available source. What else, given their situation, could they be expected to do? The essential fact of their life is the life-and-death struggle to achieve freedom. How can we turn our backs on their fight, which ultimately is our fight?

"Soviet global adventurism, in southern Africa and elsewhere, threatens developing and developed nations alike with its totalitarian rule."

Some say the U.S. should not "march to Pretoria's tune" by assisting a revolution South Africa supports. But this is a case of logic in reverse. With the Clark Amendment's repeal [in 1985] and our long-delayed financial help, UNITA need not rely on South Africa. Our obligation to help people fighting for freedom does not disappear just because a government we don't like is on the same side. That is a rationalization for shirking our responsibility.

Moreover, one major South African excuse for not dismantling apartheid is the communist threat. This excuse would carry less weight if communist regimes in the region, such as Angola and Mozambique, were replaced by genuine democracies—in fact it would become one more force for South African racial reform.

Global Adventurers

Soviet global adventurism, in southern Africa and elsewhere, threatens developing and developed nations alike with its totalitarian rule. Oppressed by a system of apartheid so reprehensible that no decent American dare defend it, South African blacks still find it possible to appeal to the United States to pressure their country for peaceful change. But to whom will black South Africans or anyone else appeal if Soviet global ambition achieves its goal of world domination? The Reagan doctrine is our effort to prevent that domination and preserve the possibility of freedom where it hardly exists today.

Those who favor and those who oppose assistance to Savimbi equally hope that diplomacy can end the conflict and bring freedom to Angola. But if the negotiation process succeeds, it is because of UNITA pressure on the Marxists to move toward free and fair elections and to secure withdrawal of all outside military forces. Assist the freedom fighters and negotiate—we can *and* should do both.

In foreign policy you deal with one evil at a time, as great democratic leaders recognize. Washington achieved American independence by seeking aid from the autocratic French King Louis XVI; Churchill and Roosevelt defended democracy by an alliance with Stalin to defeat Nazism and fascism.

It falls to each and every one of us, reader by reader, to decide what we would do in the context of this African liberation struggle. We are lucky: We are citizens of the one country endowed with leadership because of our natural wealth and extraordinary human industry. Personally, I would not have it any other way. Reality dictates that we take account of two overriding considerations in foreign policy issues—the demands of our moral conscience, and the imperatives of our nation's interest.

Bankrupt Marxist Policies

Those who believe that we should be neutral in this struggle illustrate the school of foreign policy that might be called "the new isolationism." That school already has the decimation of Kampuchea to its credit. I do not want to see Angola added to the list. In the world competition of ideas, Marxist-Leninist doctrine has demonstrated its bankruptcy over and over again as a political philosophy and as an economic model for growth and prosperity. No one chooses slavery or poverty willingly. Yet given time, the "new isolationism" could accomplish what the free competition of ideas alone will not: the incremental surrender of our interests, our allies, and finally, our faith in human rights and self-government for all peoples regardless of race or color.

For these reasons, I believe active American support for Angola's freedom fighters is essential to the progress of self-government and freedom in southern Africa and consequently to the future of the global democratic revolution.

New York Republican Jack Kemp is a member of the House of Representatives and the House Subcommittee on Foreign Operations.

"There is a lot of criticism . . . that it is the Soviet Union that commands in Angola. That is an absolute lie."

Angola Is Not a Soviet Client State

Keith Somerville

The MPLA leadership has implemented policies intended to reconstitute the broad-based national liberation movement into a disciplined and united vanguard party guided by Marxism-Leninism; to develop state control of the most vital areas of the economy; where possible, to set up state farms and agricultural cooperatives; and to launch mass health and educational campaigns, the latter being aimed at stamping out illiteracy and providing educated cadres for party, state and economic bodies. The commitment to Marxism-Leninism of the MPLA leadership under both Agostinho Neto and President Eduardo dos Santos is undeniable and it is evident that it intends to continue implementing policies, where the political, economic and military circumstances allow, aimed at creating the political, social and economic bases from which to embark on the formation of a new society.

Sabotaged Policies

But, and it is a very large but, a number of massive obstacles remain in the path of the MPLA and its socialist policies. So far, relatively little progress has been made in making socialist aims reality as a result of the devastation caused by the liberation and civil wars, the continuing military actions and sabotage by UNITA [the National Union for the Total Independence of Angola] and its South African backers, and the crippling shortage of educated and politically conscious cadres to fill both party and state positions. Until at least the first two of these obstacles are removed, progress in reconstruction and towards socialist transformation is likely to be painfully slow.

The campaign of sabotage and destabilization carried out by UNITA and South Africa has forced the MPLA to devote a high proportion of its human and material resources to the war effort rather than to pressing political and economic tasks. Only the removal of South African military units from southern Angola and occupied Namibia and an end to Pretoria's support for UNITA will enable the Angolan armed forces to defeat UNITA militarily and enable the MPLA to combat its political influence on Ovimbundu areas. Without the massive assistance it receives from South Africa, UNITA would undoubtedly crumble into impotence, as did the FNLA [Angolan National Liberation Front] and Holden Roberto following the withdrawal of extensive Zairean support. Until this battle is won, it will be impossible for the MPLA to make meaningful progress towards politicizing rural areas and winning the support of the bulk of the peasantry, particularly in the agriculturally important central and southern highlands. . . .

Firmly Non-Aligned

Internationally, the MPLA has stuck firmly to its policy of anti-imperialist non-alignment combined with the expansion of cooperation and friendship with the socialist states. Increasingly closer ties have not meant, however, that the Angolans have become Soviet clients. They have guaranteed their independence in decision-making, something demonstrated by the clear divergence of views between the MPLA and the Soviet leadership concerning talks with the United States and South Africa on the future of Namibia. On the other hand, the Luanda authorities have steadfastly refused to bow to American and South African pressure to agree to a withdrawal of Cuban troops from Angola as a precondition for Namibian independence and the withdrawal of South African troops from Namibia.

Cooperation with the socialist countries, particularly the Soviet Union and Cuba, has not prevented the MPLA government from developing excellent trade and economic relations with Western countries and multinational corporations. Although Angola has sought to increase trade and economic cooperation with the socialist countries, this has not been particularly damaging to cooperation with the West. It is a fact that, despite the poor political relations with the United States, Angola works very closely with the US Gulf Oil Company in the exploitation of oil resources. . . .

> *"Increasingly closer ties [with the socialist states] have not meant, however, that the Angolans have become Soviet clients."*

The commitment of the MPLA to Marxism-Leninism—and there can be little doubt that this commitment remains strong and is likely to be the salient feature of the party's future political orientation—did not develop as a result of the aid given to the movement during the liberation and civil wars by the Soviet Union, Cuba and other socialist states. Right from the formation of the movement, it had a strong Marxist element within it. The influence of the Marxists within the movement was strong both because many of the MPLA's founders were Marxists or were sympathetic to the ideology and because the Marxists in the MPLA were among the most highly educated of the members of the movement.

The Basis of Angolan Marxism

This opening statement begs the question: why did many of the leaders of the MPLA hold Marxist beliefs? The answer is that the early leaders of the national liberation struggle in Angola formed many of their ideas about the fight against colonialism while living outside Angola and they were influenced and guided by the ideological and political environment in which they began their political activities. . . .

In the case of the MPLA, many of the early leaders received their political education as students in Fascist Portugal. Political activity was impossible except in clandestine groups. The effect of this political environment was to polarize politics more than in other colonial states (for example, in Britain and France, where African nationalists could imbibe political ideologies ranging from Marxism to liberalism and private enterprise capitalism). In Portugal, Angolan students and intellectuals found that political activity of a form that offered support for the aims of African nationalists was to be found almost wholly on the left of the political spectrum. The nature of the Portuguese Fascist state, and the

opposition groups to which it gave rise, lent greater legitimacy to the Marxist-Leninist ideology of the Portuguese Communist Party in the eyes of African nationalists than, say, the British Communist Party did to nationalists from British colonies in Africa. In addition, the Portuguese Communist Party and related youth and trade-union organizations were more willing than other groups to accommodate and offer support to the liberation struggles and aspirations of African nationalists. Another important factor in bringing the Africans and the Portuguese communists together was the existence, in the years immediately following the second world war, of communist party cells in Luanda.

In this political and ideological environment it was hardly surprising that Angolan nationalists took on board Marxist teachings on political, social and economic analysis and Marxist-Leninist theories on political struggle. . . .

A Vanguard Party

As for the position of Angola and the MPLA in the international communist movement, both the MPLA and the Soviet Union regard developments in Angola as an integral part of the world revolutionary process. . . .

The MPLA and its leaders are very forthright in maintaining that their party is a Marxist-Leninist vanguard party committed to the transformation of society along socialist lines. It does not claim to have established even the foundations of socialism let alone communism, but it does demand to be taken seriously as a party of the working class. In our analysis so far, we have suggested that the MPLA has been consistent in its adherence to and development of Marxism-Leninism and has implemented a concerted policy of ridding the party of non-Marxist elements and ensuring the adoption of democratic centralism and other vital components of Marxist-Leninist organizational and party work practice. Vast problems may remain in the building of the party and in the preparation of the foundations of socialism, but it is hard to deny that the MPLA has the basic credentials to be labelled a Marxist-Leninist party.

The Soviet View

In the Soviet view, things are not as simple as that. Soviet party leaders and theoreticians have come up with a formulation known as 'socialist orientation' to describe the increasing number of parties and states in the Third World that adhere to Marxism-Leninism and have declared it their intention to create systems based on that ideology. Such countries include Angola, Mozambique, Benin, Congo and the People's Democratic Republic of Yemen. The formulation, used widely by CPSU [Communist Party of the Soviet Union] leaders and by Soviet theoretical journals and the media, is a function not so much of developments in the Third World states concerned as of Soviet caution over pledging support for and recognizing as Marxist-Leninist parties and governments over which the Soviet Union has no controlling political influence and which may, in the Soviet view, be only temporary in their hold over power or their ideological commitment. The concept of socialist orientation correctly identifies the aims of the states concerned and lists certain basic policies which apply to them, but it falls short of recognizing the total commitment of the states to Marxism-Leninism. It is effectively a form of ideological fence-sitting. The Soviet Union is willing to offer support to the states labelled as ones of socialist orientation and to applaud their development of vanguard parties, but it is not willing to accord them equal status as Marxist-Leninists.

The fence-sitting exercise undoubtedly resulted from the disappointment and ideological confusion in the Soviet Union over the failure of Nkrumah in Ghana, Keita in Mali, Sekou Touré in Guinea, Nasir in Egypt, and other Third World leaders of the 1960s who appeared to be moving steadily towards socialism but then were removed from power and replaced by anti-Soviet or at least anti-Marxist regimes or which, in the case of Sekou Touré and also of Siyad Barreh in Somalia, turned their backs on Marxism-Leninism or opted for a pro-Western international stance. The Soviet Union has been willing to provide extensive military and political support for Angola and Ethiopia, for example, but has not taken the step of recognizing the MPLA or the Worker's Party of Ethiopia as Marxist-Leninist parties. They remain parties and states of socialist orientation.

> "Angola's right to decide on its own future and to direct its developments free of outside influence was repeatedly stressed by [President] Agostinho Neto prior to his death."

The essence of the socialist orientation formulation was set out by the late CPSU leader Leonid Brezhnev at the Soviet party congress in February 1981. He said of the states of socialist orientation: 'Their development along the progressive road is not of course proceeding uniformly, for it is taking place under complex conditions'. . . . He went on to say that socialist orientation meant the liquidation of imperialist monopolies, the restriction of the role of foreign capital, securing for the people's states the commanding heights of the economy, an increased role for the working masses in public life and the state apparatus, and the growth of the revolutionary

party and an anti-imperialist foreign policy (*Pravda,* 24 February 1981). This analysis of what constitutes a state of socialist orientation certainly fits the conditions pertaining in Angola and the basic policies of the MPLA. However, the MPLA would not agree that it was merely a state of socialist orientation. It would demand to be taken seriously as a Marxist state in its own right, and would reject the right of the Soviet Union to sit in judgement on whether or not it had the right to label itself Marxist-Leninist.

Deciding Its Own Future

Angola's right to decide on its own future and to direct its developments free of outside influence was repeatedly stressed by Agostinho Neto prior to his death and has since been upheld by President dos Santos. In a statement in May 1977, Neto said that 'There is a lot of criticism of us abroad to the effect that Angola is subject to Soviet orientation, that it is the Soviet Union that commands in Angola. That is an absolute lie. And so long as the political leadership (of the MPLA) directs this country, we shall always defend our independence and non-alignment'.

In conclusion, there are few better descriptions of the place of Angola and similar states in the world communist system than that given by Michael Waller and Bogdan Szajkowski in their opening chapter in *Marxist Governments: A World Survey*:

> Even where, as in Angola, Vietnam, Cuba and Ethiopia, Soviet influence is particularly strong, the countervailing effects of cultural diversity and local circumstances make it increasingly difficult to make societies 'fit' a political model which draws overwhelmingly on Soviet experience. Moreover, there is ample evidence from all corners of the communist movement that the majority of the regimes that compose it are themselves not looking for the import of socialist practices from abroad. They aspire to their own original socialism. A socialism that will accord with their own circumstances.

For Angola, what now remains is to ensure that the form of Marxism-Leninism it applies to its own situation accords rather than conflicts with circumstances.

Journalist Keith Somerville has covered African and Third World affairs for Africa *magazine of London and is a regular contributor to* Africa Now *and* Modern Africa.

"The Communist team of Angola, the Soviet Union, and SWAPO will not be satisfied with any solution that does not grant them complete control of Namibia."

viewpoint 136

The Soviet Threat to Namibia Warrants US Concern

Philip M. Crane and Charles M. Lichenstein

Editor's note: The following viewpoint is taken from the Congressional Record. *It includes a speech from Republican Congressman Philip M. Crane and a statement by former Ambassador Charles M. Lichenstein.*

I believe that U.S. policy toward any country, but particularly toward Namibia, should be to try to ensure the well-being and freedom of the Namibian people and to protect vital U.S. interests. In this instance, both of these goals can be achieved only by following one policy—that of assuring that the Soviets and their SWAPO henchmen are unsuccessful in obtaining control of Namibia. But in recent years it has become painfully obvious that the Communist team of Angola, the Soviet Union, and SWAPO will not be satisfied with any solution that does not grant them complete control of Namibia. Such an occurrence would have disastrous consequences not only for the Namibian people and the region of southern Africa, but also for the rest of the world, for Namibia has the largest known uranium deposits in the world, as well as strategic waterways along its western coast.

In order to avoid SWAPO domination of Namibia, our policy must be altered. The time has come to dissociate ourselves with the U.N. designation of SWAPO as the "sole and authentic" representative of the Namibian people, for this amounts to declaring a winner before the elections are even held. Rather, we must stand up for the principles of antiterrorism, self-determination, and peaceful resolution of political differences.

An Alternative to SWAPO Terrorists

This does not mean that U.N. Resolution 435 needs to be abandoned for a reasonable solution can be reached under it. Recently, the Government of

Philip M. Crane, "Keeping Namibia Free from Communist Oppression," *Congressional Record,* vol. 132, no. 55, April 29, 1986.
Charles M. Lichenstein, statement submitted to the *Congressional Record* by Philip M. Crane, vol. 132, no. 55, April 29, 1986.

South Africa granted the request of the Multi-Party Conference of Namibia for autonomous local self-government pending implementation of U.N. Resolution 435. This transitional government, made up of representatives of numerous political parties and all races, represents a viable and necessary alternative to the SWAPO terrorists who have waged a long and insidious campaign of violence to gain control of Namibia. Supporting this transitional government in its efforts to bring independence to the beleaguered Namibians requires no expenditure of government funds; all it requires would be recognization by the United States. This would elevate these dedicated, pro-Western leaders of the transitional government to the same level as the Communist terrorists of SWAPO.

I hope the United States will take this important and historic step and thereby signal an end to the preferential treatment of SWAPO. The cause of stability, liberty, and self-determination will be served by such a move. Much blood has already been spilled, and much time has been wasted, but the chance to achieve our goals is within sight.

In this light I recommend the following statement made by Ambassador Charles M. Lichenstein, the former U.S. Deputy Ambassador to the United Nations. He speaks from personal experience about the situation in Namibia, having recently returned from there. I commend his remarks to my colleagues.

Faulty Preconceptions

In late January [1986], I was the guest of the Transitional Government of National Unity, in office since June 1985, on a week-long fact-finding tour of South West Africa—more generally known these days as Namibia. My preconceptions about this last-remaining colonial territory in southern Africa, in trust to the South African government since the end of the First World War, had largely been formed during incessant debates in the U.N. Security Council where I served as the deputy U.S. representative from 1981 to 1984.

Not surprisingly, considering the virtually ritualistic nature of these debates—vicious polemics, in fact, aimed at what is typically called in that chamber of horrors "the racist regime in Pretoria"—my preconceptions turned out to be in major part wrong. And because most of what most Americans think they know about "the problem of South West Africa" is a by-product of U.N.-generated disinformation, public understanding of that territory and indeed of the entire southern African region is basically and tragically flawed. Rational U.S. policy is a further victim of this discontinuity between reality and perception.

I do not mean to minimize the severity or complexity of the obstacles in that region to peaceful and reasonable outcomes—outcomes that serve U.S. strategic interests and, even more important, outcomes that might serve the interest of the people, all the people of southern Africa. The obstacles are formidable. Deprivations of fundamental human rights are real, and they are harsh. The status quo in all probability cannot be preserved for any term much longer than a few years or a decade, nor should it be. At the same time, however, evolutionary processes are under way—now, this very day—that hold out the promise of productive outcomes. There are no grounds for euphoria. There are grounds for cautious hope—if everyone directly, genuinely and, yes, constructively involved, not least our own government, seize upon the opportunities now at hand.

And in South West Africa these opportunities are real: the million or so people of that emerging nation are building a new reality there, a multiracial and multiethnic reality.

The daunting problems of the region cannot of course be wholly decoupled from the evolutionary process now under way in South West Africa. But this process demands our particular focus and our understanding. On its own merits, it deserves our encouragement. The payoff, for us and for the people of the region, potentially is enormous.

Obvious Facts

Let me back off a few steps and restate what is obvious to all of us.

As the Soviet Empire has expanded all around the periphery, relentlessly and until recently unopposed—in Asia, the Middle East, Africa, deep within our own hemisphere—the Soviets have relied more and more on surrogates to carry the fight, to do their dirty work. The international terrorist network, "National Liberation Movements" in the nomenclature of Soviet disinformation, is at the very core of this Soviet imperial aggression. Two of the principal such liberation movements, both of them

officially sanctified by the United Nations as the "sole and authentic representatives" of the people whose legitimate interests the Soviets thus cynically exploit, are of course the Palestine Liberation Organization (PLO), the terrorist spearhead of Soviet and radical Arab interests in the Middle East, and the South West Africa Peoples Organization (SWAPO), whose terrorist guerrilla forces based in Angola—now in major part pinned down by Jonas Savimbi's UNITA—are attempting to seize control of South West Africa. I'll come back to this point but, for the moment, I add just a footnote: it is ironic (and worse) that the U.N., whose world mission it is supposed to be to defuse and resolve conflict without recourse to force of arms, by its precertification of such groups as SWAPO in effect overrides the normal democratic political process and creates disincentives for entering into peaceful negotiation. The U.N. already has declared SWAPO the winner in South West Africa—so why indeed should SWAPO take part in the evolutionary process now unfolding there? Why should SWAPO assume any of the risks of the competitive democratic politics?

Getting the Minerals

The Soviet strategy in southern Africa, typically, is no secret at all. Leonid Brezhnev stated it openly as recently as 1973. Soviet world strategy, he said, is to gain control of the two great treasure houses on which the West depends—the energy treasure house of the Persian Gulf, and the mineral treasure house of central and southern Africa.

"The international terrorist network, 'National Liberation Movements' . . . is at the very core of this Soviet imperial aggression."

These parallel Soviet thrusts need little embellishment. Various committees of Congress have examined U.S. vulnerability in the area of strategic minerals. Platinum is a lot more than just a precious bauble in a jewel box: it has wide-ranging significance industrially. With its five associated metals—palladium, osmium, ruthenium, iridium and rhodium—it is a vital component of essential technologies. It doesn't take a lot of it, but defense industries from fighter planes to space craft would virtually shut down if our access to platinum were interrupted or cut off altogether. Our food supply would be affected. So too would air pollution: there would be more of it! Platinum in fact is used in the manufacture of about one in five of our industrial products—and the further fact is that we are close to 100 percent import dependent for platinum.

In 1983, the Congressional Budget Office reported to Congress on U.S. strategic minerals vulnerability. According to the CBO, "U.S. import dependence is almost total for minerals such as . . . the platinum group metals. Moreover, U.S. dependence is increasing." The CBO report went on to say that the extremely high concentrations of platinum in southern Africa "renders this group of metals one of the most critical of all potential mineral contingency problems, both in terms of supply interruption and deliberate price escalation." The Soviet threat, in other words, proceeds on twin tracks: Soviet control of South West Africa along with Mozambique and Angola, even apart from the actual threat during a military confrontation, would subject the U.S. to the equal if not greater threat of "diplomatic blackmail" on a global scale.

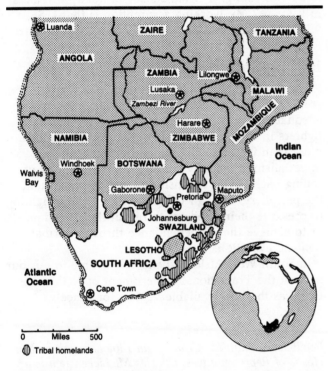

Robert Mansfield, *Great Decisions '87* © Foreign Policy Association, New York, NY. Reprinted with permission.

This potential Soviet-controlled triad in southern Africa—Angola and Mozambique, now possibly South West Africa—defines the strategic challenge we must confront. Angola has been a Soviet puppet for the more than ten years of its putative "independence." The MPLA [Popular Liberation Movement of Angola] ruling cadre is propped up by some 40,000 Cuban troops and 5,000 Soviet and East German "advisors." Angola is the staging base, moreover, for the transport of troops from Cuba to still other components of the Soviet African empire, to Mozambique and Ethiopia, for example. And the SWAPO terrorists, trained, financed, and directed by the Soviets, pursue their fight for control of South West Africa from bases in southern Angola. Should

SWAPO succeed—whether by arms or by a U.N.-sanctioned "diplomatic" takeover—the Soviet Noose would tighten over U.S. access to platinum and such other strategic minerals as chromium and cobalt which are available to us almost exclusively in this region of the world.

The U.S. interest in South West Africa goes beyond access to strategic resources. This is a country about twice the size of California with a population of slightly more than one million—consisting of 12 major ethnic groups who speak eight languages and 29 dialects and who range on the scale of socioeconomic development literally from the Stone Age to the highest rungs of, say, the London Inns of Court. It is a fascinating blend of the First and Third Worlds—and heir to the problems of both. Along with its strategic minerals, it contains the world's largest uranium mine and one of the largest gas fields. It is, as I've been saying, a major target of Soviet expansionism, one last stop from the borders of the Republic of South Africa itself.

Forming the Transitional Government

In 1985, that country—in technical violation of Resolution 435 of the U.N. Security Council, which demands immediate independence for Namibia with SWAPO virtually guaranteed political control—transferred all powers of local self-government, save only national defense, from its own Administrator-General to a Multi-Party Conference of Namibian political leaders representing every major group within South West Africa, including the dominant Ovambo people of the north (by most estimates about half of the total population) who are presumed to constitute the base of SWAPO strength. (I might note in passing that the leaders of SWAPO-D, the breakaway group of Ovambos, dedicated to peaceful evolution to independence, seemed to me fully prepared to contest this proposition at the ballot-box.) The Multi-Party Conference in turn established a Transitional Government of National Unity [in June 1986] . . . and invited SWAPO to lay down its guns and join in the peaceful evolution of an independent and democratic Namibia. SWAPO rejected the invitation, as it has consistently rejected all offers of negotiation and peaceful reconciliation. SWAPO continues to pursue its objective of total domination with guerrilla, terrorist warfare across the border from southern Angola.

I am, I concede, simply an "eight-day expert" in the politics of South West Africa—backed up, however, with almost four years' involvement in the international diplomatic process. My recent visit left with me some indelible impressions, and some grounds for cautious optimism.

The Transitional Government is working. It appears to be in full control of day-to-day administration. And it is taking on many of the hard issues: during my visit, the Minister of Education presented a controversial plan for a unitary national educational system, which would have the effect of reallocating locally-generated resources from the minority white to the majority black communities. Interestingly, and encouragingly, there are both blacks and whites on both sides of the debate.

Consciously designed to reflect the full range of the ethnic diversity of South West Africa, and its multiracial composition, the Transitional Government includes the leaders of every major group. It is multiracial: I met personally and at considerable length with every one of its eight cabinet members, five of whom are black. Roughly the same distribution is to be found within the National Council (the legislature) and the Constitutional Council, which is hard at work on a representative constitutional system, leading in due course to competitive democratic elections and ultimate *de jure* independence. The chairman of the Constitutional Council, a respected South African jurist and legal scholar, is publicly committed to a unitary electoral system, probably embracing some form of national lists and proportional representation. The Administrator-General, for his part, seemed to me to be dedicated to working himself out of a job at the earliest possible date.

"Soviet control of South West Africa along with Mozambique and Angola . . . would subject the U.S. to the . . . threat of 'diplomatic blackmail' on a global scale."

I repeat: this Transitional Government is in place, and it is working. The invitation to SWAPO to join in is on the table. The Lusaka agreement between South Africa and Angola prohibiting cross-border operations—by SWAPO to the south, by the South Africa Defense Forces to the north—appears to be holding, more or less. The essential elements of a peaceful evolution to Namibian independence, in short, are at hand.

US Aid Is Needed

What is most conspicuously lacking, in my judgment, is official recognition by the U.S. Government that this "new reality" in South West Africa presents all the players in southern Africa with genuine new opportunities. Our government seems to be frozen into the "Resolution 435 formula" at precisely the moment when a fresh approach is called for. I am not suggesting that the U.S. turn its back on Resolution 435: construed with flexibility, and with the crucial exception of the guaranteed dominance awarded to SWAPO, it does

provide a rough framework for peaceful evolution to Namibian independence. I am suggesting—indeed I am strongly recommending—that at the same time our government develop practical, working links to the Transitional Government in Windhoek. Modest amounts of U.S. assistance, particularly in agriculture and fisheries (economic development generally) and in the area of education, could make a vast difference. Official U.S. encouragement to the private sector, encouragement to potential investors and to nonprofit entities alike, could be just as important: in the course of my visit, I was struck again and again with obvious possibilities for partnerships between U.S. and Namibian schools and colleges and (of special relevance to local needs) vocational training facilities. And these are just the obvious possibilities for the mutually productive relationships we ought to be cultivating. In what sense "mutually"? What's in it for us? My working assumption is that U.S. interests are served by peaceful change in southern Africa.

Rolling Back Soviet Expansion

The emerging Reagan Doctrine in U.S. foreign policy is built on the foundation of U.S. support—adequate support, timely support—for freedom-fighters in every part of the world. It contemplates more than just the containment of Soviet imperialism: it actually perceives the possibility of rolling back Soviet expansion at key points around the periphery, through U.S. support for those fighting to preserve their freedom, to regain their freedom—or to achieve their independence through normal political evolution.

In South West Africa, I believe it is time to put our bets on the Transitional Government of National Unity as the best available vehicle for peaceful change.

Republican Philip M. Crane is an Illinois member of the House of Representatives. Charles M. Lichenstein is a former US deputy ambassador to the United Nations.

"Swapo's importance . . . has never been in doubt, except for those who have swallowed South Africa's story that the movement is . . . controlled by the Soviet Union."

viewpoint **137**

The Soviets Do Not Threaten Namibia

John A. Evenson

Portius Blasius is 15 years old. He attends what passes for a secondary school near his home village of Onhema, in the "operational zone" of northern Namibia. On June 6, [1986] after school, he was sitting outside a closed liquor store when 12 soldiers from the South African Defense Force (SADF) drove up in a truck. Portius was ordered to open the shop. He tried to explain that the owner was away and he had no keys, but the soldiers were not satisfied. They seized the boy, threw him into the truck, and drove away.

"They took me to an unknown place where they accused me of being a 'stupid little Swapo' and asked me about Swapo fighters. Some soldiers started to beat me while others, pulling my hair, held my face against the exhaust pipe.

"Although I was screaming very loudly, those merciless white devils did not care, and even left me there in the bush with much pain."

Portius was helped by a neighbor to the closest medical facility, the state-owned Oshakati hospital. A photographer for *The Namibian*, an independent English-language weekly, was in the region and went to the hospital, but medical personnel tried to keep him from seeing the boy. After some hours of persistence, he managed to get to Portius' bedside, where he found the boy lying in dirty, unwashed sheets, waiting to be treated for his burns.

A Forgotten Cause

[Since 1984], . . . events in the Republic of South Africa have often dominated the foreign and domestic news pages. But during this period, the ostensible reason for the U.S. policy of "constructive engagement," the independence of Namibia, has been conveniently forgotten. Even in the early days of the Reagan administration—days punctuated by

over-optimistic reports from U.S. Assistant Secretary of State Chester Crocker and his aides—very little was said about what was actually happening inside the 318,261 square mile territory.

Instead, we were treated to an endless litany of "progress is being made", "a breakthrough is near', and "prospects are reasonably good", as reporters dutifully took down the words of U.S. and South African officials. The United States had embarked on a negotiating policy that regarded South Africa as the aggrieved party in the Namibian affair, and life for Namibians under South African rule went on as usual.

There is little to suggest that Washington's policy-makers have ever had much concern . . . about South Africa's occupation of the territory. While the exhaust pipe incident is but one of thousands of acts of arbitrary violence occurring each year in the territory, it would appear that our current policy has been to disregard the valid human rights expectations of the Namibian people in favor of South Africa's insistence on the imposition of an East-West scenario.

And yet it is the human rights expectations of the Namibian people that are at the core of the struggle that is Namibia. To disregard or to treat lightly these legitimate yearnings has resulted in a devaluation of America's moral pretenses as leader of the "free world."

Independence Is Past Due

Listening to Namibians from all walks of life, there is an overwhelming consensus that independence is long, long overdue. The trust mandate granted by the League of Nations to "His Brittanic Majesty, to be administered by the Union of South Africa" was revoked by the United Nations in 1966. The mandate revocation was upheld by the International Court of Justice (ICJ) in 1971. There is no serious dispute over the standing of Namibia in international

John A. Evenson, "The Question Still Stands," *Africa Report*, September/October 1986. Reprinted by permission of *Africa Report*. Copyright © 1986 by the African-American Institute.

law. The fact can be simply stated: South Africa is illegally occupying the territory of Namibia.

The mandate was revoked for a reason. South Africa was no benevolent trustee. It had applied the full weight of apartheid in its rule of the territory, resulting in the predictable gross differences in infant mortality, life expectancy, education, and income between black and white.

To insure that its laws are upheld and its sovereignty protected, South Africa has installed an army and police force of considerable size in the territory. This army, especially in the northern "operational zone" (where one-half of Namibia's 1.4 million people live), is given full emergency powers. Like other armies of occupation, it has purchased the cooperation of a minority of the population, but in the main the SADF and the local forces it recruits are hated and feared.

South Africa's Opponents

There are two principal movements opposing the South Africans in Namibia. The first is the South West Africa People's Organization (Swapo), a multi-ethnic liberation movement with wide support whose small army, PLAN, has been attacking South African installations in the country since 1966. The second is the Christian church, which like its counterparts in the Philippines and Poland, has taken a clear stand on the side of the common man and woman against a totalitarian ruler.

The lightly armed Swapo guerrillas have concentrated their attacks on South African installations and mobile troops. Trained and armed by the Eastern bloc, these young people have found help and sustenance in the homes of rural Namibians. They are "the boys," the sons of friends, the hope of a new Namibia. Thousands left the country in the late 1970s as teenagers. Now they are returning, and if the body counts of the SADF are to be believed, many to almost certain death. But they continue to return home to try and dislodge the South African army of occupation.

There is a certainty about their effectiveness, not in defeating the South Africans in open battles, but in their ability to harass, to make the occupation costly, and to show that there are Namibians willing to die for freedom. Landmines are planted, telephone poles blasted, and rockets launched into white areas of South African administrative and military centers. In recent months, Swapo soldiers have attacked numerous bases, including the SADF headquarters at Oshakati, and have shot down at least one South African helicopter.

The South African response to Swapo "incursions" has been to increase its repression of the civilian population. Thus on July 23, [1986,] President   tha Botha stepped into the legal process in Namibia, authorizing his appointed "interim government" in Windhoek to quash a murder trial against four white

SADF soldiers who had killed a 48-year-old father of five last November. The trial was halted because it was "not in the national interest."

To Namibians, it is the SADF, the "Koevoet" death squad, and the troops of Unita who train in Namibia who are the terrorists. The people of the north say evening prayers in their kraals, asking God to "defend us from all the perils and dangers of this night." As many Namibians from "the operational zone" have told the author: "We are always thinking, is this the night that the Boers will come again?"

"Our current policy has been to disregard the valid human rights expectations of the Namibian people in favor of South Africa's . . . imposition of an East-West scenario."

In a war, there are casualties among the military and civilians alike. But in the war in Namibia, methods of brutality against the civilian population are clearly associated with the repression of an unwilling populace. Bishop Kleopas Dumeni, leader of Namibia's large Evangelical Lutheran church, said that the level of violence had increased dramatically. While he recognized that the violence came from both sides, Dumeni stated that the killings continue "simply because the South African government refuses to sign a ceasefire agreement between its troops and Swapo."

That is the opinion of most Namibians. They see one basic reason for their suffering: the continued illegal occupation of their country by the government of South Africa. In the minds of the vast majority of Namibians, there is no other issue. They are not afraid of Cuba, nor of Angola, and they are certainly not afraid of their political party of choice—Swapo.

No Soviet Threat

Swapo's importance in the struggle for independence has never been in doubt, except for those who have swallowed South Africa's story that the movement is a terrorist organization controlled by the Soviet Union. Swapo's roots are in the anti-colonial feelings that have been passed down from grandparents who remembered life before the Germans came in the 19th century. The Namibians did not need a European textbook to teach the difference between justice and injustice.

Like many other liberation movements, Swapo went first to the West in its search for aid. And as with other liberation movements, the United States, Great Britain, and France showed Swapo the door. The West's trusted ally, the Republic of South Africa, was the "bird in the hand," and a white bird after all. But the Swapo leaders who went into exile found help from churches and individuals even in these countries—assistance and support that continues to this day.

Funds for its refugee work (more than 60,000 Namibian refugees are currently in Angola and Zambia) and education bursaries come from churches, aid agencies, the United Nations, and a diverse list of Western, non-aligned, and Eastern bloc countries. Young Namibians attending school in Europe, North America, Africa, and Asia are trained in a variety of trade and scientific skills, preparing for the needs of an independent Namibia.

Swapo's leader, Sam Nujoma, is an old-time patriot, a now grandfatherly figure who has kept the movement together through many difficult trials. Criticized by Chester Crocker's staff as not having the intelligence or sophistication of a Robert Mugabe, one suspects that Nujoma has the common sense, rural directness, and clarity of purpose that foreign service officers cannot manipulate.

South African-Created "Governments"

South Africa has tried many means to cripple Swapo. It repeatedly establishes "governments" to create the illusion that the territory is self-governing without Swapo. Each dispensation of this ploy, little different than the homeland governments it has set up in the Republic, has floundered for want of popular support. The current government, appointed June 17, 1985, has suffered from continuous squabbling between anti-Swapo black Namibians who need some changes in the apartheid laws to establish their credibility, and "baster," white, and Coloured ministers who like things just the way they are.

"[South Africa] repeatedly establishes 'governments' to create the illusion that the territory is self-governing without Swapo."

The parties that make up this "interim government" would likely win no more than 15 percent of the vote in any free election. The largest component is the white National Party, and most other groups in the "Multi-Party Conference" are rooted in tribally based homeland governments financed by South Africa.

To convince others of its democratic inclinations, the interim government passed a "bill of rights" early on. But to its consternation, Swapo and the churches have used this legislation to overturn some of South Africa's laws restricting freedom of assembly. Apart from the fact that it is not representative of the people, the interim government lost any credibility it might have had by assuming responsibility for implementing South Africa's draconian detention laws.

Coupled with this attempt to politically isolate Swapo are the military adventures of the SADF in Angola. Since 1975, South Africa has maintained a presence in southern Angola, both with its own battalions and through its support for Jonas Savimbi's Unita troops. Neither South Africa nor Unita has any compunction as to whom they attack, be it unarmed civilians, church mission stations, or refugee camps. Many families in Namibia learn months later that a child or brother or sister has died in Angola in an attack by the SADF or Unita.

South Africa's one-two punch of censorship and heavy investment in propaganda has paid dividends in Western capitals. By restricting journalists' movements in northern Namibia, the story of its repressive measures is not being told. Instead, compliant reporters are flown to Oshakati, the main SADF base in the operational zone, and shown the bodies of Swapo "terrorists" and stacks of captured weapons. Outside the SADF fortresses— unreported—Namibians are mourning their dead.

South African Propaganda

South Africa has also financed a propaganda effort specifically supporting its government in Namibia. Under the direction of Sean Cleary, former South African diplomat and chief of staff of Botha's administrator-general in Namibia, public relations offices in Bonn, Paris, London, and Washington provide a steady stream of "anti-communist" stories hailing the interim government as Namibia's answer to apple pie.

Through right-wing organizations such as the International Society for Human Rights, South Africa has attempted to mount a campaign citing human rights violations in the Swapo camps. Except with extremist politicians in West Germany, Great Britain, and the United States, these flimsily documented attempts at smearing Swapo have not met with any success. But the communist label they have bestowed on Swapo has frightened off many otherwise sympathetic legislators.

Inside Namibia, where it counts, events continue to show that there is overwhelming support for parties and groups that refuse to collaborate with the interim government. One indicator, the churches, are a potent force because they have overcome both ethnic and theological differences to work together for independence and human rights.

The Power of the Churches

More than 70 percent of the 1.4 million population are active members of Lutheran, Roman Catholic, Anglican, and African Methodist Episcopal churches. Through the Council of Churches in Namibia, they have a history of publicly attacking the human rights violations of the SADF, the police, and the various interim governments. As far back as 1971, immediately following the ICJ decision, the two major Lutheran churches issued a scathing open letter to then-Prime Minister Vorster challenging South Africa's activities in the country.

As bishops, pastors, and priests have continued to reveal South Africa's human rights violations, the Church has not gotten away unscathed. British, Finnish, and German missionaries have been deported, priests imprisoned, church services disrupted, church buildings destroyed, and active lay officials detained and tortured. The headquarters of the Council of Churches was firebombed [in] January [1986], and the government refuses to grant some church leaders travel documents.

Swapo Christians

The churches' influence extends into the Swapo ranks in exile. Swapo refugee camps in Angola and Zambia are staffed by chaplains from Lutheran, Roman Catholic, and Anglican churches. Many Swapo soldiers receive instruction in the faith, and many have been baptised by pastors serving the refugee community.

The churches have strongly reacted to South Africa's claim that in fighting Swapo it is resisting communism. Says Bishop Dumeni: "It is propaganda. Who is Swapo? Let me tell you. Swapo are members, men and women, daughters and boys of our families, members of our churches. They are Christians. But the question is why they left the country. Precisely because of the hardships of the war situation, apartheid, separate development, and injustice." . . .

"The United States has . . . given South Africa a reason for not leaving Namibia . . . [and has become] a partner of Jonas Savimbi, South Africa's surrogate in Angola."

The most dramatic indication of what would occur if free elections were held came in July [1986]. Sometimes, even in Namibia, white judges can surprise the government. On July 3, the Windhoek Supreme Court threw out a 1981 law that effectively banned public meetings of Swapo. On July 27, free from fear of arrest, more than 13,000 people gathered in Katutura, the black township outside Windhoek, to attend the liberation movement's first legal meeting in many years.

In the mid-1970s, when the UN General Assembly was demanding sanctions because of South Africa's intransigence, the Western members of the Security Council stepped in and assumed responsibility for Namibia's independence. With the adoption in 1978 of UN Security Council resolution 435 and its accompanying detailed plans for a ceasefire, peace-keeping force, and elections, Namibians had real hope that their independence was near. After all, as one church official said: "The leaders of the free world had taken an interest in our cause."

Hypocritical US Policy

Eight years later, Namibians are still dying, living under apartheid, and seeking the implementation of the Western plan for their independence. But now they have no champion for their cause among the leaders of the free world. Namibian independence is not even on the agenda of the sanctions debate. The United States has not only given South Africa a reason for not leaving Namibia, namely the presence of Cuban troops in Angola, but has even made that irrelevant condition impossible to fulfill by becoming a partner of Jonas Savimbi, South Africa's surrogate in Angola.

In a Swapo refugee camp, a young Namibian said to me: "I've read your declaration of independence. That's what we want. Why won't America help us?" The question still stands.

Journalist John A. Evenson is the director of the Namibia Communications Centre, a London-based news agency working with churches in Namibia.

*"The communist FRELIMO regime in
Mozambique has been one of Moscow's
staunchest allies in Africa."*

viewpoint **138**

The US Must Oppose Soviet
Influence in Mozambique

William Pascoe

Since gaining independence from Portugal in 1975,
Mozambique has been one of Moscow's closest allies
in Africa. This alliance was forged ten years ago,
when Mozambique signed a 20-year Treaty of
Friendship and Cooperation with the Soviet Union.
In return for military advisers and a large arsenal of
Soviet weapons, Mozambique's communist regime,
known as the Front for the Liberation of
Mozambique (FRELIMO), has given the Soviet navy
access to ports, has supported Soviet-backed
insurgents, and allowed Moscow's allies preferred
access to Mozambique's natural resources.

Soviet weapons and advisers are used to fight the
nine-year-old insurgency of the Mozambique
National Resistance, or RENAMO. Its 22,000
pro-Western freedom fighters have waged an
increasingly successful guerrilla campaign against the
FRELIMO regime. RENAMO now controls 80
percent of the countryside.

Committed to Communism

Mozambique faces other problems: economic and
military pressure from neighboring South Africa, a
famine that threatens 5 million Mozambicans, and
the normal problems associated with a leadership
change, after President Samora Machel was killed
last October [1986] in a plane crash. He was
replaced by Joaquim Chissano, who promptly
reconfirmed his regime's commitment to Marxism-
Leninism and to the Soviet bloc.

Many observers believe that RENAMO is so close
to victory that it could become the Third World's
first triumphant anti-communist insurgency. A main
obstacle to this, strangely, is the Reagan
Administration. Instead of invoking the Reagan
Doctrine and supporting the democratic resistance
forces, as the Reagan Doctrine seemingly would

William Pascoe, "Mozambique Merits the Reagan Doctrine," The Heritage
Foundation *Backgrounder*, March 31, 1987. Reprinted with permission.

require, the U.S. has sided with the Soviet-backed
communist regime. For the last six years, the State
Department ostensibly has sought to "wean away"
the FRELIMO regime from the Soviet bloc by
providing FRELIMO with political, diplomatic, and
economic support. Since 1981, the U.S. directly has
provided Mozambigue $78 million in bilateral
assistance and has voted for another $154 million in
multilateral assistance.

Mozambique's communist rulers, however, refuse
to be weaned. They are no closer to the West and no
further from Moscow than they were six years ago.
It is thus time for the U.S. to recognize that its
Mozambique policy has failed. As such, Washington
should end all bilateral assistance to Mozambique.
The U.S. also should demand the withdrawal of all
foreign forces from Mozambique and pressure
FRELIMO leaders to negotiate with RENAMO to
devise a plan for national reconciliation and
internationally supervised elections. If FRELIMO
refuses, Washington should consider providing
Reagan Doctrine assistance to RENAMO's
democratic resistance forces.

FRELIMO's Assumption of Power

Eduardo Mondlane founded the Front for the
Liberation of Mozambique in Tanzania in 1962. He
organized FRELIMO out of several groups working
to end Portuguese rule of its African colonies. One
of these groups, forced out of Portugal by the
Portuguese secret police, had resettled in newly
independent Algeria. This "Algeria Group" contained
the most radical members of the FRELIMO
leadership: Marcelino dos Santos (who led the
group), Joaquim Chissano, Pascual Mocumbi, Sergio
Veira, Oscar Monteiro, Aquino de Braganca, and
Jorge Rebelo.

Between 1962 and 1969, rival factions battled for
power. The issue: black nationalism vs. radical
communism. In February 1969 Mondlane, a black

nationalist, was assassinated. The Algeria Group put Samora Machel in power. Soon after, Soviet bloc assistance to FRELIMO increased.

By the time of the April 1974 coup in Lisbon, which toppled the Caetano regime, FRELIMO was Mozambique's only opposition movement. When Portugal's new rulers decided to abandon their centuries-old African colonies, they merely turned power over to FRELIMO, without any election. FRELIMO took power on June 25, 1975.

Machel quickly nationalized major segments of the economy, and then the state took control of all private property (some of which has been returned). He also launched a campaign to collectivize agriculture. At a FRELIMO party congress in February 1977, Machel transformed his "liberation movement" into a full-fledged vanguard communist party. He declared "Our struggle is to destroy all vestiges of feudalism and colonialism, but fundamentally to crush capitalism, which is the most advanced form of exploitation of man by man."

The Moscow-Maputo Connection

Cuban agents first courted FRELIMO in Algeria in the early 1960s. FRELIMO participated in the January 1966 Tricontinental Congress in Havana, where Fidel Castro brought together representatives of revolutionary movements from all over the world. During the 1960s, FRELIMO members were sent to Cuba for military training. FRELIMO also joined other Soviet bloc fronts, including the World Peace Council and the Afro-Asian People's Solidarity organization.

"Washington should consider providing Reagan Doctrine assistance to RENAMO's democratic resistance forces."

By the time Machel visited Moscow in May 1976, he already had signed Treaties of Friendship and Cooperation with Bulgaria, Czechoslovakia, Romania, and North Korea. In Moscow, his Soviet patrons apparently told him that before they would give him such a treaty, he would have to demonstrate his commitment to Marxism-Leninism by formally transforming his movement into a vanguard communist party. As a promise of good things to come, Moscow signed an arms agreement. Machel accepted these conditions, and the transformation took place in February 1977. One month later, he was rewarded with a 20-year Treaty of Friendship and Cooperation.

Since then, Soviet military assistance to Mozambique has been substantial. Moscow sold FRELIMO $978 million worth of arms on very favorable credit terms between 1977 and 1983,

including MiG-21 jet fighters, MI-24 helicopter gunships, and T-54/55 tanks. . . . [Since 1985], Moscow has upgraded Mozambique's arsenal. Following a March 1986 Machel visit to Moscow, the Soviets signed a five-year arms agreement that for the first time would provide FRELIMO forces with MiG-23 jets and heavy T-62 tanks. And [in March 1987] the Soviets signed a new arms agreement with FRELIMO, the details of which are still unknown.

The Soviets reap benefits from their alliance with FRELIMO. Soviet ships use the Mozambican ports at Nacala and Maputo. FRELIMO meanwhile supported Soviet-backed anti-government insurgents operating in Rhodesia (now Zimbabwe) and South Africa. The Soviet bloc also has been allowed preferred access to Mozambique's natural resources: Moscow takes fish; East Germany, agriculture products (mainly citrus fruit and rice), textiles and coal; Cuba, tobacco, sugar and coffee; Romania, cotton; and Bulgaria, wheat, maize, rice, and beef.

Immediately following Machel's death, Soviet leaders gathered to review Soviet policy toward Mozambique. They apparently decided to speed arms deliveries. Another 100-man contingent of Soviet bloc advisers was dispatched to Maputo, the Mozambigue capital. And Red Army General Yevgeny Ivanovsky, deputy defense minister and commander-in-chief of Soviet ground forces, was sent to Machel's funeral to demonstrate publicly Moscow's commitment to Mozambique's defense.

The "Turn to the West"

By 1980, socialist economic policies and mismanagement had so devastated Mozambique's economy that Machel asked to join the Council for Mutual Economic Assistance (COMECON), the Soviet bloc economic organization. Moscow, itself financially strapped, turned down Machel's request. He then turned to the West for assistance.

U.S. Assistant Secretary of State for African Affairs Chester Crocker responded enthusiastically. If Machel was willing to accept Western economic assistance, Crocker apparently believed, perhaps he would be willing to drop his ties to the Soviets as well. And, over time, Machel would come to realize that while Moscow could provide him with military aid, only the West could provide him the economic aid he needed. Faced with such a choice, Crocker hoped, Machel would choose the West.

Accordingly, the U.S. sponsored Mozambique for membership in the International Monetary Fund and the World Bank, and gave Mozambique direct bilateral assistance. Coupled with the economic assistance was a diplomatic campaign aimed at achieving a treaty between Mozambigue and South Africa. The Nkomati Accord, signed in March 1984, committed South Africa to end its support for the RENAMO freedom fighters; Mozambique agreed to expel Soviet-trained cadres of the African National

Congress, which had used Mozambique as the headquarters for their actions against South Africa.

The zenith of the U.S. campaign to woo Mozambique came in September 1985, when Machel visited Washington. There he met with Ronald Reagan, who called him "amigo," or "friend." The Administration even asked Congress to give Mozambique $4.6 million over two years in military assistance. To date, the U.S. has provided $78 million in direct bilateral assistance to Mozambique, and has voted for $154 million more in multilateral loans.

But the "turn to the West" has not been genuine. The Machel regime never gave up any of its fundamental communist beliefs or its ties to the Soviet Union. Too many observers err in calling Machel—and other Third World communists—"Marxists." In fact, these leaders are not so much "Marxists" as they are "Leninists." That is, they care less about organizing their national economies than about achieving and maintaining power. Their attraction to the Soviet model is not to its economic system, which has proved disastrous, but to its political system, which offers a guaranteed method of obtaining and keeping power. And their attraction to Moscow and Havana is to regimes that provide support for their power consolidation.

As long as Leninism flourishes in Mozambique, nothing fundamental has changed. The FRELIMO regime's willingness to accept Western economic aid in no way signals any lessening of its commitment to Leninism or of its ties to the Soviet bloc.

In fact, it may reflect a new stage of Soviet strategy for the Third World: use whatever means are neccesary and appropriate to establish communist regimes in the Third World, then encourage them to accept Western economic assistance. This accomplishes three goals: it releases Moscow from the economic burden of supporting its burgeoning Third World empire, it seduces the West into expending its own scarce resources in the elusive search for a communist regime that can be weaned away from the Soviet bloc, and it stabilizes Soviet-backed regimes which otherwise would deteriorate because of ruinous economic policies.

The New Government

After weeks of deliberation following the October [1986] death of Samora Machel, FRELIMO chose former foreign minister Joaquim Chissano as the new president. The reasons: First, Chissano was known to have supported Machel's "turn to the West," and clearly was viewed as the contender most likely to guarantee continued Western assistance to the regime. Second, he was younger than the other candidates, and was believed to have the vitality necessary to shoulder the triple tasks of heading the party, government, and armed forces. Third, Chissano was black, and was not subject to increasing anti-*mestico* (i.e., mixed race) resentment

in Mozambique.

Chissano's selection was greeted with relief by liberals and diplomats in the West. They portrayed him as a moderate. *The Washington Post*, for instance, headlined its story "Moderate Marxist Succeeds Machel," and called Chissano "Mozambique's pragmatic, westward-leaning foreign minister."

The truth is that Chissano was a member of the original group of radicals, the Algeria Group. According to his official FRELIMO biography, he was sent "out of the country" (presumably to either Cuba or the Soviet Union) for military training twice between 1964 and 1966. He holds the rank of major general in the Mozambique Armed Forces, granted for his service as FRELIMO's security chief during the war, when he purged the party of non-communists.

"The Machel regime never gave up any of its fundamental communist beliefs or its ties to the Soviet Union."

In his first speech as party Chairman, Chissano reaffirmed his Marxist-Leninist commitment. He declared: "We are going to strengthen our FRELIMO party . . . we will be instransigent with deviations that are contrary to party policy. . . . Our party has defined the construction of socialism the objective of Mozambican society . . . because only a socialist society guarantees to the people as a whole equal rights and opportunities." In case anyone doubted his commitment to the Soviet bloc, he added: "The FRELIMO party will continue to follow the principles contained in its Statutes and in its relations with the Marxist-Leninist parties and with other socialist states."

[In March 1987], another regime official specifically rejected the notion of Mozambique's "turn to the West." Information Minister Teodato Hunguana declared in London that "Mozambique is not shifting from one side to the other, from West to East." "The Soviet Union has been a historic ally," he said, adding that this had not changed.

The Founding of RENAMO

The Mozambique National Resistance (RENAMO) was established in April 1977 by Andre Matsangaisse, with the help of disaffected FRELIMO militants, Portuguese exiles, and the Rhodesian Central Intelligence Organization (CIO). Rhodesia backed RENAMO to retaliate for Machel's support for anti-Rhodesian guerrillas. Matsangaisse was killed in 1979, and his lieutenant, Afonso Dhlakama, took control of RENAMO.

When Robert Mugabe successfuly wrested power from Ian Smith in Rhodesia, he immediately cut off assistance to RENAMO. South African Military Intelligence (SAMI) took on the task of aiding the insurgency, and through the early 1980s, RENAMO continued to grow.

RENAMO first unveiled its political platform in August 1981. In effect it is a draft constitution for post-FRELIMO Mozambique. Its seven chapters deal with politics, economics, justice, constitutional matters, health and education, public services, and foreign policy. It calls for the dissolution of the communist system of government, and guarantees "the people's right to choose and freely vote on the country's political, social and economic system."

"FRELIMO has not reduced its ties to the Soviet bloc; it merely has taken U.S. aid . . . and quite likely will continue to do so as long as it is offered with no political strings."

The Nkomati Accord of March 1984 ending South African support stunned Dhlakama. But RENAMO did not dissolve, as Samora Machel had assumed it would. Dhlakama proved that he was not a "South African puppet." In fact, RENAMO became even stronger, carrying the war for the first time into all ten of Mozambique's provinces. RENAMO increased its combat contacts with FRELIMO forces over the next three years: in 1983, RENAMO averaged 100 contacts per month; in 1984, 150 per month; in 1985, 200 per month; and by 1986, the average approached 250 per month. Moreover, in an important indicator of trends in a guerrilla war, RENAMO began initiating an increasing share of the contacts, from 60 percent in 1984 to 85 percent by mid-1986.

Regional Allies

As FRELIMO's position weakened, Machel began consulting his regional allies. Returning from one such meeting, his plane crashed on South African territory. In the debris, South African authorities found documents outlining a conspiracy by Mozambique, Zimbabwe, the Soviet Union, and Cuba to overthrow the neighboring Malawian government. Though these nations denied the charges and claimed the documents were forgeries, Zambian President Kenneth Kaunda reportedly confirmed their authenticity.

Zimbabwe, which already had contributed an estimated 10,000 troops to defending the Beira Corridor (which runs from the Mozambican port of Beira to the Zimbabwean capital, Harare) pledged more assistance. Zambia and Tanzania also increased their commitments to FRELIMO. The Soviets speeded the delivery of arms already promised, and there are unconfirmed reports that two battalions of Cuban combat forces have arrived in Beira, with another five expected shortly.

Following Chissano's installation as President, rumors spread through Mozambique and Lisbon that he would soon open negotiations with RENAMO. Though Chissano continues publicly to deny the rumors, the evidence is strong. Senior members of the Mozambican Armed Forces are in contact with RENAMO, and have pressed Chissano to open talks. They also are believed to have warned RENAMO leaders secretly of upcoming government attacks on RENAMO bases.

The Failure of Constructive Engagement

"Constructive engagement" has been Assistant Secretary of State Chester Crocker's policy of dealing diplomatically with all the governments of southern Africa. He believed that by reducing conflict in southern Africa, he could reduce Soviet influence. The flaw was in the premise: not all reductions in violence decrease Soviet influence. Crocker's mistake was in identifying U.S. interests with a particular regime, instead of with the nation as a whole. In Mozambique, that meant aligning the U.S. with a self-proclaimed Marxist-Leninist regime closely tied to the Soviet Union. If that meant downplaying FRELIMO's ideological beliefs, so be it. In congressional testimony, Crocker said "We do not consider the Government of Mozambique to be . . . a communist government." He continued: "The Government of Mozambique has been working systematically in the past four or five years to move away from its previously close embrace with Moscow."

But FRELIMO has not reduced its ties to the Soviet bloc; it merely has taken U.S. and other Western nations' economic assistance, and quite likely will continue to do so as long as it is offered with no political strings. An estimated 3,500 Soviet, Cuban, and East German military advisers still are in Mozambique, and the Chissano regime recently requested—and received—even more to help fight RENAMO. Delegations from the Soviet Union, East Germany, and North Korea were in Maputo simultaneously, all negotiating increased support levels with FRELIMO. FRELIMO is not moving away from the Soviets; the Mozambican communists are moving closer. Clearly, the campaign to wean away Mozambique from Moscow has not worked.

A New US Policy

A new U.S. policy is needed. The U.S. should:
• *Terminate economic assistance to FRELIMO.* The State Department justification for aiding FRELIMO is that it will entice FRELIMO into coming closer to the West. But making FRELIMO's economy run more efficiently is not enough; that simply would

mean helping to create a lean, efficient communist regime in Mozambique. FRELIMO's putative movement away from Marxism is not nearly as important as its break with Leninism. As long as the regime maintains its Leninist political structure, nothing fundamental has changed.

• *End famine assistance.* The U.S. recently announced it would provide FRELIMO $50 million in famine aid. The most recent U.S. experience with famine aid to a communist government in Africa was disastrous. Some U.S. aid actually contributed to the death toll in Ethiopia. Until U.S. famine relief officials can guarantee that aid to FRELIMO will not be misused in a similar fashion, it should be held up. If FRELIMO cannot make such guarantees, the program should be terminated.

• *Launch a public diplomacy campaign.* The West, and the U.S. in particular, has been fooled by the FRELIMO regime. FRELIMO is as rigidly communist as it ever was, and will continue to be so. The U.S. should launch a diplomatic campaign aimed at exposing the true nature of the FRELIMO regime and at persuading other Western allies to terminate assistance to FRELIMO.

• *Upgrade contacts with RENAMO.* No high-level U.S. policy maker has ever met a RENAMO representative. This has resulted in a profound lack of knowledge about RENAMO's structure, political goals, and military strategy, that has manifested itself in the current flawed policies. The Administration should immediately send a high-level envoy to RENAMO-held areas of Mozambique to report back on the real situation.

"After six years and $78 million, U.S. influence has not increased and Soviet influence has not decreased."

• *Demand withdrawal of all foreign forces.* Only the combined forces of the Soviet Union, Cuba, East Germany, North Korea, Zimbabwe, Zambia, and Tanzania keep the Chissano regime in power. Their withdrawal would force the regime to open national reconciliation talks and would be the best indicator of the regime's sincerity in its professed desire to "turn to the West."

• *Push for national reconciliation.* RENAMO will not go away. It will not allow political and economic stabilization in Mozambique unless its goals are met. The only way to end the strife in Mozambique is to negotiate an end with RENAMO. The U.S. should push FRELIMO to begin negotiations immediately.

• *Consider Reagan Doctrine assistance to RENAMO.* If the Chissano regime refuses to negotiate with RENAMO, the U.S. should signal strongly its break with the communists and place itself squarely on the side of the democratic resistance forces. Such action, in the context of U.S. assistance to the UNITA freedom fighters in Angola, would restore consistency to U.S. policy in southern Africa. As in Angola, RENAMO's greatest needs are the anti-aircraft missiles necessary to deprive regime forces of air superiority.

Applying the Reagan Doctrine

For ten years the communist FRELIMO regime in Mozambique has been one of Moscow's staunchest allies in Africa. It has provided support to Soviet-backed insurgents operating against pro-Western governments, given the Soviets access to ports on the Indian Ocean, and allowed Soviet bloc nations preferred access to Mozambique's natural resources. Meanwhile, a pro-Western insurgency has waged an increasingly successful guerrilla war against the regime, and now controls 80 percent of the countryside. The communist regime is so weak that it must depend on 16,500 foreign troops and military advisers to keep it in power.

U.S. policy toward Mozambique has been a failure. Instead of pursuing the promising path of the Reagan Doctrine, and supporting the democratic resistance forces, Ronald Reagan and George Shultz have listened to those who claim they can wean away the communist FRELIMO regime from its close ties to the Soviet Union. For six years, the U.S. has tried this strategy, providing political and economic support to the Mozambican communist regime, while specifically rejecting the cause of the pro-Western RENAMO insurgents. After six years and $78 million, U.S. influence has not increased and Soviet influence has not decreased. Clearly, it is time for a new policy—one aimed at winning freedom for Mozambique and one that affirms the Reagan Doctrine.

William Pascoe is a policy analyst specializing in the Third World for The Heritage Foundation, a conservative Washington think tank.

"With continuing war and drought and economic manipulation by external powers, Mozambicans and their independence will be the losers."

Soviet Influence in Mozambique Is Not the Issue

David Munro

It isn't just Ethiopia. Ignored by the spotlight of television and the press, at least seven other African countries are suffering the plagues of famine and war. In Mozambique food trucks can only move with military escorts to protect them from rebels known as the M.N.R. Like the Contras in Nicaragua, the M.N.R., or RENAMO as they are also known, have no real political motivation, and in fact are just another proxy army, their pay-masters being the South African government who wish to make life unbearable for Mozambicans and FRELIMO, their socialist government.

During the war of independence to end illegal white minority rule in neighboring Rhodesia, Ken Flowers, Ian Smith's head of the Rhodesian Central Intelligence Organization, decided to set up a private army, a kind of fifth column, which would operate from within Mozambique and be composed mainly of Mozambicans. In 1974 Mozambique, a former Portuguese colony, was all but independent after ten years of ruinous and merciless war, and Mozambicans who had been part of PIDE, the colonial secret police (which like the Guardia Nacional in Nicaragua had served their masters' whims in the years of blood-letting), fled to Rhodesia, fearing post-independence vengeance. These men together with members of the elite and hated G.E.P. paratroop force, whom the Portuguese had also formed, were recruited by Flowers for two specific tasks. Firstly, they were to attack Mozambican-based units of Robert Mugabe's liberation army, and secondly, since independent black states were anathema to Flowers and Ian Smith, this private army was to begin a process of armed destabilization of FRELIMO.

South Africa does not like black independent states

on her doorstep either, for the same reason that the U.S. has no love of independent states in Central America—if they are successful they might be an example to others, and that would never do—so when Zimbabwe finally won her independence in 1980 and Flowers could no longer pay the M.N.R., Pretoria took over these bandits, paying them to attack vital economic and strategic installations and increase the internal pressure on FRELIMO.

The Name of the Game

Of course, it is not Pretoria's intention that the M.N.R. should win and become a government (the M.N.R. is capable of neither anyway), but simply that they make life and post independence development impossible. Furthermore, the situation has the tacit approval of certain western governments because FRELIMO has an ever-growing military and economic relationship with the Soviet Union, which has her own motives for being there. So hurting Mozambique hurts Moscow. And that in the end is the name of the game.

From 1980 onwards the South African government poured money into the M.N.R. providing equipment, training and logistical support to bandits operating from bases both in South Africa and within Mozambique itself. As the war intensified whole provinces were cut off from Maputo, the capital; roads and tracks were mined and travelers ambushed. The vital rail link from the oil port of Beira, on which land-locked Zimbabwe depends, was cut, as was the line which comes from Zambia and runs through Tete province to the coast. Vast stocks of coal, normally a lucrative export, built up at the pit heads in Tete because the trains couldn't run. At the same time South Africa cut back 75 percent of her use of the port of Maputo, thereby reducing Mozambique's foreign earnings (though Pretoria must have instructed the M.N.R. not to touch the rail line that comes from South Africa because it is

From *The Four Horsemen: The Flames of War in the Third World* by David Munro, © 1987. Published by arrangement with Lyle Stuart.

still carrying South African coal for export through Maputo, which is a cheaper route than using her own Port Elizabeth).

In the two years 1982/83, the M.N.R. destroyed 840 schools, 212 health posts, a minimum of 200 villages and over 900 shops. Through those two years the war in all of its forms cost Mozambique over eighteen hundred million dollars. All of this, combined with the effects of economic sabotage by the departing Portuguese colonists, forced Mozambique in effect to declare bankruptcy in 1984 by asking to reschedule payment of her foreign debts, which were then in excess of $1.4 billion, saying that she would not be able to service the interest of $714 million until 1990.

Then came the drought that has hit so many countries in sub-Saharan Africa and in early 1984 a cyclone that destroyed roads and powerlines and swept away vital top soil. Mozambique was on its knees; the elements and destabilization were working.

The Nkomati Agreement

It would have been impractical and not politically expedient to turn to Moscow for combat troops, and economic help was being denied her by COMECON. Finally, with no other alternative, Mozambique was forced to sign the Nkomati agreement of March 1984 with South Africa. On the surface it might seem fine to make a "non-aggression" pact with so powerful a neighbor, the terms of which were that South Africa would end her control and support of the M.N.R. and in exchange Mozambique should expel members of the A.N.C. (the African National Congress that is fighting to abolish apartheid in South Africa and is to Black South Africans what the P.L.O. is to Palestinians). However, for a front-line state to sign any agreement with Pretoria is nothing short of defeat, and of course while Mozambique did, with great pain, expel the A.N.C., South Africa continued active support and direction of the M.N.R.

All of this increased Mozambique's military dependence on Moscow, with more and more Soviet military advisers coming in to help run the war and thereby giving Moscow the chance to exert some influence over access to Mozambican resources.

By 1984/85 the famine had really taken hold and M.N.R. attacks made the task of getting food through to the starving at times almost impossible.

A Matter of Survival

Though the details may be different from the Horn of Africa, the overall problem remains the same. The will of the so-called "free world" to put pressure on Pretoria to end the war and help feed Mozambicans is not conditioned by their need but by "geo-political interests."

"Do you have the milk powder, the maize, etc., that you need?"

REV. LLOYD THOMAS and NURSE GILLIAN WRIGHT, Volunteer Aid Workers from South African Baptist Church: "No we have nothing. They get a government supply of maize meal but they actually need things like milk, milk powder and general high protein foods . . . they have nothing, they have nothing. . . ."

"Have you asked for that or has the camp asked for that?"

"The government is doing its best but the enormity of the need is the problem. Even if the medical supplies and food are brought into the area, getting it to the people is a major problem."

"In the once-rich Portuguese resort town of Beira they have no electricity, no water, little food and no beer."

"How much are the efforts of the government and people like yourselves being hampered by the war, by the existence of the M.N.R.?"

"They have attacked this camp more than once in the past month. Most of their banditry is geared towards taking food and just terrorizing the population."

"But the M.N.R. claim that they are representing the population of Mozambique, that the population supports them."

"When someone holds a gun to your head I don't think you have much political choice. It's a matter of survival." . . .

Nothing Can Move

Mozambique is a large country and communications between Maputo and the northern provinces are bad at the best of times. But with the M.N.R. constantly cutting the roads, nothing can move. People can't trade; kids can't go to school, so the future is also being ransomed. In countries like this—Nicaragua or Vietnam, for example—either at war or living with the legacy, it is easy as a foreigner to be overwhelmed by the situation, to be taken over by the statistics and the politics, to be so concerned with the overall issues that one misses, if one is not careful, the minutiae. But it is the little things that really show what the situation means to ordinary people. For example, the first words that a foreigner will hear from a Mozambican are, "Have you got any soap?"

In the once-rich Portuguese resort town of Beira they have no electricity, no water, little food and no beer. The Hotel Don Carlos, in the past a favorite with the colonials, can offer you a bed, but nothing else, and in the center of town even the "Dollar Shop"—that Alladin's cave where foreigners and well-to-do Mozambicans alike can normally spend their greenbacks on imported goods, foodstuffs and ice-cold canned beer—is closed because the shelves are bare.

There are trucks here to transport food to the interior of the province, but since the oil terminal in the docks was hit by the M.N.R. there is no fuel for them, and anyway the roads into the interior are mined.

DR. EVO GARRIDO, Maputo General Hospital: "The people is suffering from hunger and from war at the same time. You cannot do anything to develop Mozambique if you don't stop the war. If you try to put in a pump, they come and destroy the pump. If you try to build a house, they come and destroy the house. If you try to make some crops, they put fire on the crops. If you send a motor car with something to the people, they stop the car, they destroy the car. It's impossible. First of all you must stop the war. We must have peace."

Development is the key word, but development might just help the Mozambicans towards real independence. . . .

Nkomati Accord Violated

The security situation in some provinces is so bad that the only way to get relief to the starving is with an aging DC-3. The irony is that while South Africa pays the M.N.R. to wage war in Mozambique, the Mozambican Red Cross has to pay a South African company for the use of the plane.

CONGRESSMAN TED WEISS: "Well, when we were there in August of 1983, it was quite clear that South Africa in fact was engaged in all-out war against the Front-Line nations and it was using a variety of actions to destabilize the governments of those countries, either to keep them off-keel or make them so vulnerable economically that they would in fact enter into negotiated agreements with South Africa. And South Africa points to those agreements as an indication that, in fact, it does too get along with its neighbors: 'Look at the agreements we are able to negotiate with them.'"

DR. CHESTER CROCKER, U.S. Assistant Secretary of State, Africa: "The Nkomati agreement was a series of undertakings in which the Mozambicans agreed that they would not serve as a springboard for A.N.C. activity directed against South Africa, and South Africans in a reciprocal manner undertook not to become involved in serving as a springboard for M.N.R. activity into Mozambique. It is our general impression that both sides have lived up to their commitments in that regard. The fact that the war inside Mozambique has not come to an end, that there is no ceasefire, is of great concern to us and as long as that situation continues will be of great concern to us, because clearly one of the fruits of the Nkomati process was to bring about stability and peace and development for Mozambique, but I think it would be going well beyond that fact to argue that

the reason that that war continues is . . . as simple as your question implies . . . that cross border supply of the M.N.R. by South Africa hasn't ceased."

CONGRESSMAN TED WEISS: "The Mozambicans in fact adhered to the commitments that they made. The South Africans, for whatever reason, have not been able to implement their side of the bargain and there can be an argument as to whether it's in fact the government of South Africa or whether it's the military within South Africa, whether it's the Portuguese nationalists who are calling the shots either in Portugal or in South Africa. The fact is that Mozambique did not get what it bargained for and the United States again has been of the opinion that working behind the scenes it could be more effective with South Africa than publicly condemning it."

DR. CHESTER CROCKER: "No doubt there's been private trafficking and so forth, but I don't think that the South African armed forces are likely to violate the stated policy of the State President of South Africa, which is that this activity was supposed to cease as of the signing of the Nkomati agreement."

"Constructive engagement has been taken as a signal by Pretoria that they have carte blanche to do whatever they like . . . to their Black neighbors."

"I accept that it was supposed to cease. What is however quite apparent is that there is still cross-border supplying of the M.N.R. by the South African military, that there is contact on a daily basis between South African military personnel and the M.N.R. I know that South African military officers have entered Mozambican territory since Nkomati—I've seen photographs of them shown to me by the M.N.R. I can't believe that the Intelligence Services of the United States—which is far more sophisticated in its information gathering techniques than I am—don't have similar information."

"Well, you may have information that is not available to me. I don't have such information. My . . . information would indicate that having helped to create the M.N.R. into the rebel force that it is, the South African government has found it rather difficult . . . to bring about a pattern of control over its activities such that you'd see an actual ceasefire develop. We do not have information that would confirm your statement that the South African military is continuing to supply the Mozambique resistance."

Dr. Crocker is the architect of the Reagan administration's policy towards South Africa known as "Constructive Engagement," another fine piece of official newspeak. Constructive engagement means that rather than the imposition of effective sanctions or actual condemnation of apartheid, the White House believes that it can change the political course of events in southern Africa by on-going "dialogue." So periodically Dr. Crocker visits Pretoria and informs the South African government that the President and the people of the United States want to see an end to apartheid and the South Africans are polite but obstinate, and then Dr. Crocker goes away again. This policy ignores the fact that Pretoria has no intention of anything other than cosmetic change and that, since the implementation of constructive engagement, violence and repression have increased. In effect, constructive engagement has been taken as a signal by Pretoria that they have carte blanche to do whatever they like to their own Black dis-enfranchized majority and to their Black neighbors.

Diplomatic Lies

It continues to be a constant source of amazement to me that diplomats and politicians lie blatantly, and at times unnecessarily, particularly to the media, when they know—as Dr. Crocker must have when he said, "We do not have information that would confirm your statement that the South African military is continuing to supply the Mozambique resistance"—the lie is so transparent. Perhaps they feel that this is a necessary part of the game of deceit that officialdom plays with the public. Perhaps if Dr. Crocker admitted that he knew of the on-going support of the M.N.R. by South Africa he would feel that he was compromising the U.S. relationship with Pretoria, a relationship that is motivated by balance sheets. If that is the case, compromising the lives of ordinary Mozambicans is probably of only passing concern. If on the other hand Dr. Crocker was not lying, then the C.I.A. Station Chief for the area ought to be hauled over the coals for not being able to furnish the Assistant Secretary of State with information that was available to me and as a shaper of U.S. foreign policy he should have had.

Whatever reasons Dr. Crocker may have had for his denial, the South African government admitted their continuing and active involvement with the M.N.R. in September 1985.

Though the long-term goals for Mozambique of South Africa and the West may differ slightly, they remain fundamentally the same and to those ends they work together towards the subjugation of FRELIMO and the easing out of the Soviet Union. In 1981, South African commandos bombed a suburb of Maputo, purportedly acting on intelligence supplied to them by the C.I.A.

DEREK PARDEY, Development Agency Field Officer, Maputo: "After the Matola raid in January 1981, Mozambique exposed a C.I.A. network in Mozambique and expelled quite a few C.I.A. agents who were working in the American embassy. The American ambassador left at that time, and the Americans just wouldn't give any aid for something like two, three years until round about the time of the Nkomati Accord. There was a visit from a U.S. AID man and the situation improved. But for three years, the country that probably gives more aid than any other in the world just decided not to give any to Mozambique."

Little Help from the Soviets

During that three years probably one hundred thousand Mozambicans died of starvation. But what was the Soviet Union doing if the States would not help? The answer is precious little. They have introduced teachers and doctors and geologists, but have trained few Mozambicans in these much-needed professions and have declared that they cannot support FRELIMO because it professes to be only Marxist oriented and not a full Marxist-Leninist party. If that is the criterion then Moscow should put its own house in order. . . . Finally, they have refused Mozambique access to COMECON financial support on the grounds that they are economically unstable. They don't apply the same rules to Vietnam or Cuba, but then, unlike Vietnam and Cuba, Mozambique has declared that no foreign power, West or East, shall have military bases on her soil, and so far Moscow has not been able to turn the screw hard enough to force Mozambique to change this policy. So lacking rights to have bases in Mozambique, Moscow does not perceive any great immediate strategic gain, but being there is better than not—it keeps the door open and annoys the West. Therefore, until such time as she can exert enough pressure to gain even limited base facilities, she will simply continue to send advisors to help run the war and supply weapons to fight it; any other help will not be forthcoming. . . .

"What was the Soviet Union doing if the [United] States would not help? The answer is precious little."

Russian armaments land at Maputo port alongside Western grain; both necessary for the country's survival, as both donor blocs pressure Mozambique for its allegiance. But it may be too late. Because of the years without help and the continued backing of the M.N.R., by October 1986 the forecast was that three million people were suffering the effects of primary malnutrition and without massive grain supplies, fuel and transport they would all die. But the war goes on and as the U.S. Senate voted to overturn President Reagan's veto on their sanctions against South Africa, Mr. Pic Botha, the South African Foreign Minister, threatened in a television interview that the sanctions would cause him to effectively cut off food supplies to the Front-Lines States.

It is by no means clear who will win this square on the geo-political chess board, the West or the Soviet Union, neither is it clear who will win internally, FRELIMO or the M.N.R. But what is quite clear is that with continuing war and drought and economic manipulation by external powers, Mozambicans and their independence will be the losers.

"[The over two hundred other nations on this planet] have never individually or collectively agreed that the super powers could use it as their battleground."

DICK CLARKE, Aspen Institute for Humanitarian Studies: "American foreign policy's always difficult to figure out and I think it's particularly difficult in this administration. It seems clear to me that our practice or our policy in Mozambique really is to undermine the Soviet position, and I think the reason is that it seems fairly clear that the Soviets are giving a lower priority to southern Africa now. They've got great economic problems at home; they've got problems in eastern Europe and so forth, and they're not prepared to put the kind of money into Mozambique and perhaps into other countries in Third World areas that they once were. They haven't had the success in the Third World that I think many people thought they might have a decade ago, and so I think the American policy clearly is to get into Mozambique in every way they legally can, in the hope of winning that regime away from the Soviet Union. We don't do that in many other cases. There are other cases—Central America, for example—in which we take exactly the opposite position, but consistency has never been one of our strong points."

CONGRESSMAN TED WEISS: "George Hauser has said that Henry Kissinger's attitude towards policy in Africa was that it reflected a global strategy in which African realities were secondary to a perceived Soviet challenge, and I think that's probably accurate. It's not to say that American policy does not interest itself in the well-being of Third World populations for their own sake, but that really becomes secondary. In many places around the globe we don't get involved even though the conditions and situations may be just as critical or devastating as they are in places where we do get involved. . . . So often the only criteria for where we do get involved is that it has played some role in the East/West struggle."

DR. CHESTER CROCKER: "I don't think we have any strategic aspirations vis-à-vis Mozambique. We would like to see a non-aligned Mozambique and have a full and productive relationship there that would include active assistance programs, in the first instance, in the famine emergency, but more importantly in the field of economic development."

DICK CLARKE: "Well I'm sure that America's interest in Mozambique is anti-Soviet. I mean we've never shown any interest in any country in Africa that I know of for any other reason, certainly in southern Africa—so I'm sure it's strategic."

BEREKET SELASSIE, Professor of International Law: "Beginning from Angola in 1975, when the M.P.L.A., the Angola government, was faced with a South African invasion and the C.I.A. inspired invasion from Zaire, the feeling in South Africa and the Western allies was that there was literally a revolutionary wave sweeping down southern Africa which might overwhelm politically, ideologically that subcontinent, and they decided to stem the tide of this wave."

DR. CHESTER CROCKER. "We did believe we had to reassert Western leadership and American leadership in a region where we had been on the receiving end for six of seven years in a row. There was a negative trend for sure. We were determined to reverse that trend. *We do not accept any legitimate right of foreign intervention by our global adversary in southern Africa."* (Emphasis added.)

Who Owns the World?

Whatever Washington and Moscow and latterly Peking may want to believe, the world does not belong to them. There are over two hundred other nations on this planet and to my knowledge they have never individually or collectively agreed that the super powers could use it as their battleground. Global adversaries indeed! That may seem an over-simplistic and obvious statement but it is none the less true. However, for as long as they continue to regard each other as global adversaries, they will do nothing but add to the turmoil and carnage that is the legacy of imperial domination and interference.

British filmmaker David Munro spent fifteen months traveling and taking photographs in eight different war areas in the Third World.

"The Soviets have actively sought to limit and reduce strategic nuclear arms. They have even been willing to make unilateral concessions."

The US Should Negotiate with the Soviets

Michael MccGwire

Arms control is a value-laden term, dependent for its meaning not only on a definition of the words but on the viewpoint with which one looks at the process. Most Americans assume that the West has sought the mutual limitation of strategic nuclear weapons while the Soviets have obstructed negotiations. The record of the last two decades argues otherwise.

In truth, Americans have always been ambivalent about the value of arms control. Many believe that it works against U.S. interests. Until the late 1960s, the Soviets shared this ambivalence, believing that world war would inevitably be nuclear and that arms control agreements would impair their ability to survive such a war. Then in 1966 they concluded that nuclear war—and the devastation of Russia— might possibly be avoided. Under that assumption, arms control agreements would not only help avoid war but also promote Soviet military objectives in the event that war could not be avoided. Since then the Soviets have actively sought to limit and reduce strategic nuclear arms. They have even been willing to make unilateral concessions to achieve agreement.

The assumption that the Soviets are eager to seize any chance, however slight, to destroy the United States, coupled with the focus on our own interests and vulnerabilities, has blinded most of us to the tangible evidence of the Soviets' interest in arms control. That evidence is apparent in their strategic missile programs—and the cuts they imposed on those programs. Moreover, the Soviet readiness to negotiate is documented in the memoirs of several U.S. officials. Most recently, in his account of his time as secretary of state, Alexander Haig writes that from the earliest days of the Reagan administration, the Soviets indicated their eagerness to enter into

arms control talks on almost any basis.

American misperceptions about Soviet motivations have almost certainly resulted in missed opportunities for meaningful arms control agreements. A continued misreading of Soviet interests and aims could lead the United States to adopt policies whose results are the opposite of what it desires. The Strategic Defense Initiative is a case in point. This article explains the logic of the Soviet policy on arms control and sets out concrete evidence of the changed approach. It then examines the roots of U.S. arms control policy and the reasons for our misperceptions. Finally it considers what this combination portends for arms control in the wake of the Reagan-Gorbachev meeting in Reykjavik last October [1986].

Avoiding Devastation

Since the 1950s Soviet doctrine had held that a world war—a war they absolutely want to avoid but cannot afford to lose—would inevitably be nuclear and just as inevitably entail massive strikes on Russia. In such a fight to the finish, where defeat would be synonymous with extinction, the twin Soviet objectives were to preserve the socialist system and destroy the capitalist one. The latter objective required nuclear attacks on the United States and its allies, and to the extent these attacks could disarm the West's ability to retaliate, they would help preserve the socialist system. Soviet strategy was therefore predicated on successful nuclear preemption.

The Soviet belief that a world war would inevitably be nuclear reflected the declared Western policy of relying on "massive retaliation" and NATO's stated readiness to resort immediately to nuclear weapons in the event of war in Europe, policies that went back to the mid-1950s. The West began to move away from those policies in 1961 when the Kennedy administration introduced the

Michael MccGwire, "Why the Soviets Are Serious About Arms Control," *The Brookings Review,* Spring 1987. Reprinted by permission of The Brookings Institute.

concept of "flexible response," proposing to check a Soviet offensive in Europe for several days using conventional forces only. Initially the Soviets misread this concept as an attempt to improve NATO's ability to wage nuclear war, in part because its introduction coincided with the deployment of new U.S. nuclear weapons in Europe. By 1964, however, the Soviets were coming to recognize that flexible response implied that a war in Europe might start with a conventional phase, although they continued to assume that nuclear escalation was inevitable.

"For the Soviet Union, arms control implies limiting and reducing the size of nuclear arsenals."

It was only in the second half of 1966, probably as the result of a reevaluation following France's withdrawal from NATO, that the Soviets appear to have reached two conclusions. One was that a war in Europe would not inevitably lead to massive strikes on Russia, except in retaliation for an attack on North America. The other was that the size and diversity of the U.S. strategic arsenal meant that a preemptive strike on the United States would do little to limit the devastation of Russia. During this period the strategic opportunity presented by the NATO doctrine of "flexible response" became clear to the Soviets. If, during this initial conventional phase of a war in Europe, the Soviets could neutralize NATO's theater nuclear forces, they could remove the first rung of escalation. If they could knock NATO out of the war using nonnuclear forces, the question of intercontinental escalation might become moot.

These new considerations led the Soviets to conclude in December 1966 that a world war would not necessarily be nuclear and, even if it were, it would not necessarily include massive strikes on Russia. Under this new doctrine, it became logically possible for the Soviets to adopt the objective of avoiding the nuclear devastation of Russia. . . .

Misreading the Soviets

Given the striking evidence of Soviet interest in arms control, how does one account for the widespread perception that the Soviet Union has to be pressured into negotiations? Part of the explanation lies with the Soviets themselves. They see arms control as an incremental process and, until recently, have responded negatively to radical new initiatives. Once embarked on negotiations, the Soviets aggressively pursue relative advantage, seeking to cap Western capabilities and fence off dangerous new developments whenever possible, while protecting their own programs and possibilities

for future development. At the same time, their fear of disclosing key military objectives accentuates their natural secretiveness.

The misreading is also a function of U.S. domestic politics. To gain support for arms control from the conservative right, successive administrations have funded new weapons programs, explaining that they were necessary to bring the Soviets to the negotiating table. But the main reason for misperception lies in our mistaken assumption that Soviet arms control policy continues to mirror the ambivalence of the U.S. policy.

The United States acquired strategic superiority in World War II and has been understandably reluctant to give it up. U.S. policymakers have used arms control negotiations to limit and, if possible, reduce Soviet inventories in areas where the Soviets were catching up or moving ahead. U.S. negotiators have rejected limits in areas where asymmetries in force structure or advanced technology give the United States an edge. The Strategic Defense Initiative (SDI) is the latest variation on this theme.

During the 1960s and 1970s the emerging concepts of parity, equivalence, and sufficiency ran into tenacious resistance in the United States. In the 1980s the Reagan administration sought explicitly to restore some measure of superiority, while denigrating existing arms control agreements. The SDI reflects this logic. Defense Secretary Caspar W. Weinberger explained to the Senate Armed Services Committee on February 1, 1984, that the SDI offered the prospect of returning to the situation of the immediate post-World War II years when the United States was "the only nation with nuclear weapons and did not threaten others with [them]."

Differing Theories

However, the difference in the two sides' approaches extends beyond the level of their interest in arms control to the theoretical underpinnings of the term. For the Soviet Union, arms control implies limiting and reducing the size of nuclear arsenals. For the United States, it has more to do with crisis stability, a concept that derives from nuclear deterrence theory and its offshoot, reassurance theory. Deterrence theory, which emerged in the early 1950s and reflected the lessons of Munich and World War II, held that Soviet aggression in Europe could only be prevented by the threat of dire punishment and that the credibility of that deterrence depended on the certainty of the U.S. response. The means of retaliation, therefore, had to be held totally secure, a requirement that gave full rein to a new form of worst-case analysis as imaginative theorists sought to discover possible chinks in the armor of assured response.

In the second half of the 1950s, as the Soviets began to acquire the capability to strike at North America, other theorists focused on a danger that stemmed from the nature of nuclear weapons and did not depend on either side having aggressive intentions. In a confrontational situation, the advantage of disarming the other side by getting in the first blow was so great that a prudent national leader might be prompted to launch a nuclear strike on the mere suspicion that the other side was contemplating war. This pressure to preempt in a crisis introduced a new concern for the "stability" of deterrence. It became necessary to find ways of reassuring the Soviets in a crisis that the United States would not initiate preemptive war.

U.S. arms control theory had its intellectual origins in this recognition of the need for mutual reassurance, which was to be achieved by both sides having an assured "second strike" (or more properly, strike second) capability. Deterrence theory requires that the United States be able to launch its whole force under attack. Reassurance theory is more demanding and requires that each side should have enough weapons to survive a first strike and still be able to devastate the opponent's homeland. The theory, which underlies the concept of mutual assured destruction, also assumes that both sides would avoid weapon systems that might deprive the other of such a capability. Failing that, reassurance theory becomes a recipe for arms racing, as each side seeks to ensure that it can absorb a first strike and still retaliate.

> *"The Soviet Union cannot afford to let the United States build a space-based weapon system that could neutralize the Soviets' wartime deterrent."*

In any case, there is a world of difference between the theory of arms control as developed in the United States and arms control policy as pursued by successive U.S. administrations. American policy is a shifting amalgam of the viewpoints of the reassurers, the deterrers, and those who seek to retain military superiority. The reassurers' requirement to be able to ride out an attack links the two opponents in an upwards spiral, and concern for the credibility of deterrence provides arguments for more, different, or better offensive weapons. Both theories can be manipulated to require de facto U.S. superiority. Nor does an assured response have to depend on arms control; it can be pursued unilaterally through new weapons programs and innovative basing modes.

American Ambivalence

The American ambivalence toward arms control explains why the United States could more than triple its warheads in the years immediately surrounding the signing of SALT I. Between 1970 and 1975, the number of U.S. warheads shot up from 1,775 to 6,800. During the same period, Soviet warheads increased from 1,700 to 2,700. It explains why SALT II allowed the United States to add 3,360 air-launched cruise missiles to the strategic inventory (trading in gravity bombs and short-range standoff weapons), and why the United States refused to accept any limits on the ground- and sea-launched versions of these strategic systems. By 1979 the United States had authorized production of both versions and, besides the 464 cruise missiles already earmarked for Europe, it plans to deploy about 750 nuclear cruise missiles aboard some 80 surface ships and about 100 attack submarines. The Soviets are following suit.

There is also a fundamental difference in how the two sides view the danger of war. Deterrence theory fosters the idea that war can only come about through a premeditated Soviet attack or some other initiative that the West must counter. Reassurance theory worries about the pressure to preempt in a crisis. Both theories focus on the danger of sudden attack, and both seek to prevent war by the threat of certain punishment. The Soviets are not primarily concerned about a bolt from the blue, and by 1959 they had largely discounted the possibility of a premeditated U.S. attack. They also see little relevance in the "pressure to preempt" that underlies the American concern for crisis stability, having themselves discarded as counterproductive the concept of intercontinental nuclear preemption. The Soviets believe war is most likely to arise from a chain of events that cannot be deterred by some threat of punishment. The first requirement is, therefore, to reduce the causes of East-West tension, amongst which arms racing ranks high in Soviet, if not American, eyes.

The Stumbling Block

No one should have been surprised that the negotiations in Reykjavik last October foundered on the SDI. The Soviets immediately objected to placing weapons in space when Reagan first broached the idea in 1983. They reasserted those objections at the Geneva summit in 1985, and they implicitly conditioned a summit in Washington on progress in preventing the extension of the arms race into space. The Soviets repeatedly noted the lack of such progress in the months preceding Reykjavik, but the Reagan administration dismissed these objections as a negotiating ploy. Officials acknowledged that the SDI would cause the Soviets the expense of matching or outflanking a U.S. ballistic missile defense system, but were unable to grasp the more fundamental nature of the Soviet objections.

The SDI requires the United States to scuttle the only strategic arms limitation treaty it has ratified. Abrogation of the ABM treaty will reverse the arms control process, depriving the Soviets of their only means of effecting reductions in the U.S. nuclear arsenal, and will open up a new arena for arms racing. The SDI also makes conflict in space almost inevitable. The Soviet Union cannot afford to let the United States build a space-based weapon system that could neutralize the Soviets' wartime deterrent and spell the demise of the Soviet state. A multilayered missile defense, even if less than perfect, would have some chance of absorbing a Soviet retaliatory attack in the wake of a U.S. disarming strike. If the United States refuses to be bound by treaties banning space weapons, the Soviets will have to consider whether to prevent the assembly of the SDI components in space.

"The Soviets are prepared to make major concession to keep weapons out of space."

The Soviets must also be prepared to defeat a space-based defense system by saturating it with more warheads than it can handle. They cannot therefore afford to reduce their ICBM inventory unless the ABM treaty is strengthened to exclude permissive interpretations and unless they are convinced that the United States will abide by it. But even if these major obstacles were removed, the two sides still have quite different interests in limiting strategic nuclear weapons.

The primary mission of the Soviet force is to deter a U.S. nuclear attack on Russia in wartime. If America has no strategic nuclear weapons, Russia needs none. If nuclear weapons remain, the smaller the two sides' arsenals, the better for the Soviets. U.S. nuclear forces are intended to deter all forms of Soviet aggression, a requirement that would persist in the absence of Soviet nuclear weapons. Furthermore, even moderates in the United States consider that some 6,000 warheads are necessary to ensure that the Soviet Union is "deterred" in all circumstances.

Delivery Systems

The difference in requirements extends to nuclear delivery systems. This fact was demonstrated in the wake of Reykjavik, when the United States wanted to limit the proposed ban on nuclear weapons to ballistic missiles, whereas the Soviets were prepared to accept a ban across the board. The United States has always had a technological lead in bombers and long-range cruise missiles, as well as in defense against them, which is helped by America's geographical isolation. It refused to allow bombers to be counted in SALT I and excluded ground- and sea-launched cruise missiles from SALT II. The Soviets, therefore, cannot afford to give away their ICBMs—

one of the few negotiating levers they retain—without securing concessions in bombers and cruise missiles, where the United States has a significant advantage.

Theater systems are a separate issue. The Soviets believe that the elimination of nuclear weapons in Europe is to their operational advantage and will also reduce the likelihood that conflict will escalate to nuclear strikes on Russia. However, they have had to balance their interest in banning theater systems against the possibility that the prospect of such agreement can be used as leverage to bring the United States to the table on the SDI. I suspect that the Soviets' overall negotiating position could be improved by concluding an agreement on theater nuclear forces, even if there is no progress on the SDI. With its recent proposal to negotiate separately on theater forces, it may be that Moscow now sees the situation the same way.

The ironies surrounding the present impasse are inescapable. Since 1969 the Soviets have sought to reduce the size of nuclear arsenals but have been unwilling to divulge that aim lest it weaken their negotiating position. They have been willing to make unequal concessions, but these have not been recognized as such by a United States preoccupied with its own vulnerabilities. If we had pressed ahead within the negotiating framework agreed upon at the Vladivostok summit in 1974, we might have halted the Soviet buildup at a significantly lower level and then gone on to achieve reductions in strategic forces. Instead arms control became hostage to U.S. domestic politics. Successive administrations have embarked on new weapons systems as a way of securing the political acceptance of those agreements that have been negotiated. The Reagan administration, skeptical of any kind of arms control, now offers the implausible argument that the SDI will force the Soviets to cut back on their strategic missile force.

A second irony is that it is left to the Soviet Union, the "evil empire" berated by the United States for its aggressive behavior, to draw attention to the portentous consequences of putting weapons in space. The Soviets believe that such a step is at least comparable to the introduction of atomic weapons in 1945. There is some discussion in the United States of the SDI's implications for crisis stability but no significant debate on the advisability of opening the Pandora's box of "weaponizing" space.

Major Concessions

A third irony is that a president untutored in Western arms control theory, leading a fractious administration that is largely unsympathetic to arms control and holds outdated assumptions about Soviet doctrine, should have engendered a situation that is peculiarly favorable to reaching an agreement on major reductions in nuclear weapons. This turn of events has occurred partly because the Soviets are prepared to make major concessions to keep weapons out of space and partly because Reagan is still uniquely qualified to deliver the Senate votes to ratify such a revolutionary treaty. But it is also attributable to a new readiness in the United States to question the theories of deterrence and reassurance.

"The arms control community must now assimilate the proposals for sweeping reductions in nuclear weapons that were agreed on in principle at Reykjavik."

Having been ridiculed from the right for basing America's defense on the threat of mutual suicide and challenged from the left on the morality of threatening nuclear devastation, the arms control community must now assimilate the proposals for sweeping reductions in nuclear weapons that were agreed on in principle at Reykjavik, proposals that evoked widespread popular support. There may now be a new willingness to recognize that the West's oversophisticated theory of arms control has resulted in ridiculously high levels of armaments on both sides and to examine the merits of a less complicated approach—one that assumes that deterrence can work at a low level of threat and that concentrates on reducing the size of the two sides' nuclear arsenals. That this also happens to be the Soviet approach is no reason to reject it.

Michael MccGwire is a senior fellow in the Foreign Policy Studies program at the Brookings Institute.

"The Soviet objective in the negotiations is to obtain U.S. and Western acquiescence in a Soviet right to massive nuclear superiority."

viewpoint **141**

The US Should Not Negotiate with the Soviets

Eugene V. Rostow

The central problem . . . of world politics and of American national security remains what it has been since 1945: the Soviet program of indefinite expansion achieved by the aggressive use of force. The possibility of direct Soviet moves against Western Europe and Japan was contained and deterred during the Truman administration, and a Soviet nuclear threat against China was successfully met by Richard Nixon. In recent years, the most active part of the Soviet campaign of expansion has been directed against strategic targets in the Third World—targets of importance in outflanking and enveloping the major centers of power, the United States, its NATO allies, China, Japan, and a few other key countries.

Genteel Vocabulary

The genteel vocabulary of Western diplomacy now labels Soviet attempts to exploit or exacerbate Third World conflicts as "regional problems." Reagan sought to have this issue placed on the agenda at Reykjavik. Gorbachev wanted to confine the Iceland summit to the intricacies of nuclear arms-control negotiation. On this, Gorbachev prevailed. Except for a few formal American comments for the record about regional conflicts and human rights, the Iceland summit was limited to the problem of nuclear arms control.

The tactical reason for the Soviet desire to make nuclear arms control the centerpiece of the Soviet-American dialogue is the Soviet belief that a nearly mystical faith in arms control has become the opiate of Western opinion in general and American opinion in particular. In this view, the Soviet tacticians are right.

An enthusiasm for arms-control and disarmament agreements is an integral feature of American

Eugene Rostow, "Why the Soviets Want an Arms-Control Agreement, and Why They Want It Now." Reprinted from *Commentary*, February 1987, by permission; all rights reserved.

culture. From the beginning, the American mind, largely shaped by Low Church Protestantism, has had a special faith in law as a shaping influence in the social process. The word "covenant" has great resonance in the American language. We take a keen interest in disarmament and arms-control treaties for the same reasons which led us to draft and adopt the Constitution and endow the Supreme Court with extraordinary power as its prophet. Thus the United States proposed an agreement demilitarizing the Great Lakes as early as 1783, and for over two centuries has been a vigorous advocate of international arbitration and many other initiatives in the same spirit. Our first reaction to the nuclear weapon after World War II was to propose the Baruch Plan, to be embodied in a treaty bringing all forms of nuclear energy under the control of an international agency, and prohibiting national nuclear forces, including our own, which were then a monopoly. The American effort to obtain nuclear arms-control agreements slowed down after the Soviet Union rejected the Baruch Plan, but was revived and accelerated by the Cuban missile crisis, which we saw as a demonstration of the risks of nuclear uncertainty. Arms-control agreements, we thought, could help to bring some stability and predictability into the contentious rivalry of the great powers, and keep that rivalry from escalating into nuclear war.

With the steady expansion of Soviet power since the Cuban missile crisis, and the rising pressure of the Soviet military build-up, the traditional Western enthusiasm for arms-control agreements has become an obsession. In a mood which contains disturbing elements of hysteria, the people of the democracies are more and more attracted by the glitter of panaceas, and above all by the illusion that arms-control and disarmament agreements are assurances of peace, a ritual that could achieve peace without tears. That illusion was equally popular in the 1930s when Western governments kept pressing disarmament treaties on Hitler while Germany rearmed and began its career of conquest. The persistence of the view, despite the failures of arms-control efforts during the interwar period and the last twenty years, has offered the Soviet government a dazzling opportunity to divert attention from the real problems of Western security. The Soviet leadership has taken full advantage of this opportunity.

Soviet Propaganda

Thus the Soviet propaganda apparatus, led by Gorbachev himself, has been preaching the virtues of a moratorium on testing nuclear weapons, a comprehensive test ban, and a limited test-ban treaty confining nuclear testing both in number and in scale.

The movement for a moratorium on testing and a comprehensive test-ban treaty is a cruel and pathetic deception. Its unstated premise is that if tests are forbidden, the existing stock of nuclear weapons will die, and no new nuclear weapons could be made. Both parts of the premise are incorrect. No one knows how long existing nuclear weapons could be fired, but all are agreed that they will remain usable for many years. And new weapons modeled on existing weapons can be manufactured without further tests. But a moratorium or a comprehensive test ban would prevent the development of smaller, cleaner, and more accurate nuclear weapons, which would be less dangerous than existing weapons to the environment and to noncombatants. The United States has steadily replaced older weapons with such modern weapons and greatly cut the size of its nuclear arsenal in the process.

There was an informal test moratorium during the late 50s and early 60s which the Soviet Union broke without warning, leading President John F. Kennedy to remark that we should never make such an agreement again. During the moratorium period, many of the scientists working on the improvement of the American nuclear arsenal took more active jobs, and it required a number of years to restore the vitality of our laboratories. The Soviet Union has no such problems; its scientists do as they are told.

All the nuclear powers and many others are in fact against a test moratorium or a comprehensive test ban, although most of them give lip service to the idea. The United States has stubbornly persisted in opposing these projects and explaining why.

The ten-year-old Threshold Test Ban and Peaceful Nuclear Explosion Treaty, limiting the scale of underground nuclear tests, is another matter. Although the reports from Reykjavik do not coincide on the point, some American officials have said that the Soviet Union has accepted, others that it is ready to discuss, an American proposal on testing which it had previously rejected—a proposal to improve the

verification provisions of the Threshold Test Ban Treaty and then ratify it. Such a step would not be a serious military burden, and it might reduce the irrational clamor for a comprehensive test ban. On the other hand, it might have the opposite effect.

Beyond the level of tactics and political theater, there is a weighty strategic reason for the Soviet Union's desire to limit the Soviet-American dialogue to nuclear arms-control issues. Even though a deliberate nuclear war among the nuclear powers is the least likely of possible scenarios for the future, the state of the nuclear balance is a critical and under many circumstances a decisive factor in determining the ability of these powers to use or threaten to use conventional force. The link between the nuclear balance and the use of conventional weapons was brought out dramatically in the Cuban missile crisis. In that confrontation, the Soviet Union retreated in the face of an American threat to invade Cuba with conventional forces. The threat was backed by a nuclear arsenal obviously capable of retaliation against the Soviet Union for any use of nuclear weapons against the United States. In 1962, the United States could have controlled the possible escalation of any conflict over Cuba, so that even a local use of conventional force by the Soviet Union would have been futile.

"A . . . test ban would prevent the development of smaller, cleaner . . . more accurate nuclear weapons, which would be less dangerous than existing weapons to the environment and to noncombatants."

Soviet policy took this aspect of the Cuban missile crisis to heart. Soviet leaders perceived arms-control agreements as devices that could allow them to build a nuclear first-strike capability, and prevent the United States from matching such a capability. The Soviet Union has acted on that principle, transforming a nuclear force which was far behind that of the United States in 1962, and significantly inferior in 1972 (when the SALT I agreements were signed), to one which is larger than that of the United States in land-based ballistic missiles, and growing more rapidly than that of the United States in every other weapons category.

Soviet Superiority

In its report of July 16, 1986, *Where We Stand on Arms Control*, the Committee on the Present Danger said:

> The Soviet negotiating pattern since 1969 . . . is consistent with only one hypothesis: that the Soviet objective in the negotiations is to obtain U.S. and

Western acquiescence in a Soviet right to massive nuclear superiority, especially in land-based ballistic missiles. The 1972 Interim Agreement on Strategic Offensive Arms accepted a Soviet advantage in ICBMs, and the Soviet Union has been trying through arms control to get its superiority in ICBM warheads and throwweight recognized as a law of nature.

The consequences of an agreement based on the Soviet approach are described in these terms by the distinguished French expert, François de Rose:

> A disarming first-strike capacity of the land-based components of strategic forces would create a situation of permanent insecurity, no longer balanced by the certainty of retaliation at the same level. Under such circumstances, the victim state under threat would be faced with the choice between accepting defeat or resorting to a second strike at the risk of annihilation. . . .
>
> What Helmut Schmidt rightly called the "subliminal" political influence of such a first-strike capacity is already palpable both in Europe and in the United States. It arises from the present state of the Soviet-American nuclear balance because of the Soviet Union's heavy advantage in intercontinental and intermediate-range ground-based missiles. . . .

Falling into a Trap

The most spectacular idea broached in Reykjavik—the American proposal to abolish offensive ballistic missiles entirely within a ten-year period—demonstrates how the addiction to arms control can lead us into a Soviet trap. . . .

It is impossible to discern any convincing rationale for completely eliminating ballistic missiles during the second five years of such an agreement, even if the formidable problem of monitoring compliance could be solved.

In the first place, abolishing ballistic missiles completely is a chimera. The same physical principles are applied to launch satellites, nuclear weapons, and space vehicles. Knowledge of the relevant technology is spreading rapidly. And many countries, large and small, now possess the capacity to make ballistic missiles.

Secondly, an agreement to abolish ballistic missiles would violate the prudent policy of maintaining the "triad" in our nuclear-weapons program—the policy of developing land-based, sea-based, and air-based weapons. That policy is required by the possibility that technology might suddenly make one or another class of weapons obsolete, or partially obsolete. The maxim about not putting too many eggs in one basket remains sound. And the chances for inducing the Soviet Union to give up its policy of expansion in the near future are surely not great. If we try to anticipate the longer future, other predator nations may appear, and bid for hegemony in their turn. And there is always the risk that an irrational political leader may acquire nuclear weapons.

All that being the case, we shall continue to need a deterrent retaliatory nuclear capacity for as far ahead as we can see. The force behind deterrence will also need to be as strong and flexible as possible. Existing and prospective Soviet defensive systems can stop some of our bombers and cruise missiles, which are slow and vulnerable. Soviet defenses against ballistic missiles are not yet nearly so effective. Ballistic missiles are therefore indispensable to the fulfillment of our nuclear strategy.

Fallacy of First Strike

Some administration spokesmen have said that the United States has proposed to eliminate ballistic missiles as a class because they are the only weapons now capable of a first strike. This is surely an error. Against a non-nuclear power or an inferior nuclear power, any system for carrying a nuclear weapon is capable of executing a first strike. The only nuclear weapons thus far used in war, after all, were carried by bombers. Beyond a certain technological threshold, the principal distinction between first-strike and retaliatory weapons is their number and quality.

"An agreement to abolish ballistic missiles would violate the prudent policy of maintaining the 'triad' in our nuclear-weapons program."

It is of course true that ballistic missiles are still the most accurate, speedy, and destructive nuclear-weapon carriers, and the ones least vulnerable to defense. But their capacity to execute a first strike depends upon their number in relation to the types of targets to be attacked, the enemy's defenses, and the opposing forces capable of a response.

Manifestly it is also correct, as Secretary of Defense Caspar Weinberger pointed out in a speech on November 17, 1986, that while all nuclear weapons threaten massive destruction, only offensive ballistic missiles "threaten to overwhelm us in the blink of an eye." Therefore they should, as he said, "be at the core of arms-reduction agreements." It does not follow, however, that they can be dispensed with altogether.

It is widely assumed that we could protect our security effectively with conventional forces if nuclear forces were radically reduced or even if all nuclear weapons were eliminated. In that form, the familiar assumption is untenable. Two reasons compel the conclusion that we shall be dependent indefinitely on the threat of effective nuclear retaliation to deter nuclear or conventional-force attacks on ourselves, our allies, and other vital interests around the world. The first is that for a variety of reasons the West cannot match the Soviet

Union and its allies in conventional forces in all the relevant theaters where the Soviet Union is operating or may strike. The second is that we shall have to retain a fully effective nuclear retaliatory capacity because we can never be sure that the Soviet Union will not make an attack "with all weapons"—that is, with nuclear, chemical, or biological weapons—despite possible reductions in its nuclear forces and a possible "no-first-use" pledge. Former Secretary of Defense Robert S. McNamara made the point emphatically when proposing that the United States adopt a no-first-use policy in 1984. We should have to maintain a nuclear retaliatory capacity, he said, because we could never be confident that the Soviet Union would honor its own no-first-use pledge.

A Token Gesture

A certain number of Americans who advocate the total abolition of ballistic missiles, like some of those who favor the American proposal to abolish mobile missiles, intend only to make a propaganda gesture. They meet criticisms of the proposal by assuring their critics that the Soviet Union will reject it, so there is nothing to worry about. There can be no worse ground for supporting a policy, as Gorbachev demonstrated at Reykjavik, where he leapfrogged the American proposal to abolish ballistic missiles, without accepting it, by proposing to abolish all strategic nuclear weapons and then all nuclear weapons.

"We shall have to retain a fully effective nuclear retaliatory capacity because we can never be sure that the Soviet Union will not make an attack."

There are also many Congressmen and other Americans who believe that in the end we have enough nuclear weapons to deter an attack on the United States itself, and that protecting our interests abroad does not really matter. Yet as the experience of the Cuban missile crisis shows, the deterrence of attacks on the United States requires exactly the same measure of American nuclear retaliatory capacity as the deterrence of attacks on American allies and other interests abroad. Moreover, the United States would be unable to protect its liberty if the Soviet Union gained control of Western Europe, China, and Japan.

The same reasoning applies to the American proposal to abolish mobile land-based ballistic missiles. That proposal, now several years old, is apparently still on the table in Geneva. Yet small, mobile, land-based missiles—the Midgetman, now in development—could be an important contribution to

the essential task of restoring the nuclear balance. The Midgetman missile would make our ICBM force less vulnerable, and thus reduce the pressures for a "launch-on-warning" policy. And it would make it easier to maintain an effective nuclear deterrent.

Though Midgetman was urged as a necessity by the Scowcroft Commission appointed by President Reagan himself, it seems clear that the reason he later proposed to abolish it is that the administration despaired of persuading Congress to authorize small mobile missiles after it had killed the plan for deploying the large MX missiles in Nevada. Nevertheless, from the strategic point of view, Midgetman remains a sound idea.

A Nuclear Fantasy

As for the dream of eliminating nuclear weapons altogether, all American Presidents since Truman have declared their support in principle for ultimate abolition, and as Soviet spokesmen point out, Gorbachev's call for it again at Reykjavik revives a plan Andrei Gromyko tabled in 1946. At that time, the Soviet plan was dismissed by the West as transparent propaganda, and has been similarly treated at intervals since 1946 when the Soviet Union brought it back in one form or another. In all these forms the Soviet proposals have invariably depended on national rather than international action, with minimal arrangements for the verification of compliance. But of course without complete confidence in the enforcement of compliance, such a treaty would be a trap for the obedient. By hiding 100 weapons in a cave, a treaty violator could emerge as the overlord of world politics.

But the debate about alternative plans for nuclear abolition is irrelevant. A non-nuclear world can never be restored. Any moderately industrialized country can make nuclear weapons, and any rich country can buy them. Thus the West will always need some nuclear weapons against the chance that a strong hostile power or a state under the control of an irrational leader will obtain them. The Reagan administration is urging defensive systems as an answer to the possibility of such cheating. But SDI can never be more than a partial answer. What if the attack is made or threatened against an American ally which does not have an effective defense against nuclear weapons?

Even if a non-nuclear world could be imagined, would it be in the interest of the United States to help achieve it? If the American nuclear deterrent were to be removed, could anything prevent the Soviet Union from working its will by the use of conventional forces or the threat to use them? Recognizing that the answer to this question is no, many in Europe, the United States, and Canada nevertheless imagine that they could live as autonomous islands of peace in a world otherwise dominated by Soviet power. This idea is a suicidal illusion. The Western powers, along with China, have too much specific gravity to be allowed to flourish indefinitely as neutrals in a world order dominated by the Soviet Union. The Soviet leaders would calculate that the Western powers might, after all, wake up with a roar some morning and change their minds.

"The government of the Soviet Union has sacrificed the standard of living of two generations of its people in order to gain great military power."

When, more than a decade ago, Henry Kissinger spoke tentatively about the "linkage" between nuclear arms-control efforts and Soviet expansion, he was denounced for placing impossible obstacles in the path of peace. His critics said that we must understand and accept Soviet expansion as a fact of life. They advanced a number of theories to justify Soviet international behavior. The aggressive use of force, some suggested, was the prerogative of a great power seeking status, recognition, and legitimacy. Alternatively, other critics explained, the Soviet drive for power was a defensive symptom of nearly paranoid suspicion or the manifestation of an inferiority complex.

The Imperial Mission

Since the Soviet Union will not give up its imperial mission, Kissinger's critics concluded, we in the West must make sure that our more and more limited efforts at containment do not explode into nuclear war. At a minimum, they urged, nuclear arms-control agreements are useful ways to stabilize the inevitable competition between the two superpowers, rules of the game that could at least keep them from going over the precipice. Some went so far as to suggest that arms-control agreements could do more—that they would of themselves produce peace, and were in effect a substitute for the harsh and costly burden of having a foreign policy at all. "Linkage" became an idea politicians and bureaucrats avoided, and scholars and journalists ignored.

But the startling beams of light which pierced the fog of Reykjavik reveal once more that linkage is a reality which cannot be evaded or exorcised. Arms-control agreements, after all, are a means to an end, not an end in themselves. For the West that end can only be the goal of peace: a pluralist world order of independent states, based on a balance of power and generally governed by the rules of international behavior set out in the United Nations Charter. The

end sought by the Soviet Union is altogether different. The Soviet Union is not trying to establish a balance of world power but to escape from its restraints. It is steadily building an alternative state system based not on equilibrium but on Soviet dominance—a true Pax Sovietica. The nuclear weapon is and will remain a key factor in the continuing struggle between these rival conceptions of world public order: for the West, the ultimate deterrent of Soviet expansion; for the Soviets, the ultimate deterrent of any Western defense against their own expansionist moves.

What is also clear from Reykjavik, finally, is that Soviet foreign policy under Gorbachev has ceased to be patient and long term. Gorbachev wants answers now. Taught to believe that the correlation of military forces will determine the future of world politics, Gorbachev is demanding that the United States draw the obvious conclusion from the fact that the Soviet Union is a stronger military power than the United States, and that its military strength is growing more rapidly than ours, despite our rearmament efforts of the last ten years. Gorbachev knows as well as we do that the Bolshevik Revolution has failed economically, socially, politically, and ideologically. He knows that the government of the Soviet Union has sacrificed the standard of living of two generations of its people in order to gain great military power. He knows that it is now on the verge of achieving overwhelming strength, and the momentum to generate much more strength, especially in its nuclear arsenal and its command of outer space. He is determined to utilize this military superiority before it evaporates. Thus his violent rush to intimidate Reagan at Reykjavik.

In concentrating almost entirely on arms control to the virtual exclusion of the issue of Soviet aggression, and in flirting with proposals that would give the Soviets a clear-cut first-strike capability, the Iceland meeting left the world with a single question: is the West still "containing" the expansion of Soviet power, or is the Soviet Union "containing" (and dividing) the industrialized democracies, steadily forcing them into a narrowing perimeter by the pressure of nuclear blackmail?

Eugene V. Rostow served as director of the Arms Control and Disarmament Agency from 1981 to 1983 and as under secretary of state for political affairs from 1966 to 1969.

"We have deep, continuing concerns about Soviet noncompliance with the ABM [anti-ballistic missile] Treaty."

The Soviet Union Violates Arms Control Treaties

Ronald Reagan

At the request of the Congress, I have provided four reports to the Congress on Soviet non-compliance with arms control agreements. These reports include the Administration's reports of January 1984, and February and December 1985, as well as the report on Soviet noncompliance prepared for me by the independent General Advisory Committee on Arms Control and Disarmament. Each of these reports has enumerated and documented, in detail, issues of Soviet noncompliance, their adverse effects to our national security, and our attempts to resolve the issues. When taken as a whole, this series of reports also provides a clear picture of the continuing pattern of Soviet violations and a basis for our continuing concerns.

In the December 23, 1985, report, I stated:

> The Administration's most recent studies support its conclusion that there is a pattern of Soviet noncompliance. As documented in this and previous reports, the Soviet Union has violated its legal obligation under or political commitment to the SALT I [strategic arms limitation talks] ABM [Anti-Ballistic Missile] Treaty and Interim Agreement, the SALT II Agreement, the Limited Test Ban Treaty of 1963, the Biological and Toxin Weapons Convention, the Geneva Protocol on Chemical Weapons, and the Helsinki Final Act. In addition, the U.S.S.R. has likely violated provisions of the Threshold Test Ban Treaty (TTBT).

I further stated:

> At the same time as the Administration has reported its concerns and findings to the Congress, the United States has had extensive exchanges with the Soviet Union on Soviet noncompliance in the Standing Consultative Commission (SCC), where SALT-related issues (including ABM issues) are discussed, and through other appropriate diplomatic channels.

I have also expressed my personal concerns directly to General Secretary Gorbachev during my

Ronald Reagan, "Soviet Noncompliance With Arms Control Agreements," an unclassified report presented to the Speaker of the House of Representatives and the President of the Senate, March 10, 1987.

meetings with him, both in 1985 in Geneva and then again this past October [1986] in Reykjavik.

Another year has passed and, despite these intensive efforts, the Soviet Union has failed to correct its noncompliant activities; neither have they provided explanations sufficient to alleviate our concerns on other compliance issues.

Compliance is a cornerstone of international law; states are to observe and comply with obligations they have freely undertaken.

UN Resolution

In fact, in December 1985, the General Assembly of the United Nations recognized the importance of treaty compliance for future arms control, when, by a vote of 131-0 (with 16 abstentions), it passed a resolution that:

• Urges all parties to arms limitation and disarmament agreements to comply with their provisions;

• Calls upon those parties to consider the implications of noncompliance for international security and stability and for the prospects for further progress in the field of disarmament; and

• Appeals to all UN members to support efforts to resolve noncompliance questions "with a view toward encouraging strict observance of the provisions subscribed to and maintaining or restoring the integrity of arms limitation or disarmament agreements."

Congress has repeatedly stated its concern about Soviet noncompliance. The U.S. Senate, on February 17, 1987, passed a resolution, by a vote of 93 to 2, which:

> declares that an important obstacle to the achievement of acceptable arms control agreements with the Soviet Union has been its violations of existing agreements, and calls upon it to take steps to rectify its violation of such agreements and, in particular, to dismantle the newly-constructed radar sited at Krasnoyarsk, Union of Soviet Socialist Republics,

since it is a clear violation of the terms of the Anti-Ballistic Missile Treaty. . . .

Compliance with past arms control commitments is an essential prerequisite for future arms control agreements. As I have stated before:

> In order for arms control to have meaning and credibly contribute to national security and to global or regional stability, it is essential that all parties to agreements fully comply with them. Strict compliance with all provisions of arms control agreements is fundamental, and this Administration will not accept anything less.

I have also said that:

> Soviet noncompliance is a serious matter. It calls into question important security benefits from arms control, and could create new security risks. It undermines the confidence essential to an effective arms control process in the future. . . . The United States Government has vigorously pressed, and will continue to press, these compliance issues with the Soviet Union through diplomatic channels.

The ABM Treaty

I must report that we have deep, continuing concerns about Soviet noncompliance with the ABM Treaty. For several reasons, we are concerned with the Krasnoyarsk radar, which appeared to be completed externally in 1986. The radar demonstrates that the Soviets were designing and programming a prospective violation of the ABM Treaty even while they were negotiating a new agreement on strategic offensive weapons with the United States.

"The Soviets were designing and programming a prospective violation of the ABM Treaty even while they were negotiating a new agreement."

The only permitted functions for a large, phased-array radar (LPAR) with a location and orientation such as that of the Krasnoyarsk radar would be space-tracking and national technical means (NTM) of verification. Based on conclusive evidence, however, we judge that this radar is primarily designed for ballistic missile detection and tracking, not for space-tracking and NTM as the Soviets claim. Moreover, the coverage of the Krasnoyarsk radar closes the remaining gap in the Soviet ballistic missile detection and tracking screen; its location allows it to acquire attack characterization data that could aid in planning the battle for Soviet defensive forces and deciding timely offensive responses—a standard role for such radars.

All LPARs, such as the Krasnoyarsk radar, have the inherent capability to track large numbers of objects accurately. Thus, they not only could perform as ballistic missile detection and tracking radars, but also have the inherent capability, depending on location and orientation, of contributing to ABM battle management.

A Clear Violation

LPARs have always been considered to be the long lead-time elements of a possible territorial defense. Taken together, the Krasnoyarsk radar and other Soviet ABM-related activities give us concerns that the Soviet Union may be preparing an ABM defense of its national territory. Some of the activities, such as construction of the new LPARs on the periphery of the Soviet Union and the upgrade of the Moscow ABM system, appear to be consistent with the ABM Treaty. The construction of the radar near Krasnoyarsk, however, is a clear violation of the ABM Treaty, while other Soviet ABM-related activities involve potential or probable Soviet violations or other ambiguous activity. These other issues, discussed fully in the body of the report, are:

• The testing and development of components required for an ABM system that could be deployed to a site in months rather than years;

• The concurrent operation of air defense components and ABM components;

• The development of modern air defense systems that may have some ABM capabilities; and

• The demonstration of an ability to reload ABM launchers in a period of time shorter than previously noted.

Soviet activities during the past year [1986] have contributed to our concerns. The Soviets have begun construction of three additional LPARs similar to the Krasnoyarsk radar. These new radars are located and oriented consistent with the ABM Treaty's provision on ballistic missile early warning radars, but they would increase the number of Soviet LPARs by 50 percent. The redundancy in coverage provided by these new radars suggests that their primary mission is ballistic missile acquisition and tracking.

This year's reexamination of Soviet ABM-related activities demonstrates that the Soviets have not corrected their outstanding violation, the Krasnoyarsk radar. It is the totality of these Soviet ABM-related activities in 1986 and earlier years that gives rise to our continuing concerns that the USSR may be preparing an ABM defense of its national territory. The ABM Treaty prohibits the deployment of an ABM system for the defense of the national territory of the parties and prohibits the parties from providing a base for such a defense. As I said in last December's [1986] report:

> [This] would have profound implications for . . . the vital East-West . . . balance. A unilateral Soviet territorial ABM capability acquired in violation of the ABM Treaty could erode our deterrent and leave doubts about its credibility.

The integrity of the arms control process is also

hurt by Soviet violations of the 1925 Geneva Protocol on Chemical Weapons and the 1972 Biological and Toxin Weapons Convention. Information obtained reinforces our concern about Soviet noncompliance with these important agreements. Progress toward an agreement banning chemical weapons is affected by Soviet noncompliance with the Biological and Toxin Weapons Convention. Because of the record of Soviet noncompliance with past agreements, we believe verification provisions are a matter of unprecedented importance in our efforts to rid the world of these heinous weapons—weapons of mass destruction under international law.

"The Soviet Union repeatedly violated the SALT II Treaty and took other actions that were inconsistent with the Treaty's provisions."

The Soviets have continued to maintain a prohibited offensive biological warfare capability. We are particularly concerned because it may include advanced biological agents about which we have little knowledge and against which we have no defense. The Soviets continue to expand their chemical and toxin warfare capabilities. Neither NATO retaliatory nor defensive programs can begin to match the Soviet effort. Even though there have been no confirmed reports of lethal attacks since the beginning of 1984, previous activities have provided the Soviets with valuable testing, development, and operational experience.

Nuclear Testing

The record of Soviet noncompliance with the treaties on nuclear testing is of legal and military concern. Since the Limited Test Ban Treaty (LTBT) came into force over twenty years ago, the Soviet Union has conducted its nuclear weapons test program in a manner incompatible with the aims of the Treaty by regularly permitting the release of nuclear debris into the atmosphere beyond the borders of the USSR. Even though the debris from these Soviet tests does not pose calculable health, safety, or environmental risks, and these infractions have no apparent military significance, our repeated attempts to discuss these occurrences with Soviet authorities have been continually rebuffed. Soviet refusal to discuss this matter calls into question their sincerity on the whole range of arms control agreements.

During their test moratorium, the Soviets undoubtedly maintained their sites because they quickly conducted a test soon after announcing

intent to do so. Furthermore, there were numerous ambiguous events during this period that can neither be associated with, nor disassociated from, observed Soviet nuclear test-related activities.

Soviet testing at yields above the 150 kt limit would allow development of advanced nuclear weapons with proportionally higher yields of weapons than the U.S. could develop under the Treaty.

The United States and the Soviet Union have met on four occasions during the past year [1986] for expert-level discussions on the broad range of issues related to nuclear testing. Our objective during these discussions consistently has been to achieve agreement on an effective verification regime for the TTBT and PNET [Peaceful Nuclear Explosions Treaty]. I remain hopeful that we can accomplish this goal.

The Helsinki Final Act

In 1981 the Soviet Union conducted a major military exercise without providing prior notification of the maneuver's designation and the number of troops taking part, contrary to its political commitment to observe provisions of Basket I of the Helsinki Final Act.

During the past year [1986], we have reached an accord at the Stockholm Conference on Confidence- and Security-Building Measures that contains new standards for notification, observation, and verification of military activities, including on-site inspection. We will be carefully assessing Soviet compliance with these new standards, which went into effect January 1, 1987.

At the end of 1986 and during the early weeks of 1987, new information pertaining to some of the issues in this report became available, but it was judged that the data did not necessitate a change in any of the findings. This was partially due to the developing nature of the information at the time and certain ambiguities associated with it. Furthermore, the Soviet Union resumed underground nuclear testing on February 26, 1987.

SALT II

The Soviet Union repeatedly violated the SALT II Treaty and took other actions that were inconsistent with the Treaty's provisions. In no case where we determined that the Soviet Union was in violation did they take corrective action. We have raised these issues in the SCC and in other diplomatic channels.

The Soviets committed four violations of their political commitment to observe SALT II; they were:

- The development and deployment of the SS-25 missile, a prohibited second new type of intercontinental ballistic missile (ICBM);
- Extensive encryption of telemetry during test flights of strategic ballistic missiles;
- Concealment of the association between a

missile and its launcher during testing; and
- Exceeding the permitted number of strategic nuclear delivery vehicles (SNDVs).

In addition, the Soviets:
- Probably violated the prohibition on deploying the SS-16 ICBM;
- Took actions inconsistent with their political commitment not to give the Backfire bomber intercontinental operating capability by deploying it to Arctic bases; and
- Evidently exceeded the agreed production quota by producing slightly more than the allowed 30 Backfire bombers per year until 1984.

Concerning the SALT I Interim Agreement, the Soviets used former SS-7 ICBM facilities to support deployment of the SS-25 mobile ICBM, and thereby violated the prohibition on the use of former ICBM facilities.

Soviet Noncompliance

On June 10, 1985, I expressed concern that continued Soviet noncompliance increasingly affected our national security. I offered to give the Soviet Union additional time in order to take corrective actions to return to full compliance, and I asked them to join us in a policy of truly mutual restraint. At the same time, I stated that future U.S. decisions would be determined on a case-by-case basis in light of Soviet behavior in exercising restraint comparable to our own, correcting their noncompliance, reversing their military buildup, and seriously pursuing equitable and verifiable arms reduction agreements.

"The Soviets are in the process of deploying illegal additions to their force that provide even more strategic capability."

The December 23, 1985, report showed that the Soviets had not taken any actions to correct their noncompliance with arms control commitments. In May 1986, I concluded that the Soviets had made no real progress toward meeting our concerns with respect to their noncompliance, particularly in those activities related to SALT II and the ABM Treaty. From June 1985 until May 1986, we saw no abatement of the Soviet strategic force buildup.

The third yardstick I had established for judging Soviet actions was their seriousness at negotiating deep arms reductions. In May 1986 I concluded that, since the November 1985 summit, the Soviets had not followed up constructively on the commitment undertaken by General Secretary Gorbachev and me to build upon areas of common ground in the Geneva negotiations, including accelerating work toward an interim agreement on INF [intermediate-range nuclear forces].

In Reykjavik, General Secretary Gorbachev and I narrowed substantially the differences between our two countries on nuclear arms control issues. However, the Soviets took a major step backward by insisting that progress in every area of nuclear arms control must be linked together in a single package that has as its focus killing the U.S. Strategic Defense Initiative (SDI). Furthermore, it became clear that the Soviets intended to make the ABM Treaty more restrictive than it is on its own terms by limiting our SDI research strictly to the laboratory.

End of SALT II Observance

It was, however, the continuing pattern of noncompliant Soviet behavior that I have outlined above that was the primary reason why I decided, on May 27, 1986, to end U.S. observance of the provisions of the SALT I interim Agreement and SALT II. The decision to end the U.S. policy of observing the provisions of the Interim Agreement (which had expired) and the SALT II Treaty (which was never ratified and would have expired on December 31, 1985) was not made lightly. The United States cannot, and will not, allow a double standard of compliance with arms control agreements to be established.

Therefore, on May 27, 1986, I announced:

> in the future, the United States must base decisions regarding its strategic force structure on the nature and magnitude of the threat posed by Soviet strategic forces and not on standards contained in the SALT structure, which has been undermined by Soviet noncompliance, and especially in a flawed SALT II treaty, which was never ratified, would have expired if it had been ratified, and has been violated by the Soviet Union.

Responding to a Soviet request, the U.S. agreed to hold a special session of the SCC in July 1986 to discuss my decision. During that session, the U.S. made it clear that we would continue to demonstrate the utmost restraint. At this session we stated that, assuming there is no significant change in the threat we face, the United States would not deploy more strategic nuclear delivery vehicles or more strategic ballistic missile warheads than does the Soviet Union. We also repeated my invitation to the Soviet Union to join the U.S. in establishing an interim framework of truly mutual restraint pending conclusion of a verifiable agreement on deep and equitable reductions in offensive nuclear arms. The Soviet response was negative.

In my announcement, I had said the United States would remain in technical observance of SALT II until later in the year when we would deploy our 131st heavy bomber equipped to carry air-launched cruise missiles. The deployment of that bomber on November 28, 1986, marked the full implementation of that policy.

Now that we have put the Interim Agreement and the SALT II Treaty behind us, Soviet activities with respect to those agreements, which have been studied and reported to the Congress in detail in the past, are not treated in the body of this report. This is not to suggest that the significance of the Soviet violations has in any way diminished. We are still concerned about the increasing Soviet military threat.

Illegal Additions

A number of activities involving SALT II constituted violations of the core or central provisions of the Treaty frequently cited by the proponents of SALT II as the primary reason for supporting the agreement. These violations involve both the substantive provisions and the vital verification provisions of the Treaty. Through violation of the SALT II limit of the one "new type" of ICBM, the Soviets are in the process of deploying illegal additions to their force that provide even more strategic capability.

Soviet encryption and concealment activities have, in the past, presented special obstacles to verifying compliance with arms control agreements. The Soviets' extensive encryption of ballistic missile telemetry impeded U.S. ability to verify key provisions of the SALT II Treaty. Of equal importance, these Soviet activities undermine the political confidence necessary for concluding new treaties and underscore the necessity that any new agreement be effectively verifiable.

Soviet noncompliance, as documented in this and previous Administration reports, has made verification and compliance pacing elements of arms control today. From the beginning of my Administration, I have sought deep and equitable reductions in the nuclear offensive arsenals of the United States and the Soviet Union and have personally proposed ways to achieve the objectives in my meetings with General Secretary Gorbachev. If we are to enter agreements of this magnitude and significance, effective verification is indispensable and cheating is simply not acceptable.

Ronald Reagan is president of the United States.

"[The Soviet Union] has methodically deactivated strategic nuclear weapon systems to meet the limitations . . . imposed by the SALT I and II treaties."

viewpoint 143

The Soviet Union Does Not Violate Arms Control Treaties

Matthew P. Gallagher

Editor's note: The following viewpoint is excerpted from an article Matthew Gallagher wrote for The Defense Monitor.

Arms limitation treaties are not based on mutual trust, but on self-interest. The Soviet Union entered the SALT I and II treaties because it believed that they would contribute to its security. It accepted the restraints imposed by the treaties as the cost of insuring that the United States would observe similar restraints. The United States made the same judgment and accepted the same tacit bargain. Compliance is not a matter of good will but of practical self-interest.

The Reagan Administration alleges that the Soviet Union has systematically violated the treaties. Such charges run in the face of clear and consistent evidence that the Soviet Union has been careful to observe all the principal requirements of the SALT I and II treaties. It has done so, moreover, at the cost of dismantling or retiring far greater numbers of strategic weapons to stay in compliance than has the United States.

The Administration's action is prompted by its long-standing ideological biases and political purposes, as well as by legitimate concerns about Soviet treaty compliance. Administration spokesmen made clear from the beginning that they were determined to do away with what candidate Reagan called the "fatally flawed" SALT II treaty. The Administration has been equally determined to make big increases in military spending as a means both of restoring what it claimed was an "eroded" security position and of forcing the Soviet Union to the bargaining table on U.S. terms.

Unfortunately, the Administration's campaign has had the effect of misinforming the American people

Matthew P. Gallagher, "Soviet Compliance With Arms Agreements: The Positive Record," *The Defense Monitor*, vol. 16, no. 2, 1987. Reprinted with permission.

about the complexities of the nuclear relationship and the role that arms talks have played in moderating and controlling the U.S.-Soviet nuclear weapon competition. This [issue of] *Defense Monitor* clarifies the record.

"Let them back up their words with deeds . . ." is a challenge that the President and other Administration spokesmen have frequently used to suggest that when it comes to arms limitation the Soviet Union is all talk, no action. Apparently they haven't been watching very closely, because in fact the Soviet Union has put its missiles where its mouth is. It has methodically deactivated strategic nuclear weapon systems to meet the limitations on launchers and various categories of weapons imposed by the SALT I and II treaties. . . .

Soviet Compliance

Between the entry into force of SALT I on October 3, 1972 and President Reagan's announcement on May 27, 1986 that the United States was no longer bound by the agreements, the Soviet Union has withdrawn or dismantled 1,324 strategic nuclear missiles to stay in compliance. The corresponding U.S. total is 896. The Soviet Union has also withdrawn or dismantled 21 nuclear-missile carrying submarines, 14 of them modern, comparable to the U.S. Polaris. The U.S., by comparison, dismantled 11. As for bombers, the number of Soviet deactivations is in dispute, with the Soviets claiming 51, and the U.S. conceding only 15. The United States itself has not deactivated any bombers.

This record of Soviet compliance with the numerical ceilings of the SALT agreements is hard to reconcile with the Administration's charges of systematic and widespread non-compliance by the Soviet Union. Why would the Soviet Union cheat for relatively insignificant military advantages, as the Administration charges, when at the same time it is adhering to the major provisions of the treaties that require militarily significant restraint and substantial economic costs? The Administration offers no explanation for this imputed inconsistent behavior because it studiously avoids acknowledging that the Soviet Union has indeed been observing the SALT ceilings. . . .

A series of reports published by the Reagan Administration since 1984 accus[es] the Soviets of systematically cheating on arms agreements. The specific charges differ greatly in degree of gravity and in the certainty with which the accusations are made. Many of them are couched in highly tentative language, and are surrounded with such qualifying adjectives and phrases as: "the evidence . . . is ambiguous," "the evidence . . . is insufficient to fully assess," "the U.S.S.R.'s actions . . . constitute an ambiguous situation," "there are ambiguities concerning the data," and so on.

Moreover, they virtually all represent "worst case" analyses of evidence that is always difficult to assess. A "worst case" analysis places the most alarmist interpretation on a set of data. As Secretary of Defense Caspar Weinberger said in 1983, "Compliance issues are always very difficult, in part because existing agreements often contain vague or equivocal language of which there can be, in the nature of the case, no authoritative interpretation."

"The Soviets reportedly offered to halt construction on the radar if the U.S. would do the same on two . . . that it is installing in Greenland and the U.K."

The United States has reason to be concerned over some Soviet SALT-related activities and should pursue them with the Soviet Union to a satisfactory solution. The new Soviet radar under construction near Krasnoyarsk, the new Soviet SS-25 ICBM, and the Soviet use of encryption to conceal missile test telemetry are among the issues that warrant serious investigation and discussion with the Soviets.

The Krasnoyarsk radar is a large phased-array radar of a type associated with early warning functions which also has some inherent ABM capabilities. The radar's purpose cannot be determined conclusively because it is not yet operational. The Administration believes that it is an early warning radar because it closely resembles other Soviet radars of this type. If so, it would be in violation of the ABM treaty which provides that such radars must be located on the periphery of the national territory and facing outward. The Administration also argues that the Soviets intend to use the radar in a future nationwide ABM system,

which, of course, would violate the ABM treaty even more flagrantly.

The Soviets contend that the radar is intended to perform space tracking functions which is allowed by the ABM treaty. Space tracking would involve monitoring its own and other countries' satellites as well as the great amount of space debris that has accumulated since the 1950s. The signals emitted by the radar when it is turned on will help to resolve the issue because the power required for space tracking is much less than that required for ABM functions. In the meantime, the Soviets reportedly offered to halt construction on the radar if the U.S. would do the same on two early warning phased array radars that it is installing in Greenland and the U.K. Whether the U.S. explored the offer is not known, but it seems clear that the Administration's high voltage publicity on the issue is not calculated to encourage the Soviets to push their offer further.

Disputed Data

The SS-25 is a solid-fueled, single warhead ICBM, capable of mobile deployment, that was first tested in 1983. The Administration charges that it is a violation of SALT II on two counts. First, it is alleged to be a second new ICBM, the one new one allowed by the treaty, the SS-24, having already been designated by the Soviet Union as its authorized missile. Second, even if it is a permitted modification of the SS-13 as the Soviets claim, it is said to violate certain technical parameters established by the treaty to inhibit the addition of warheads to single warhead ICBMs.

The Soviets deny both charges, claiming that they are based on faulty data. In fact, the U.S. data on the SS-13 were derived from tests some 20 years ago and are less detailed than those that can be collected today. In addition, say the Soviets, the U.S. has not made proper allowances for the fact that the SS-25 nose cone included an instrumentation package, whereas the SS-13's targeting mechanism is carried in the third stage rather than the nose cone as with other missiles. As a result the SS-25's throw weight appears higher and the SS-13's lower than they are in fact. To support their contentions, the Soviets fired two SS-13s in 1985 to give the United States the opportunity to recalculate the missile's characteristics. The United States has never publicly acknowledged these demonstration firings, something it might be expected to have done if the data confirmed the Administration's charges. *Newsweek* reported that the CIA found that the new data supported the Soviet case, but that the Pentagon remained unpersuaded.

The Soviets fought hard in the SALT negotiations to avoid restrictions that would have prevented them from deploying the SS-25. Assistant Secretary of Defense Richard Perle has deplored this type of negotiating practice, saying that it amounts to designing loopholes in the treaty. It could be argued with equal merit that the Soviets' refusal to accept language that they knew they could not honor demonstrates their respect for the treaty.

As for what this issue tells us about the Soviet compliance record, a key point is that the Soviets have been dismantling an SS-11 for each SS-25 they deploy. Thus they are deploying one single warhead missile for another, and destroying the latter's costly launcher. It is difficult to see how the modest increase in military capability they stand to gain from such an exchange would justify jeopardizing SALT.

Encryption

Telemetry encryption refers to the practice of denying electronic information transmitted by missiles in test flight to monitoring stations of the other side. Both sides intercept the telemetry of the other's test flights as a means of verifying missile characteristics, such as launch weight, throw weight, number of stages, and so on. The United States argued for restrictions on telemetry encryption in the SALT II negotiations on the grounds that this was required by the SALT I undertaking "not to use deliberate concealment measures which impede verification." The Soviets resisted any limitation on their right to protect military secrets as best they saw fit. Eventually the Soviets proposed and the United States accepted a formula which stated that information essential to verifying the treaty should not be encrypted, but left it to the encrypting side to decide what kinds of information this would be.

That the Soviets have used encryption increasingly in recent years seems to be agreed between the Administration and its critics. The issue is whether this practice is a blatant violation of the treaty or simply a case of the Soviets making use of ambiguous treaty language. When the Administration finally raised this issue in the diplomatic forum set up to deal with compliance complaints, the Standing Consultative Commission (SCC) in 1983, it was told by the Soviets that they would modify their practices if the U.S. would specify what types of telemetry information it needed to verify treaty compliance.

With Catch-22 logic, the U.S. has declined to specify what is needed on the grounds that to do so would reveal too much of its intercept capabilities. Since the Soviets already have detailed knowledge of U.S. electronic surveillance capabilities, it appears that the U.S. position is more likely to prevent than to promote a resolution of the problem.

Nuclear Tests

In addition to these substantive cases, the Administration's list of compliance violations includes many issues of a more problematic character. Two of the Administration's favorites concern underground nuclear testing and the overall

ceilings on nuclear delivery vehicles set by the no-undercut-of-SALT II commitments.

The nuclear testing issue concerns Administration charges that the Soviet Union has violated both the 1963 Limited Test Ban treaty (LTBT) and the 1974 Threshold Test Ban treaty (TTBT) in its underground testing. Charges under the first count concern the alleged venting of nuclear materials into the atmosphere. Charges under the second concern tests which allegedly have exceeded the 150 kiloton limit provided by the treaty.

As for venting, both sides agreed that occasional unintended venting once or twice a year would not be considered a violation of the treaties, and this agreement was made a part of the public record of the TTBT. The Administration does not mention this understanding, nor the fact that the U.S. has also been guilty of occasional accidental ventings.

"The Reagan Administration practices a demonology that attributes a large part of the blame for various kinds of trouble in the world to Soviet mischief."

As for violations of the 150 kiloton limit, the accuracy of the U.S. charges has been called into question by many eminent seismologists. For example, Dr. Roger Batzel, Director of the Lawrence Livermore National Laboratory, said in 1985 that the Soviets appear to observe a yield limit and that "Our best estimate of this yield limit is consistent with TTB treaty compliance." Professor Charles Archambeau, a seismologist at the University of Colorado, expressed the scientific community's opposition more bluntly saying, "No rational scientist would draw the conclusions that the present administration is drawing. It's fairly evident that there is a lot of politics involved in this."

Over strong objections from the Department of Defense, the CIA in 1986 accepted a new methodology for estimating yields of Soviet nuclear tests, belatedly acknowledging the different geological structures of U.S. and Soviet testing sites. This lowered the estimate of Soviet test yields by an average of 20 percent, in effect wiping out the statistical basis for many of the U.S. charges.

As the basis for the U.S. charges has eroded, Administration spokesmen have tended to shift their position from complaining about Soviet violations to insisting that the U.S. must continue to explode nuclear weapons to maintain the reliability of its nuclear arsenal. For example, Richard Perle, in a television interview in San Francisco on May 9, 1986, dismissed the seismologists' views on the grounds that they were simply trying to advance their own professional interests. When reminded that a Defense Department panel of experts also agreed with the seismologists, Perle responded that he didn't particularly care what their opinion was. "It doesn't have any profound bearing on our policy," he said. Both he and other Administration spokesmen have made it clear that the United States intends to continue testing, regardless of the adequacy of verification measures. . . .

Stretching the Facts

Compliance issues are often judgmental in character. Those disposed to expect the worst of the Soviet Union can usually find evidence to support their suspicions; those who take a less alarmist view of Soviet intentions can likewise offer less disturbing interpretations of the same evidence. The biases and political purposes of the Reagan Administration are thus legitimate considerations to bear in mind in assessing the charges of Soviet non-compliance.

The Reagan Administration practices a demonology that attributes a large part of the blame for various kinds of trouble in the world to Soviet mischief. Besides reflecting Ronald Reagan's deep-seated ideological biases, this view of the world provides broad support for the Administration's foreign policy and military buildup by stressing the omnipresence of a Soviet threat. As Assistant Secretary of Defense Richard Perle explained it, "Democracies will not sacrifice to protect their security in the absence of a sense of danger. And every time we create the impression that we and the Soviets are cooperating and moderating the competition, we diminish that sense of apprehension."

"The controversy over Soviet compliance has as much to do with . . . political partisanship as it does with the realities of Soviet behavior."

The Administration has kept up a drumbeat of agitation on the compliance issue which has vastly inflated the formal charges. The Administration's main spokesmen on defense and arms control matters, Secretary of Defense Weinberger, Assistant Secretary Perle, and Arms Control and Disarmament Agency chief Kenneth Adelman, routinely represent the alleged Soviet violations as constituting a broad, persistent, and deliberate policy of deception. Weinberger first described the Soviet violations as a "policy" in his 1985 letter to the President on the eve of the Geneva summit recommending "proportionate" responses to Soviet actions. Perle describes alleged Soviet violations as a "strategy of erosion." Adelman uses the phrase "systematic non-

compliance."

In addition to overstating their case against the Soviet Union, Administration spokesmen have stretched and distorted evidence. For example, in the above-mentioned letter, Weinberger said that the Soviets would be required to dismantle only 558 strategic weapons as compared to 1320-2240 for the U.S. under the dismantling requirements of SALT II. In fact, the argument disingenuously used *missile* numbers to calculate the Soviet requirements while using *warhead* numbers to calculate the U.S. total. The true comparison, if warhead numbers had been used in both cases, would have been 2350 for the Soviets as against 1320-2240 for the U.S.

Other examples of stretching the evidence include a statement by Mr. Perle that the Soviets vented radioactive materials into the atmosphere "about 40 or 50 times a year." In fact, the U.S.S.R. has never exploded more than 31 nuclear devices underground in any one year. Still another example occurred when Mr. Adelman attempted to discredit the contention that the Soviet Union has dismantled or withdrawn over 1000 strategic missiles by asserting that the Soviets themselves claim only 540. He was clearly referring to a statement made a few days earlier by General Akhromeyev, Chief of the Soviet General Staff. But as Adelman must surely have known, Akhromeyev was referring only to the dismantlements required by SALT II, not the withdrawals of older missiles to make room for newer ones required by the launcher limitations of SALT I. . . .

Ideological Biases

The Reagan Administration has made no effort to disguise its disagreement with its predecessors over the issue of Soviet compliance. Indeed it has lost no opportunity to blame previous Administrations for failing to deal effectively with the Soviets on arms limitation issues. And it has insisted that the Soviet misbehavior it alleges has been of long historical standing, not something that arose for the first time on Ronald Reagan's watch. It seems fair to say, thus, that the controversy over Soviet compliance has as much to do with the Reagan Administration's ideological biases and political partisanship as it does with the realities of Soviet behavior.

Matthew P. Gallagher is an authority on Soviet military-political affairs who worked for the Central Intelligence Agency for twenty-six years.

The Reykjavik Summit Promoted Peace

George P. Shultz

I want to discuss the special significance of the President's recent meeting with General Secretary Gorbachev in Iceland. There's been a good deal said—in this country, in the Soviet Union, and elsewhere—about what really happened at Reykjavik. My own judgment is that in a few years we will look back at the meeting at Hofdi House as something of a watershed, a potential turning point in our strategy for deterring war and encouraging peace. I would like to explain why.

Before Reykjavik—for most of the postwar era—we have seen a steady buildup in the size and potency of nuclear forces. As a result, our negotiations with the Soviet Union have centered on two questions: how to *contain* this continuing growth of offensive forces; and how to reverse the gradual erosion of strategic stability.

A Qualitative Shift

At Reykjavik, however, there was a qualitative shift in the terms of debate. For the first time in the long history of arms control talks, a genuine possibility of substantial *reductions* in Soviet and American nuclear arms appeared. For the first time, we have to begin to deal seriously with the implications of a much less nuclear, if not non-nuclear, world. We have begun to discuss with the Soviets a safer form of deterrence, one based less on the threat of mutual annihilation. And the key to all of this has been the President's research program, whose investigation into defenses against nuclear ballistic missiles is our best insurance policy for a more secure future.

At Reykjavik, the President and the General Secretary broke down the complexities of these problems into a series of basic questions.

With respect to offensive arms, the important

questions are what systems to reduce and how quickly to reduce them. At Reykjavik, we worked out a formula for 50% reductions in the strategic nuclear offensive forces of both sides over a 5-year period. We agreed upon some numbers and counting rules—that is, how different types of weapons would count against the reduced ceilings.

For intermediate-range nuclear missiles—commonly known as INF—we reached agreement on even more drastic reductions, down from a Soviet total of over 1,400 to only 100 warheads on longer-range INF missiles worldwide on each side. There would be a ceiling on shorter-range INF missiles and negotiations to reduce their numbers as well.

Right there is the basis for the most significant arms control agreement ever achieved—one that doesn't just limit the future growth of Soviet and American nuclear arsenals but which actually makes deep and early cuts in existing force levels. These cuts, it was agreed, would reduce the numbers of heavy, accurate, multiple-warhead missiles that are the most threatening and the most destabilizing.

The President and the General Secretary went on to discuss a program for further reductions. The President proposed to eliminate, over time, all ballistic missiles. Mr. Gorbachev proposed to eliminate all strategic offensive forces. They discussed these and other ideas, including the eventual elimination of all nuclear weapons. This discussion proved inconclusive, but the agenda itself—and the very word "elimination"—marks a stunning development. It calls for us to think deeply and more creatively about future possibilities for arms control and defense.

Obviously, much more work needs to be done before implementation of these more ambitious ideas might be possible. For example, the drastic reduction and ultimate elimination of nuclear weapons will require that we also address the current East-West imbalance of conventional forces.

George P. Shultz, "Reykjavik: A Watershed in U.S.-Soviet Relations," in a speech delivered to the Commonwealth Club of San Francisco, October 31, 1986.

In close collaboration with our allies, we will have to pursue both negotiated reductions in the Warsaw Pact's massive and growing conventional forces and increased efforts to strengthen our own conventional defenses. We must also seek an effective global ban on chemical and biological weapons. And, of course, such substantial nuclear reductions by the United States and Soviet Union would require discussions with other nations armed with ballistic missiles, who have their own security requirements.

On the defensive side of the strategic equation, the two leaders again went directly to the basics. This meeting at Hofdi House was a real working meeting. They went right at it and talked substance throughout the entire time. So, in this case, there were two primary questions.

The ABM Treaty

First, for what period of time are the two countries prepared to commit themselves not to withdraw from the Anti-Ballistic Missile (ABM) Treaty? The President agreed to Gorbachev's proposal for 10 years, but in the context of steady reductions toward zero ballistic missiles during this period and on the understanding that either side would have the right to deploy advanced defenses unless the parties should agree otherwise.

Second, what would be the constraints on defensive programs during this period? The President proposed that both sides strictly observe the ABM Treaty and carry out research, development, and testing permitted by the treaty. Mr. Gorbachev proposed, in effect, to amend the ABM Treaty. He sought a prohibition on all testing outside laboratories—except testing of the sort of ABM system the Soviets now have around Moscow.

"At Reykjavik we reached agreement on what might be the first steps toward a more secure world at lower levels of nuclear arms."

The President could not agree to confine the Strategic Defense Initiative (SDI) program to the laboratory for 10 years. We need a vigorous SDI program, as permitted by the ABM Treaty. We need it to give the Soviets an incentive to agree now to deep cuts in offensive forces and to honor those agreements over the coming years. We need SDI to ensure the Soviet Union's own compliance with current ABM Treaty restrictions on defenses.

So what did we accomplish at Reykjavik? We got agreement on the outlines of a 50% reduction in strategic offensive nuclear weapons and reductions to equal ceilings of 100 warheads on intermediate-range missiles. The latter figure would mean that more than 90% of the SS-20s now targeted on our friends and allies in Europe and Asia would be eliminated.

On defense and space, there was considerable movement on both sides. Important differences were clarified. But there was no closure. The proposal made by the President in Reykjavik, however, is now on the negotiating table in Geneva and is being discussed by our delegation there.

On nuclear testing, both sides proposed to begin negotiations. We discussed an agenda that would meet both sides' concerns.

Obviously, there is still a long way to go. But at Reykjavik we reached agreement on what might be the first steps toward a more secure world at lower levels of nuclear arms. We went on to discuss the possible next steps.

Not bad for 2 days' work. But of course, those 2 productive days drew on the immense amount of preparatory effort that preceded them.

Other Concerns

And that wasn't all. Arms control was only one topic of discussion at Reykjavik. The President brought up the full breadth of our concerns. He cited chapter and verse on the question of Soviet human rights violations. The two leaders reviewed regional conflicts—and the President stated our firm opposition to aggression and subversion by the Soviet Union or its proxies in Afghanistan, Angola, Central America, and Indochina.

At the same time, the two sides also explored an expansion of bilateral U.S.-Soviet programs, involving greater people-to-people contact and cooperation in such areas of concrete interest to the United States as search and rescue and cooperation in space. And I might say, we've had some very productive negotiations with the Soviets in Washington, and I think we have—we haven't signed it—but basically, we have the essence of an agreement on civilian space cooperation and the number of projects identified. I consider that a real plus.

As you can see, we have entered a new stage in our dialogue with the Soviet Union. It has the potential to be exceptionally productive. But it's also a period in which conventional wisdom is being questioned. As we advance on old problems, we will face new issues and new challenges.

I would divide those lessons into three parts. The first lesson is that the negotiating progress we achieved at Reykjavik was built upon a broad base of American and allied strength and resolve. It was the result of literally years of effort.

This President, President Reagan, entered office with his eyes open about the Soviet Union and the reality of its system. He saw the clear need to establish a bilateral U.S.-Soviet relationship that would advance U.S. interests. He was determined to stop a growing tendency of the Soviet Union and its clients to pursue their regional objectives through subversion and armed intervention. He was committed to reverse destabilizing trends in the military balance. And—most significantly—he was also willing to question whether our capacity to deter Soviet aggression must be solely based upon the threat of mutual assured destruction with strategic nuclear weapons.

As you might put it, what's so good about a world that depends on our ability to wipe each other out in 30 minutes? Don't make any mistake about it—that's what their ballistic missiles can do to us, and that's what ours can do to them. [Snaps fingers.] Wiped out! It's kept the peace, but there must be a better way, the President thinks, and we're trying to find it.

Rebuilding a Strong Base

The first few years of this Administration were a period of rebuilding so that we could be in a stronger position to go forward. That meant reinvigorating our economy, restoring our military strength, and repairing our alliance ties with our friends in Europe, Asia, and elsewhere. It involved a lot of unspectacular but vital spadework.

"General Secretary Gorbachev seems to agree with us that the Reykjavik meeting was useful . . . to improve relations."

That general approach is now in place and working. Here at home, we have reestablished the American spirit of self-confidence. Our economy has rid itself of the corrosive inflation of the recent past. We are embarked on sound growth. And I have no doubt that as the marginal rates of taxation on income go down, we will see an improvement in the quality of that growth.

We have strengthened and modernized America's conventional and strategic military forces. Together with our allies, we have made progress in rebuilding NATO's defenses. In the face of intense Soviet pressure and domestic controversy, the Atlantic alliance has stood firm in support of its decision to redress a dangerous INF imbalance with the Soviet Union, both through negotiations and by deploying such forces of our own.

And the President has set out to protect us and our allies against ballistic missiles—by negotiation to the extent possible but, in any case, by learning how to construct a strategic defense against those missiles.

It was the sum of these policies, based on strength and realism, that enabled the President to propose,

in January 1984, a more intensive dialogue with Moscow. The Soviets were faced with an America confident in its renewed strength and an alliance united in its support of common objectives. They slowly came to drop their earlier policies of walkouts and stonewalling. They returned to the negotiating table. The resulting process of high-level dialogue led to [the] Geneva summit and the Reykjavik meeting.

Further Negotiations

Where do we go from here? For our part, we are energetically pursuing the promise of Reykjavik. Our negotiators in Geneva are picking up where the two leaders left off on nuclear and space issues. We are also ready to begin negotiations on verification improvements to existing nuclear testing agreements and, eventually, on further limitations on nuclear testing in step-by-step fashion in parallel with further reductions in nuclear forces.

We will be talking about these and other problems with Soviet Ambassador Dubinin in Washington and through our Ambassador in Moscow, Art Hartman. I will be meeting with Foreign Minister Shevardnadze in Vienna to continue our own exchanges—not just on arms control but on Soviet activities in the Third World, human rights, and other problems in our bilateral relationship.

Whether we can achieve concrete results and early agreements now depends on the Soviets. Some of their public statements have been modestly encouraging. General Secretary Gorbachev seems to agree with us that the Reykjavik meeting was useful and that it is important that both sides use this opportunity to work to improve relations. As he has said, they're full of energy to follow up on what he described as the "new situation" created by Reykjavik, and it is a new situation. Well, so are we. And we'll be looking to them to give concrete substance to their words at the negotiating table.

Not surprisingly, however, the Soviets are also trying to cast the details of the Reykjavik discussions along lines most favorable to them. Their efforts to link a possible INF agreement with our acceptance of their position on SDI are a good example. We've seen differing Soviet statements on this question. We don't see any reason why these issues should be linked, and we're going to proceed on that basis. In the past, we haven't accepted the proposition that negotiating progress on intermediate-range or strategic offensive systems should be held hostage to agreement with the Soviet position in another area. We won't now.

So all of this may take some time to work out—but that's to be expected in negotiating with the Soviets. Firmness, patience, and determination are necessary ingredients for success.

But we should also continue to look forward—with imagination and creativity. The President believes strongly that we need to go beyond half-measures; we shouldn't always be tied to traditional solutions that don't really get to the heart of a particular problem. Several years ago, he proposed that we seek the global elimination of Soviet and American intermediate-range missiles. Not a freeze, not token reductions, but zero-zero. He got a good deal of criticism at the time for supposedly being unrealistic and overly ambitious. Some people said making such a proposal shows that the President isn't serious about arms control.

Now General Secretary Gorbachev has agreed to reduce intermediate-range nuclear missiles on both sides to 100 warheads globally. As I noted before, that is a reduction of more than 90% in SS-20 warheads. And there will be follow-on negotiations on eliminating those 100 warheads as well. Make no mistake about it. It has been tough getting this far. Long negotiations were required; and great effort on the part of our allies was needed in getting us through some difficult times. We still have to nail down a formal agreement and put it into force. But I hope you will think about this experience the next time you hear one of this President's proposals called "unrealistic."

"The strategy of mutual assured destruction that has shaped our defense policy for decades [is] part of the old way of thinking."

So were our discussions at Reykjavik ambitious? Yes. Unrealistic? No. We think that substantial Soviet and American nuclear reductions are possible and that they can be achieved in a phased and stabilizing way. Reykjavik laid the groundwork for that process to begin.

Now we need to think hard about where we want to go next, about what kind of situation we want to create in the future. We need to look at a world with far fewer nuclear weapons. We may even need to begin thinking seriously about a world with *no* nuclear weapons.

One fact seems apparent. Even after the possible elimination of all ballistic missiles, we will need an insurance policy to hedge against cheating, against third countries, against a madman. We don't know now what form this insurance policy will take. The retention of a small nuclear deterrent force could be part of that insurance policy. What we do know is that the President's program for defenses against nuclear ballistic missiles can be a key part of that insurance policy. Such defenses for the United States and its allies will give us the options needed to approach a world with far fewer nuclear weapons.

None of this came up suddenly at Reykjavik. The President has made clear for many years his goal of eliminating ballistic missiles and—in proper circumstances—all nuclear weapons. He has made speeches on this subject; he has campaigned on this issue; he addressed it in the debates; and he launched the SDI program with this goal in mind. The President hasn't changed. What has changed is that his goal is now being taken seriously. I heard someone say that all this was fine as long as it was only campaign talk. Well, they weren't listening carefully. Now it is being discussed for real.

Freedom and Security

Obviously, we are taking on a difficult task as we move to create the conditions in which we can assure the freedom and security of our country and our allies without the constant threat of nuclear catastrophe. Progress—whether in science or foreign affairs—often has to do with the reinterpretation of fundamental ideas.

Times of reinterpretation are difficult. Hard thinking can hurt your head. But we cannot shirk the challenge. As Albert Einstein warned after the dawn of the nuclear age: "Everything has changed but our way of thinking." That's a sage observation—particularly as we continue to look at the problem of managing our long-term relations with the Soviet Union in a time of dramatic technological and strategic change.

So it just may be that nuclear weapons, and the strategy of mutual assured destruction that has shaped our defense policy for decades, are part of the old way of thinking. We have to start to wrap our minds around new interpretations and build new realities. If we do, perhaps we can shape a more secure world for everybody.

George P. Shultz is the US secretary of state.

"The Reykjavik proposals may well have set back the cause of responsible arms control by many years."

The Reykjavik Summit Hindered Peace

Brent Scowcroft, John Deutch, and R. James Woolsey

Events during the autumn of 1986 have produced greater confusion in American strategic policy than perhaps at any other time in the nuclear age. After unveiling its startling proposal at the Reykjavik summit meeting in October that the United States and the Soviet Union agree to ban all ballistic missiles within a decade—a proposal that was a major departure from NATO strategy that has kept peace in Europe for 40 years—the Reagan Administration has hesitantly begun to develop a rationale for that position. At the same time, the Administration is seeking to persuade the nation not only to maintain at least some nuclear deterrent, including ballistic missiles, but also to make improvements in the survivability of its ICBM force. Administration officials are not finding the intellectual task of squaring this circle an easy one. . . .

Creating an Enemy

In 1986, . . . the key decision-makers in the executive branch developed a single-minded approach to seize the national and international agenda. To accomplish this, a single enemy had to be identified. The decision-makers felt that offensive nuclear weapons could be painted as the problem—the fewer the better. Moreover, the deeper the reductions, the more politically popular they would be.

The decision-makers had flirted with such an idea before, but in this new exhilarating environment two sets of interests came together to produce a powerful force that pushed through a breathtaking series of proposals at Reykjavik—including one to ban all ballistic missiles within a decade. The first was the President's philosophical conviction that offensive nuclear weapons are evil, and his ebullience about

the future if their numbers could be deeply cut, to the vanishing point if possible. Several of his senior advisers shared this vision. The second was the desire of some of the President's defense and arms-control advisers to use proposals for drastic cuts as a negotiating lever for tough bargaining—or even as a device to make agreement with the Russians impossible.

In this spirit of enthusiastic confusion and mixed purposes, the Administration developed a theory that also had a patina of technical respectability: the agreed abolition of ballistic missiles and the development of a Strategic Defense Initiative (known to its opponents as Star Wars), now to be an "insurance policy." This theory held that trashing the strategy of deterrence would not interfere either with the pursuit of peace or the protection of freedom. It was reportedly one word away from becoming the common policy of the United States and the Soviet Union; only the Russians' insistence on the word "laboratory" as the key to limiting the S.D.I. testing program prevented the new dawn from breaking. . . .

Damaging the Triad

Abandoning ballistic missiles, as proposed at Reykjavik would eliminate two legs of the American triad—made up of land-based, sea-based and airborne nuclear weapons—a structure designed to enhance the mutual survivability of the three parts of American strategic forces.

It would mean the total elimination of submarine-launched ballistic missiles, which can both survive a Soviet attack and penetrate Soviet defenses.

The American bomber forces at their bases would be especially vulnerable to Soviet cruise missiles, which could presumably replace the ballistic missiles on Soviet submarines. The United States does not currently have the capability to detect such an attack, much less to defend against it.

True, the United States bomber and cruise-missile force is much more capable than the Russians'. But, unlike ballistic missiles, bombers and cruise missiles would be forced to penetrate massive Soviet air defenses to reach their targets. And they would have to do so unaided by ballistic-missile attacks designed to suppress such air defenses. The United States, on the other hand, has essentially no air defense.

And what about verification of a ban on ballistic missiles, much less one on all nuclear weapons? At an agreed level of zero for anything—ballistic missiles, nuclear weapons—when a few can convey great advantage, complete verification becomes extraordinarily important. And when ICBM's can fit onto 18-wheel trucks, it also becomes exceedingly difficult. A Soviet state in which the United States could verify with even a modicum of confidence the total absence of ballistic missiles, much less the abolition of all nuclear weapons, would have to be a state very different from the Soviet Union of today.

Imperfect Solution

The Administration admits such an agreement would not be perfect. But, officials argue, the Strategic Defense Initiative will be an insurance policy if the Russians cheat. Though S.D.I. under the proposal would be doubly weakened from its most robust form—a highly classified, multitiered American system—the Administration would have us believe that it could still overcome any Soviet cheating. Though the Russians would be provided with S.D.I. technology, the program is to be so perfect that presumably no level of knowledge could hurt it. Further, a system designed only as "insurance" against Soviet cheating would be less capable than one designed to defend against current Soviet forces.

"The zero option would leave Western Europe naked to the 600 or so Soviet shorter-range missiles."

At the same time the United States is undertaking these offensive cuts and defensive redirections, the Administration will apparently be trying to convince the public that the country also needs a major conventional and chemical military buildup and a massive air-defense system. The new air defenses would have to be more effective, one would suppose, if the Russians and Washington were permitted bombers and cruise missiles under the agreement. But even if Washington agreed to sign the unrealistic ban-all-nukes Soviet proposal discussed in Reykjavik, covert nuclear weapons can fit into suitcases—which means they can be carried

by Aeroflot or even the drug-smuggler aircraft that flood America's night-time skies. The United States would need heavy air defenses in either case, and they would have to be perfect too, for the Administration would have trashed the most survivable and effective part of the country's offensive deterrent. . . .

The Future of Arms Control

Where does this leave the prospect for arms control? In the current environment, there are doubtless some senior officials who regard the Administration's zero ballistic-missile proposal at Reykjavik as a sincere effort to establish a radically new basis for United States-Soviet relations. But there are others for whom tactics are paramount, and this can produce extreme demands.

In any negotiations, there is an imprecise border between mere tough bargaining and an intentional thwarting of an agreement by the statement of wholly unacceptable terms. If you cross the border you may lose the deal. In bartering to buy something, you often have nothing to lose by taking a tough stance; perhaps you were ambivalent about the purchase anyway. The best way to get a good price from a rug merchant is to half-convince yourself that you don't really want the rug; the merchant may cut the price just as you're walking out.

But in strategic-arms negotiations, there is a symmetry to most agreed-upon limitations. If Washington proposes that Moscow have zero intermediate-range missiles in Europe, or zero mobile ICBM's, or zero ballistic missiles, it can expect the same demand in return. Tough bargaining proposals here should be ones that you are prepared to live with, because you can lose not just the deal itself but—by undermining public support for your programs—also lose what you already have.

Tough bargaining helped lead to the "zero option"—the proposal to deploy no American or Soviet intermediate-range missiles in Europe. When it was first proposed, in 1981, this may have seemed unacceptable to the Russians; it had some attractive features for Americans, however, since the United States had not yet deployed intermediate-range missiles and would have been trading potential United States systems for existing Soviet ones.

The Zero Option

Now, however, the Russians have agreed to a version of the zero option, and it is a very different matter. Today, zero intermediate-range on each side in Europe means completely withdrawing the intermediate-range missiles that the United States and its allies have recently worked hard to deploy. The current zero option would leave Western Europe naked to the 600 or so Soviet shorter-range missiles that are essentially unmatched by United States systems. A sounder American proposal—for each side to keep 100 intermediate-range warheads in Europe (in addition to a similar number in Asia and the United States)—was apparently scrapped and the zero option for Europe resuscitated in the heady atmosphere of Reykjavik.

Another, more troubling United States position is the proposal—set forth in Reykjavik, and now tabled in Geneva—to ban all ballistic missiles within 10 years. This proposal would mean that the United States, in order to maintain a deterrent, would have to rely solely on its bombers and cruise missiles to penetrate the numerous Soviet radar installations, surface-to-air missiles and fighter interceptors that constitute the world's most massive air-defense network.

"The United States can ill afford suddenly to cast off the strategy that has, however precariously, preserved peace for 40 years."

Underlying this tactical negotiating approach is the view of some Administration officials that the American people cannot be counted on to support reasonable modernization of strategic forces for offensive use and careful, gradual arms control. This fear, which may in part be based on the unwise but temporary efforts by Congress to restrict United States strategic programs in the mid-1970's following SALT I, is overblown.

Admittedly, politicians need to do a better job explaining major strategic notions—the degree to which NATO rests on nuclear deterrence, for instance, and the fact that modernization is needed to improve the survivability of weaponry and to deter Soviet conventional and nuclear attack—not to add to the size of our arsenal. Explanations are harder when events—Vietnam, Watergate, the Iran-contra imbroglio—disrupt executive-legislative and Republican-Democratic cooperation. But Americans are generally far more willing to support sensible strategic programs and careful arms-control talks than some would suggest.

Publicity Hounds

In addition to domestic politics, sincere beliefs and negotiating tactics, another factor contributing to the Administration's trashing of deterrence has been a propensity for flashy, staged public events and for proposals that attract television news cameras. There is certainly nothing wrong with presenting national strategy in a favorable light, but if one begins and ends strategic planning with an eye to the next evening's news and polls, one courts eventual disaster—especially considering that the opponents,

the current world chess champions, plan many moves ahead.

For all these reasons, there is now a great deal of uncertainty about our nation's strategic policy. It is unclear whether the Administration has fundamentally undermined the country's ability, and the public's support of that ability, to maintain nuclear deterrence. It is also unclear whether it is too late to drop back into a more modest, careful, gradual approach toward strategic modernization. It is clear, though, that thus far S.D.I. has already protected the United States, by preventing an agreement at Reykjavik that would have: destroyed the American ballistic-missile deterrent within a decade; left American bombers and cruise missiles facing extensive air defenses and the Russians facing essentially none; weakened the announced S.D.I. rationale (because it would become only an "insurance policy"); removed United States intermediate-range forces from Europe and left some 600 Soviet shorter-range missiles unopposed; allowed the Russians to maintain their advantage in conventional and chemical forces, and undercut the West's support for maintaining its defenses.

The Reykjavik proposals may well have set back the cause of responsible arms control by many years. Since the early 1970's, leaders of both parties (when not running for office or addressing blatantly antinuclear groups) have been urging a more realistic approach to arms negotiations. While recognizing the understandable public urge for a dramatic and simple agreement that would transform the nuclear competition, most leaders have urged more modest expectations for formal agreements. They have felt that agreements should focus on stabilizing measures that reduce the probability of nuclear war and not on expected earthshaking breakthroughs between two competing superpowers. The Administration's initiative at Reykjavik has now been seized upon by both the right and the left, for different reasons, as demonstrating that it is possible for the leaders of East and West, merely by signing the right paper, to bring lasting peace.

Patience

One of the many unfortunate aspects of this illusion is that it could undermine the willingness of many in the West to be patient about deterrence just as patience is beginning to pay off. The Soviet Union faces many problems, which should lend us some reasonable hope that firmness, strength, and careful arms-control proposals could help produce a positive trend. Under Mikhail Gorbachev, there have been some signs of change in Russia. Information on disasters and riots has been provided more openly than in the past, and a few prominent dissidents have been freed. But we must be cautious here.

From Peter the Great to Nikita Khrushchev, Russian leaders who have been domestic reformers have often been the most aggressive in foreign policy. Moreover, leaders who dare to sponsor bold changes can be ousted if internal reaction is strongly negative; this happened to both Georgi Malenkov and Khrushchev. If domestic reform or—less likely—both domestic reform and foreign-policy retrenchment should be on Gorbachev's mind, this could happen to him as well—and happen faster than we could rebuild an abandoned deterrent. Further, by undermining the case for modernizing and making more survivable our offensive weaponry, the Administration has risked creating an unstable environment for its successor. A later President who might want to return to a policy of careful negotiation and strategic-force modernization—whatever his policy on S.D.I.—could find that path more difficult. And a President who wanted S.D.I. to be something more than an insurance policy could find his hands tied. . . .

Stop and Regroup

It is time to stop and regroup. The United States can ill afford suddenly to cast off the strategy that has, however precariously, preserved peace for 40 years. Congress must have a central role in any effort to return to moderation. Because of its structure and organization, however, Congress has no naturally coherent view of defense and arms-control policy. It is currently divided among those who passionately believe that the military competition between the United States and the Soviet Union is a ghastly mistake; those who support realistic policies to deal with difficult defense questions, and those who—like the Administration—have great faith in single solutions. There is considerable strain among these groups, notwithstanding the fact that some Congressmen are at various times adherents of more than one of them.

It is, of course, in the executive branch that foreign policy and national-security policy should be crafted. But when the executive branch proposes to cripple the nation's deterrent, as it did at Reykjavik, the security of the nation, indeed of the world's democracies as a whole, demands that Congress demonstrate great responsibility and exert its constitutional powers wisely and carefully. This is no time to try to take advantage of the apparent confusion in the executive branch or to impair even further America's deterrent posture. It is time, rather, for Congressional statesmanship of the highest order to repair the damage already done.

Brent Scowcroft was national security advisor from 1975 to 1977. John Deutch was under secretary of energy from 1977 to 1979. R. James Woolsey was under secretary of the navy from 1977 to 1979.

"In the secret espionage war there is no such thing as detente. The secret war conducted by Soviet intelligence is perpetual."

Soviet Spying Is Rampant

Stanislav Levchenko

During the last two years [1985-87], the U.S. Department of Justice has prosecuted a dozen important espionage cases. Most of them involved American citizens recruited by Soviet intelligence services to betray the secrets of their country. Some of the cases, such as John Walker's, Jerry Whitworth's and others, were extremely damaging to U.S. national security, and it will cost American taxpayers tens of millions of dollars to undo the damage.

The latest case, involving at least two U.S. Marine Corps guards stationed at the American Embassy in Moscow, is truly sensational.

If it is true that the Marines had been recruited by the Soviets and that they let them into the most secret part of the embassy—the communications center—it will mean that the Soviets managed to monitor both extremely sensitive conversations among embassy personnel and diplomatic messages to and from Washington.

The real extent of damage from this apparent breach of security is still being evaluated.

Sophisticated, Successful Spies

All these cases show that the activities of Soviet intelligence services against this country are conducted on a large scale and can be considered highly successful. But what is the Soviet intelligence apparatus?

Most of us have watched movies about the notorious KGB and have read spy novels. Unfortunately, many of them do not present a realistic picture. If every Soviet intelligence officer had iron teeth, looked like an obvious villain, dressed sloppily and was as silly as some of those portrayed in the movies, the task of uncovering Soviet spies would be very easy.

The reality, however, is quite different, and most

people in this country are unaware of the scope and the methods of the Soviet espionage effort against the United States.

Not far from the Kremlin in Moscow, on Dzerzhinsky Square, stands a huge, stolid, grayish building. No sign suggests its purpose. In the center of the square, condemned to eternal solitude, stands a bronze statue of "Iron Felix"—Felix Dzerzhinsky, the first chief of the infamous Soviet security police.

The building behind his back houses the largest intelligence and counterintelligence organization in the history of mankind—the State Security Committee, known to the whole world as the KGB. It was organized in December 1917, two months after the Great October Revolution, and its initial task was strictly domestic: to eliminate domestic opposition to the new Soviet regime.

During the Red Terror campaign in the first few years of Soviet power, hundreds of thousands who disagreed with the Bolsheviks were executed. From 1937 to 1953, under Soviet dictator Josef Stalin's orders, the security police staged another wave of bloody terror, unprecedented in the history of modern civilization, in which perhaps as many as 20 million Soviet citizens perished.

The KGB Is Above the Law

The security-police operation became a main pillar of the socialist regime. It was put above the law. It became the ruthless mechanism of the Soviet socialist dictatorship for the subjugation of its own people, in the interests of the Communist Party elite and government bureaucracy spawned by the October Revolution.

This mentality of being above the law and unaccountable to anyone except the highest authorities of the regime it served spilled over into the KGB's foreign intelligence operations, including its operations in the United States, which started in the early 1920s.

Stanislav Levchenko, "Inside the KGB: A Soviet Defector Describes the KGB's Secret War Against the West," *The San Diego Union*, April 12, 1987.

During its almost 70 years of existence, the KGB has developed a highly professional external intelligence service that also is the world's largest—the First Chief Directorate. It is accountable only to the Soviet Politburo. Its finances are enormous. Nobody, except the Soviet leaders, tells the FCD what is moral and what is not. What matters is the product, the results, and almost any method to achieve it is acceptable.

The FCD employs highly educated officers, graduates from the best Soviet universities and colleges, most of whom are fluent in foreign languages, including exotic tongues.

"Soviet intelligence officers are looking for people with vulnerabilities that make them susceptible to recruitment, such as greed, political sympathy toward the Soviet Union, . . . or disagreement with official U.S. policy on certain issues."

The general staff of the Soviet army also has its own external intelligence service, the GRU, which collects military and high technology intelligence on a global basis. In many respects, the KGB's and the GRU's tasks are similar, except that the KGB's operations are broader and include, in addition to military and technical intelligence, such areas as political and economic intelligence and disinformation operations designed to influence public opinion abroad and to shape the domestic and foreign policies of other countries.

All Over the World

Both the KGB's FCD and the GRU have undercover officers in every country in the world. From 35 to 40 percent of all Soviet officials stationed abroad are full-time KGB or GRU officers. Practically all other Soviet citizens abroad also are involved in collecting intelligence as co-opted agents. There is no country in the Free World that has such an enormous intelligence apparatus.

The KGB and the GRU have networks of foreign nationals working for them in every country.

I was stationed in Japan as a KGB political intelligence officer from 1975 to 1979, under cover as Tokyo bureau chief of the Soviet weekly magazine "New Times." The KGB network in Japan at that time consisted of about 200 Japanese nationals recruited by the Soviets. Among them were such prominent figures as Ishida Hirohide, former minister of labor and an influential leader of the ruling Liberal Democratic Party, several socialist members of Parliament, and a personal adviser to

the owner and later the managing editor of Takuji Yamane, the largest conservative newspaper in Japan, with a circulation of more than 3 million copies.

The KGB thus was able to obtain classified documents from many sensitive offices of the Japanese government, including secret cables of the Foreign Office. The Soviets managed to recruit prominent journalists in most of the Japanese newspapers. They also were running highly sophisticated, large-scale operations to influence Japanese public opinion.

The Soviets' Main Enemy

What the Soviets were doing in Japan in my time, they also were doing, and still are, in most other countries of the world.

There is, however, one country that always remains the main target of KGB and GRU activities. It is the United States, which in the early 1950s, a few years after World War II, was named by the Soviet Politburo as "the main enemy" of the Soviet Union. Today, 30 years later, that definition is still in effect.

Soviet intelligence has been operating in this country since the 1920s. Until the late 1930s it was conducting its clandestine activities here virtually unopposed—the FBI started its anti-espionage efforts only shortly before World War II. Historically, the Soviets have managed to achieve spectacular operational successes in the United States. One of the most important ones was the acquisition of atomic bomb secrets in the 1950s from a group of agents consisting of Americans and Canadians.

The KGB and the GRU have vast experience in recruiting and handling Americans. Soviet intelligence officers are looking for people with vulnerabilities that make them susceptible to recruitment, such as greed, political sympathy toward the Soviet Union or other countries, or disagreement with official U.S. policy on certain issues.

Egomania, dissatisfaction with one's career and promiscuity are also among the features Soviet intelligence officers consider as bases for possible recruitment.

The Walker Ring

Convicted Soviet agent John Walker, for instance, had been motivated by greed. But he also reportedly liked the thrill of espionage. Another convicted member of Walker's espionage ring, Jerry Whitworth, also loved money. Cool-mindedly, without any pangs of conscience, he sold the Soviets, through John Walker, highly classified information on the cryptosystems of the U.S. Navy.

There are reasons to believe that for about 10 years the Soviets were able to read large parts of the secret communications of the U.S. Navy. The KGB handled the Walker ring in such a sophisticated manner that he was able to work for them without being detected for almost two decades.

In spite of numerous successful recruitments conducted on the territory of this country, continuous improvements in FBI counterintelligence activities have made it increasingly difficult for the Soviets to establish new contacts and to "run" them in the United States.

That is why for the past several years the KGB has preferred to conduct personal meetings with its American agents on the territory of other countries. For instance, Walker had to fly to Austria, Morocco and possibly other countries to get instructions from his KGB case officer.

The Soviets also prefer to recruit Americans while the latter live or visit abroad. Tens of thousands of American citizens—military personnel, foreign service officers, businessmen, students—reside in many foreign countries, and in some of these countries it is easier for the KGB to operate without being detected than on the territory of the United States.

Thousands of Recruiters

The main task of the KGB and GRU stations—"residencies" in Soviet parlance—in any country is to recruit U.S. citizens. For successful recruitment of an American, Soviet intelligence officers are awarded the highest Soviet medals and get automatic promotions. Reportedly, during the last 18 years, several of John Walker's handlers were rewarded generously by the Supreme Soviet of the U.S.S.R.

Not surprisingly, the wildest recruitment efforts against Americans are undertaken by the KGB and the GRU in the Soviet Union itself, where Soviet intelligence feels at home and can operate with virtual impunity. Thousands of KGB and GRU officers are involved in targeting U.S. citizens on the territory of the U.S.S.R. Many more thousands of secret informers report on the activities of foreigners to Soviet intelligence and counterintelligence agencies, and many of these informers are actively involved in entrapment efforts against Americans in Moscow and other Soviet cities.

Bearing in mind that the KGB includes a vast apparatus for domestic oppression, it is easy to understand why most Soviet citizens, when approached by the KGB or the GRU with the offer of "cooperation," prefer not to refuse it because they know that a rejection of such an "offer" would get them into deep trouble.

Women agree to involve foreigners in sexual relationships.

Black market profiteers who are engaged in illegal currency trading or speculation would gladly set traps for foreigners pointed out to them by the KGB in exchange for "protection" for the rest of their operations.

The KGB and the GRU never hesitate to compromise visiting Americans and to recruit them through ruthless blackmail. Unfortunately, some U.S. citizens disregard security regulations and make themselves vulnerable to the Soviet intelligence efforts. Several U.S. Marine Corps guards at the U.S. Embassy in Moscow allegedly violated their instruction not to fraternize with Soviet women. They probably thought the KGB would not outsmart them, but they were, of course, tragically wrong.

The KGB's best officers are members of the "American target task force." In Moscow, the KGB even has a special group of veterans whose specialty is breaking into the U.S. Embassy or apartments or hotel rooms where Americans live. Members of this group are capable of opening any type of safe and planting electronic listening devices in any equipment within minutes.

"The KGB and the GRU . . . . use any relaxation in the climate in relations between Moscow and Washington to enhance their recruitment efforts."

With the exception of cases when Americans volunteer to cooperate with Soviet intelligence—and the sad truth is that in the majority of espionage cases the Americans involved did offer their services to the Soviets for money—the KGB or GRU officers do not introduce themselves as intelligence officers. They use a great variety of covers and cover stories. They introduce themselves as "clean" diplomats, trade mission officers, journalists, scholars, public relations officers, etc., when they approach foreign nationals.

It is also important to realize that most of the Soviets visiting this country to study in American universities, or as members of scientific, cultural, sports and trade exchange programs, are involved in gathering intelligence. Many of them are not professional spies, but are co-opted by the KGB or the GRU. If any Soviet citizen refuses to fulfill the intelligence requirements, he or she will never be permitted to travel abroad.

Detente

The KGB and the GRU are extremely aggressive and cynical intelligence services. They use any relaxation of the climate in relations between Moscow and Washington to enhance their recruitment efforts.

I was in Tokyo when the Helsinki Agreement, which started the so-called period of "detente," was signed. A few days later I read a top secret cable signed by FCD Director General Kryuchkov. This cable ordered every KGB officer stationed in every country in the world to double recruitment efforts against Americans and citizens of other NATO countries immediately.

Mr. Kryuchkov wrote: "Americans and other foreigners tend to be tranquilized by better relations between our countries; at such times they tend to consider the Soviet Union as a trustworthy partner and therefore are less reluctant to establish social and business contacts with us."

There is no doubt that the Soviet intelligence services are using the policy of so-called "openness" instituted by General Secretary Mikhail Gorbachev for the same purpose. They present the limited reforms begun by the Soviet leader as a sign that the Soviet system is experiencing a period of true "democratization," that there is no such thing as the "Soviet threat" anymore, in order to weaken the vigilance of the citizens of the Free World countries.

Of course, improved relations between the superpowers can be a positive political achievement. Better relations can reduce the threat of another war. But we have to realize that in the secret espionage war there is no such thing as detente. The secret war conducted by Soviet intelligence is perpetual.

Urbane, Charming Spies

Soviet embassies, consulates, trade missions and tourist offices do not display signs warning "Beware of Spies," and nobody expects to find them. Many people who have a chance to meet Soviet officials are surprised how urbane and even charming they can be—a picture so far removed from the goons portrayed in the movies.

That makes Soviet intelligence officers even more dangerous. And all of us should be aware that the number of Soviet spies is large, and that their job is to steal information or high technology. It is their duty, assigned to them by the Kremlin leaders.

Stanislav Levchenko, a former KGB officer, defected in 1979 and was granted political asylum in the US. He is the author of On the Wrong Side: My Life in the KGB.

"When a [spy] scandal does arise, the U.S. tries to milk it for maximum propaganda value."

Soviet Spying Is Exaggerated

Jim Naureckas and Charles Krauthammer

Editor's note: Part I of the following viewpoint is by Jim Naureckas; Part II is by Charles Krauthammer.

I

Secretary of State George Shultz's recent mission to Moscow to discuss arms negotiations was overshadowed by intense controversy over alleged Soviet espionage. Reports of Soviet infiltration and bugging of the U.S. Embassy in Moscow were taken so seriously that 70 senators voted that Shultz should not travel to Moscow at all because his security could not be guaranteed. A chance at improved U.S.-Soviet relations seemed to be lost because of an unfortunate coincidence.

Spy Scandal History

But was the timing of the latest spy revelations a coincidence? The history of U.S. spy scandals suggests that their relationship to American foreign policy objectives may not be entirely accidental. Consider the following:

• In February 1976, when Gerald Ford was under heavy pressure . . . to back away from the Soviets, reports were leaked that the KGB was bombarding the U.S. Embassy in Moscow with microwaves. Initially portrayed as an espionage technique, the broadcasting later seemed more like an attempt to jam U.S. electronic surveillance. In any case, U.S. officials said they had known about the microwaves for 15 years, but the leaks still produced an uproar over Soviet spying.

• Jimmy Carter's "get tough" policy toward the Soviets, unveiled in June 1978, was accompanied by a "spy war" touched off when two Soviet United Nations employees, Rudolf Chernyayev and Valdik

Jim Naureckas, "Forget Irangate, Forget Arms Control We Got Sex! We Got Spies!" April 22-28, 1987. Excerpted from *In These Times*, 1300 W. Belmont, Chicago, IL 60657, (312) 472-5700. Published weekly. Annual Subscription: $34.95.
Charles Krauthammer, "Spy Hysteria," *The Washington Post National Weekly Edition*, May 4, 1987. © 1987, Washington Post Writers Group, reprinted with permission.

Enger, were arrested and convicted in an FBI sting operation. "The U.S.," wrote *Time*, "had deliberately violated an informal understanding between Soviet and American intelligence services that each other's spies will be discreetly ferreted out of the country when they are caught."

• The August-September 1985 "spy dust" scare was set off when the U.S. State Department announced that the KGB was sprinkling the Moscow embassy with NPDD, a supposedly carcinogenic substance visible only under infrared light. The State Department admitted knowing about this "revelation" for nine years, but it chose to reveal it the week the U.S. began major Star Wars testing, which officials feared might have put the U.S. at a disadvantage at the November 1985 summit in Geneva.

• Gennadi Zakharov, a Soviet who worked for the U.N., was set up and arrested by the FBI in August 1986. The arrest, the *New York Times* reported, was approved by then-National Security Council chief John Poindexter. As in the 1978 case, the U.S. violated protocol by keeping Zakharov in custody, and the Soviets retaliated by arresting reporter Nicholas Daniloff. The affair was not settled until September 30, [1986] putting the Soviets on the defensive at the Reykjavik summit which began 10 days later.

Were these scandals carefully stage-managed public relations efforts? That's what the Soviets claim. A Soviet diplomatic spokesman told *In These Times*, "Whenever the possibility for improved relations between the Soviet Union and America arises, certain circles in the U.S. try to undermine that possibility." The State Department had no comment on the Soviet charge. But the very least that can be said is that when a scandal does arise, the U.S. tries to milk it for maximum propaganda value.

The U.S. Embassy in Moscow is now at the center

of another spy scandal—or rather, of two scandals. The first involves Clayton Lonetree, the Marine sergeant who told his supervisors last December [1986] that he had slept with a Soviet woman, Violetta Seina, when he was a guard at the embassy in 1985 and early 1986. Lonetree's confession made no mention of letting Seina or anyone else into the embassy. That allegation came from one of Lonetree's fellow Marine guards, Cpl. Arnold Bracy, who told investigators he stood guard while Lonetree allowed KGB agents to enter sensitive embassy areas. However, according to Lonetree's lawyer, William Kunstler, Bracy has recanted this statement. Kunstler told *In These Times* that polygraph tests given to Bracy support his present claim that he and Lonetree did not allow anyone into the embassy.

"The Soviets called the American reaction to the embassy story 'spy hysteria.' . . . Hysteria it is."

Kunstler described the case against his client as "a combination of his fantasy and their fraud. . . . The administration wants to hang somebody," he said. "It's a pretty good way to drive contragate off the front pages." Both the State Department and the Marine Corps declined to discuss the Lonetree case with *In These Times*, but press reports say unnamed administration officials admit the government has no evidence of the embassy violation beyond Bracy's recanted statement.

Even if Bracy's earlier story is true, the extent of security damage remains unclear. Seina was an embassy employee at the time and so had regular access to much of the facilities. Alexander Cockburn reported in a *Wall Street Journal* column that classified areas of the embassy have combination locks and are not accessible to the guards. The State Department acknowledged to *In These Times* that "in certain embassies guards do not have access to certain communications areas."

But U.S. politicians had a strong bipartisan reaction to the alleged breach of security: Reagan was calling it "outrageous" while Senate Majority Leader Robert Byrd (D-WV) declared Lonetree and Bracy "not fit to live." The uproar culminated in the Senate's formal recommendation that Shultz not go to Moscow, for fear that Seina had planted bugs that are still uncovered, more than a year later, in every part of the embassy.

The US Embassy Scandal

The other scandal concerns the new embassy complex, of which completion is now more than three years overdue. Charges have been leveled that the new embassy has been riddled with

eavesdropping devices by Soviet construction crews, and may never be secure. Congressional critics suggest the U.S. should tear down the building and start over, which could result in the U.S. moving out of its present embassy in 1995 or later.

These allegations, like others that have been raised about the U.S. Embassy in Moscow, are nothing new. The U.S. was concerned from the beginning of the project that the Soviets would attempt to implant listening devices in the structure. In fact, in 1983 the *New York Times* reported that Soviet construction workers had walked off the job at the new embassy site, saying that the X-ray device the U.S. was using to check the building for spy devices was a health hazard.

"They've known from the start that we were going to check every square inch of those buildings for bugs," the *New York Times* quoted an embassy source as saying at the time.

Behind the Controversy

Part of why this scandal has caused such a widespread uproar is the desire of congressional critics to embarrass the president. Among those senators voting against the Shultz trip to Moscow were such arms control advocates as Alan Cranston (D-CA) and John Chafee (R-RI). But part may be attributed to administration factions who wanted to be able to explain the disappointing Shultz trip on the "pall" cast over negotiations by Soviet espionage.

Shultz went to Moscow bearing some unfriendly proposals. A struggle between the hardline anti-arms control Department of Defense (DoD) and the slightly more dovish State Department was won by the Pentagon. It was the DoD's position that Shultz presented to his Soviet counterparts: the period over which proposed arms reductions took place would be lengthened, the period for which the Anti-Ballistic Missile Treaty would be adhered to (even under Reagan's perverse interpretation) would be shortened and the Soviets' offer to improve the partial nuclear test bans would not be taken up. Shultz was also directed to keep on the table a Defense Department proposal that would eliminate mobile ICBMs—which was another U.S. proposal that would require the USSR to destroy existing weapons, while the only U.S. weapons affected were still on the drawing board.

Most important, however, Shultz apparently told Gorbachev that the U.S. did not want to remove all missiles from Europe after all, despite the much-publicized "Zero Option" of 1981. The administration blames Western Europe for the switch, claiming that U.S. allies worry about a debatable Soviet superiority in conventional weapons.

Despite efforts by both sides to put an optimistic spin on the talks, both sides remain far apart on the most important issues—long-range missiles and Star

Wars. To the extent that the U.S. posture changed, it was away from the Soviet position.

II

Remember the Soviet brigade in Cuba? In the summer of 1979, President Carter submitted the SALT II treaty to the Senate for ratification. At which point Sen. Frank Church, chairman of the Foreign Relations Committee, discovered a Soviet brigade in Cuba. To meet the "crisis," SALT II hearings were postponed. The president was put on the defensive, the atmosphere was poisoned, the treaty was delayed and then sunk by the Soviet invasion of Afghanistan. Then it turned out that the brigade had been there for 16 years. It was the nonissue of the decade. But it did its damage.

Bogus Hysteria

Every decade has its bogus Cuban brigade. Now we have ours: the embassy spy hysteria. The greatest deliberative body in the world is again in an arms control mood, pushing for treaties—test ban, the Strategic Defensive Initiative, even a revived SALT II—from a weakened president. So, a weakened president, desperate to shore himself up politically and within sight of a Euromissile treaty, prepares to dispatch his Secretary of State to Moscow for crucial arms control talks. And what happens? The Senate discovers that the Soviets have been spying on our embassy in Moscow and that our new embassy there is riddled with bugs. Shocked, it passes a resolution urging George Shultz to cancel his talks with the Soviets if they don't agree to a last-minute change of venue, something they plainly would not agree to.

The Kremlin Is Right

The Soviets called the American reaction to the embassy story "spy hysteria." The Kremlin is not often right. This case is an exception. Hysteria it is. There is absolutely nothing new here. The Soviets have been building their hilltop, spy-nest Washington embassy for 10 years. Anyone who drives by can see the forest of antennas atop the buildings from which the Soviets can listen in on any conversation they please. And we have long known that our new Moscow embassy was bugged right down to the concrete foundation. Sen. Daniel P. Moynihan, for one, has been complaining about the embassy problems for years. Every administration since Nixon has ignored it. What happens? A couple of U.S. Marine guards in Moscow are alleged to have betrayed their country and let in the Soviets in exchange for the favors of a KGB Mata Hari, and Washington goes bonkers.

"Whereas the Soviet Union has totally compromised the security of our embassy in Moscow . . ." intoned the Senate, 70 to 30. Not exactly. The Marines did the compromising. The Soviets merely walked through an open door. For that they are vilified.

"Sordid tricks," an "affront," an "assault on U.S. embassy security," complained *The Wall Street Journal*. A "rape of our national privacy," gasped William Safire. This country is "damned upset," claimed Secretary Shultz. The Soviets have trespassed "beyond the bounds of reason," agreed the president of the United States. And my favorite: [columnists] Evans and Novak bravely called for "a full-scale exposure of Soviet [spy] practices whatever the impact on arms control." Since they generally view arms control as an infection in need of a vaccine, they win the 1987 Br'er Rabbit ("Please please please don't fling me in dat briar patch") Award.

Miss Manners Espionage

"The Soviets," complained Lawrence Eagleburger, "just go too far." Really? The FBI tried to tunnel into the basement of the Soviet consulate in San Francisco in the early '70s. I wish they had made it. If FBI counterintelligence is not trying to seduce, blackmail and "turn" Soviet agents in this country, it should have its appropriations rescinded. Espionage does not play by Miss Manners. No wonder the Soviets, who operate generally by conspiracy, believe that American naiveté must be feigned and there are darker reasons for the spy hysteria.

"In fact we are just protesting . . . [Soviet] success at a game both of us play."

Even the shocked acknowledge, rather illogically, that the story is old. A decade old, admit Evans and Novak. *The Wall Street Journal*, allowing its indignation to be contradicted by its pride, boasted that it had run the bugged embassy story last October [1986].

Yet Washington has reacted as if the Soviets had, say, taken over a small Central American country. (Bad example: Washington is fairly calm about that prospect. Say, as if the Soviets had cheated at Olympic hockey.) The Senate, joined by a bevy of columnists, urges Shultz not to go to Moscow for arms control talks. Why? Because the embassy is not secure? But it has never been secure. To register a protest against Soviet "penetration" of our embassy (an unfortunate metaphor, given the circumstances)? But in fact we are just protesting their success at a game both of us play. I've even heard it said that our plans at Reykjavik were compromised. But until [this Marine-espionage incident], at least, the conventional wisdom in Washington was that Reykjavik was a wreck precisely because we had no plans there.

To his credit, Shultz went to Moscow and made considerable progress. The hysteria will now shortly blow itself out. What will remain are questions not about American security but about American seriousness. If Congress pretends to make high national policy on such things as arms control, it had better stop these absurd about-faces. Just when negotiations are heating up, to suggest boycotting talks over an issue that would be utterly peripheral if it were not phony is a demonstration of high unseriousness. Good thing the Cuban brigade syndrome strikes only once a decade.

Jim Naureckas is a research assistant for In These Times, *a socialist newspaper in Chicago. Charles Krauthammer, a senior editor at* The New Republic, *is a well-known political commentator and columnist.*

viewpoint 148

US Intelligence Is Effective

Scott D. Breckinridge

If it ain't broke, don't fix it.

There is no question that the United States government will, for the indefinite future, continue to need a complex and comprehensive intelligence system as a critical part of its national security apparatus. As long as the world continues in its present restless state, there will be a basic requirement for good factual knowledge and objective reporting on the questions that confront policymakers and planners.

Difficult policy decisions inevitably reflect political, economic, and military judgments—and occasionally subjective bias. The more difficult the decisions, the more likely they are to be controversial. It follows that information assembled by the nation's intelligence system—often the basis for policy judgments—may also be controversial, in its substance as well as with respect to the organization that produced it. The intelligence system will be the forum for many such controversies, and itself will sometimes be the target of those who seek to influence the source for the views they espouse.

Most observers would agree that if a national intelligence system did not exist, one would have to be created. Were a new system to be designed starting from scratch, managerial arrangements and bureaucratic controls would probably differ materially from those now in effect. Whatever the new administrative alignments, the basic missions and programs now in existence would have to be provided for. Those programs would carry with them certain imperatives for coordination and control that would compel procedures closely parallel to those now in use. Although all this would produce differences, many similarities would also be present, for the substance of the intelligence business would be essentially the same, whatever the organizational arrangements.

A Sprawling System

The sprawling nature of the existing system is tempting to those who feel certain that there could be better arrangements and procedures for directing and controlling things. There are so many people working at so many different problems, sometimes at odds in purpose and viewpoint, that in the abstract it seems there is considerable room for improvement. As a result, it is not at all unusual to hear, within the Intelligence Community, general discussion of how better to order the workings of the entire system. It was interesting, in this respect, to observe that DCI [Director of Central Intelligence William] Casey put into effect a reorganization of CIA's Intelligence Directorate on a geographic basis, in place of the long-standing organization based along substantive and functional lines. . . .

First, the fears of those who foresaw a militarist incubus in our government—one that would make political judgments subject to military reporting—should be allayed. Firm provision has been made for civilian control: The President and his senior cabinet officers in the National Security Council preside over the general national security program, of which intelligence is an important part; civilians can be designated as Director of Central Intelligence; and when a military officer holds the post, he or she is barred from certain types of ties with the military. "National intelligence" cannot be dominated by military "departmental" interests.

Beyond the narrower issue of military control over national intelligence, a major strength of the present system is the centering influence of the DCI. The absence of pre-World War II arrangements for sharing intelligence and coordinating its analysis was highlighted in the inquiries into the Pearl Harbor debacle. That was one of the basic reasons for establishing a central intelligence service. The [National Security Act of] 1947 requires the sharing of intelligence between the services—something once resisted by the military—and authorized the DCI to ensure that this provision is observed. . . .

Flexibility Is Necessary

The Intelligence Community is not arranged as a command organization, with neat lines of subordination and command being provided for every unit. When important issues surface that do not lend themselves to easy resolution, the apparent sense of disorder becomes disturbing to many outsiders, who would change existing arrangements so that the system would function with less difficulty.

Some believe—as does this author—that the vital missions assigned to the departments and agencies that house the intelligence organizations produce attitudes and purposes that must not be stifled in a rigid chain of command. Disagreement is healthy if handled professionally by individuals who know why they are taking particular positions. It simply is not always easy to mesh specialized departmental views with broader national views. Yet if a truly balanced and comprehensive national posture is to be achieved, it must be the product of responsible, considered judgments and not the arbitrary decisions that sometimes are the product of organizational unity. A monolithic system carries with it many weaknesses as well.

Perhaps the most important attribute of the present system is that it works. Given the different interests and missions within the system, it is fair to say that it works very well. . . .

Improving the System

The present system contains the necessary structure and procedures for continuous improvement. The technical specialists work on their problems, reduce data to sensible intelligence, and pass it on to those who need it. In comparing views with one another, the area specialists develop something of an informal consensus before an issue ever moves up the chain of command. Where problems cannot be agreed upon, usually among agencies, provisions for dissent are entirely adequate. Where there is substantive dissent, that should be enough of a signal for those at policy levels to call for a thorough review of the issue at stake. Nothing is suppressed, and views tend to find expression within the system.

Key to the functioning of the current system, which works remarkably well despite the opposing biases that exist in a large government, is the unrecorded myriad of informal channels of communication that have developed over the years. Formal procedure does not take over from reason,

and form is easily modified for special situations. Were some major attempt at reorganization to occur, with significant changes in command and control within the system, all the strongly functioning informal channels would be done long-lasting harm. They might never be reestablished. Crowding large analytical organizations into one place would create more havoc than enlightenment. . . .

The requirements for intelligence coverage continue. A major part of that coverage is timely—"real time" in the intelligence world—reporting on critical situations around the world. The nation cannot afford to let down its guard while it gets a new blueprint for handling the difficult problems that currently exist [and] would remain for any successor organization that might be created. The present system soundly meets the requirements of running the intelligence business. It should not be changed recklessly, just because it suffers the malady common to all administrative systems—imperfection. In short, evolutionary change has met past needs, and should be allowed to continue as new requirements and conditions demand.

Continued Attention to Details

Instead of major organizational change in the Intelligence Community, what is needed is continued close attention to the substantive content of the various programs conducted by its members. The numerous intelligence organizations are the first line of managerial responsibility, and they will be held accountable in their departments, as well as within the Intelligence Community, for their performance. The DCI—with his Intelligence Community Staff—has the organization and procedures for providing a coherent overview of activities. The Congress, in its legislative oversight capacity, should focus on this aspect of the work.

"The present system contains the necessary structure and procedures for continuous improvement."

The two costly and important collection programs—Signals Intelligence and Overhead Reconnaissance—should be kept under continuing review to ensure that they are complying with Community guidance and that they have the capabilities needed to provide the intelligence required by national policymakers and planners. The present system provides for this assurance. The Congress's interest should address the question of capabilities, executive direction, and results. Judgments about the systems must take into consideration not only the needs for peacetime but also the capabilities that would be essential in times of war. In this latter respect, operational resources for wartime are analogous to the general military readiness of our national defense. They must exceed purely peacetime needs in order to accommodate wartime expansion. The determination that no *unnecessary* redundancy exists is an appropriate area for congressional study.

Soviets in the Third World

Clandestine collection has always been the subject of changing perceptions. After CIA developed its resources and skills, its activities were shifted about the world as policymakers judged changing needs. Witness the emergence of Third World decolonization after World War II and the growing Soviet interests there. While CIA once began to focus its clandestine efforts against the so-called classical target of the Soviet Bloc, it soon became clear that policy levels wanted reporting of events in other parts of the world as well. For example, collection and reporting were insufficient for adequately judging the deterioration of the Iranian government prior to the fall of the Shah. The extent of reporting interests must be determined clearly and set for the long term; clandestine resources cannot be made to appear at the wave of a magician's wand. A long-range view with adequate programming is needed.

Analysis must continue to be organized on a comprehensive basis, not unlike its current arrangement, with attention given to the personnel and equipment resources needed to cope with a wide range of subject matter. This is important for State, Defense, and the military services, as well as for CIA.

There seems to be a growing requirement for both the traditional counterintelligence work directed against hostile espionage and the related activity of identifying and blocking terrorists. In the past few years, a growing number of official Soviet representatives have been expelled from various countries in which they were posted. Their expulsion could be a reflection of increased aggressiveness by the KGB and GRU [Soviet army intelligence agency] during the time that Yuri Andropov—former head of the KGB—was at the helm in the USSR. In our own country FBI Director William Webster has stated that the United States currently has "more people charged with espionage . . . than at any time in our history." This phenomenon is attributed by Webster to a combination of increased Soviet technological espionage and the emergence of an attitude among many individuals, devoid of loyalty to the United States.

Indications of mounting terrorist activity have also been observed throughout the world. Terrorism ranges from localized individuals and splinter groups disaffected with society and strike out in an almost random way at those around them, through elements of larger groups acting independently, to centrally trained and directed activities. The limited or informal organization of radical splinter groups makes such terrorists a difficult and less recognizable intelligence target than the international terrorist groups.

An Obvious Problem

Both the KGB and GRU have training facilities in Czechoslovakia for terrorist activities. Third World students attending the Patrice Lumumba University in Moscow return to their homes trained in political activities and organization and prepared to work with activist organizations to subvert their own governments. These people can be identified for attention by the security forces of their homelands, which are often in cooperation with U.S. intelligence organizations. There is a continuing trail of Soviet connections with such individuals. Arms of Soviet Bloc manufacture are usually used in terrorist acts. Some arms shipments have been intercepted. Financial support is not always mysterious; banks may be robbed, but Soviet support is clear. The fact that the political ideology of the international terrorist is often characterized by some form of Marxist thought constitutes more than symbolic coincidence. The track record of Marxist infiltration of groups organizing to oust an incumbent regime is quite clear. If ties to the Soviet Union are not always clearly demonstrable under rules of evidence in an Anglo-Saxon court, they are obvious to those who must work with the problem. . . .

"There seems to be a growing requirement for both the traditional counterintelligence work directed against hostile espionage and the related activity of identifying and blocking terrorists."

The type of terrorist activity that is part of an armed insurgency against an incumbent government, such as in Central America today, sometimes presents special problems. The Congress must come to grips with the problem, unencumbered by ideological confusion and artificial legalistic concepts that relate only peripherally to the facts. If the Congress is unable to clear its mind on this point, serious repercussions for our long-range national interests could occur.

Success Depends upon Secrecy

When the substantive content of the U.S. intelligence program is understood in terms of the world we live in, a clearer attitude on its work and needs will be necessary, in place of the confused ambivalence that often is apparent in congressional debate.

Finally, to quote George Washington:

> The necessity of procuring good Intelligence is apparent & need not be further urged—All that Remains for me to add is, that you keep the whole matter as secret as possible. For upon Secrecy, Success depends in Most Enterprizes of the kind, and for want of it, they are generally defeated, however well planned & promising a favourable issue.

The members of the Executive branch who know the classified facts on a controversial subject must restrain themselves from leaking information that supports their view. Perhaps some measure must be taken to ensure that they observe this requirement. Members of the Congress too often seem not to understand the underlying requirement for security, taking public stands that compromise basic programs and the national interest. They must consider carefully what is involved and how to handle issues *within the structure of the Congress*. And the Congress, as an institution, must determine the extent to which it will exercise restraint on its own members, by depriving them of positions with access to sensitive information when they prove unable to respect it. Congressional staff employees can be dismissed out of hand, and should be, but members are another problem. A few of them seem to feel that their membership in the select club they inhabit at the will of their constituents carries with it a right to violate security, regardless of the larger national interest.

"Our national intelligence system . . . has been put together remarkably well and functions with great effectiveness."

If this country is to have an intelligence system, there are certain conditions that must be accepted. A few elected officials should not feel free to attack the system publicly on peripheral issues when the Congress, in the larger sense, has approved the system. Our elected representatives are authorized to act for all of us and are accountable to their constituents. But not all the actions they take are, or always should be, in public.

Deserving of Support

Some secrecy is essential in the conduct of international diplomacy and in national defense programs. Similarly, the secrecy characteristic of the intelligence activities that support U.S. foreign policy and national defense are necessary to their success. The tendency of some Americans to expose in detail the secret activities of their government is a source of concern to our allies, who share secrets with us. We have not found the balance between necessary

public disclosure and unnecessary revelations, even though our political system ensures fully adequate accountability for both elected and appointed officials. And within our Executive branch there is an array of procedures and mechanisms for ensuring that programs are constructed and handled with reasonable responsibility.

As one takes a long look at the development of our national intelligence system, the broad judgment must be that it has been put together remarkably well and functions with great effectiveness. Indeed, it warrants a degree of support that it has not always received.

Scott D. Breckinridge has worked for the US Central Intelligence Agency for twenty-six years, both overseas and in Washington. He has twice been awarded the Distinguished Intelligence medal.

"Serious security deficiencies exist in a number of areas within the U.S. intelligence community."

US Intelligence Is Inadequate

Permanent Select Committee on Intelligence, House of Representatives

Over the past several years, a dangerous upward trend in successful espionage operations against the United States has occurred. Present and former U.S. Government employees with access to sensitive classified information have played the key roles in each operation. Damage to U.S. national security has been significant and is still being estimated. . . .

From its early days, the Administration has focused considerable attention and effort on improving the effectiveness of U.S. counter-intelligence. Concomitantly, the House and Senate Intelligence Committees have authorized significantly increased funding for counterintelligence and urged that counterintelligence concerns assume a higher priority within the intelligence community. These efforts have elevated the morale, status and numbers of counterintelligence personnel, helped cope with security investigation backlogs and encouraged new initiatives in some operational and policy areas. Nonetheless, it has become apparent that historical inadequacies in counterintelligence and countermeasures are so deep-seated and pervasive that fundamental problems remain. These must be addressed now with renewed determination and vigor.

Serious Problems

From its hearings and interviews, the Committee has determined that serious security deficiencies exist in a number of areas within the U.S. intelligence community. These deficiencies include faulty hiring practices, inadequate and inefficient background investigations, lack of full coordination and information exchange between agencies, insufficient adherence to the "need-to-know" principle, over-classification of security documents and proliferation of personnel clearances, thoughtless

Report by the Permanent Select Committee on Intelligence, House of Representatives, "United States Counterintelligence and Security Concerns—1986." Washington, DC: US Government Printing Office, 1987.

firing practices, and over-reliance on polygraph exams.

The Committee recognizes that the intelligence community has acknowledged some of the problems addressed in this report and that some of the solutions suggested herein already are being implemented. The Committee applauds these efforts, but urges still greater attention to counterintelligence issues, beginning with acknowledgment that manifest failures have reflected systemic inadequacies rather than mere aberrations or unavoidable risks. In general, within the intelligence community there appears to remain insufficient appreciation for the importance of counterintelligence concerns, an attitude often reflected in internal agency budgetary and policy prioritizations. Moreover, despite some recent improvement, the fragmented components of the counterintelligence community remain uncoordinated, divided and turf-conscious in virtually every substantive area, ranging from simple information-sharing or investigation to policy formulation and counterintelligence operations. Dramatic improvement will require fundamental shifts in attitudes as well as in approaches and practices. . . .

Summary of Findings

The Committee makes the following key findings:

(1) Security weaknesses represent a serious management failure in the U.S. intelligence community.

(2) Weaknesses in the process of selecting personnel for initial employment in U.S. intelligence agencies constitute a key threat to national security.

(3) Senior managers of U.S. intelligence agencies have downplayed the seriousness of counterintelligence and security failures and have not taken adequate measures to correct deficiencies.

(4) The polygraph is a useful tool in security

screening of personnel, but the U.S. intelligence community places excessive reliance on the value of the polygraph interview.

(5) The attitude prevalent among intelligence community personnel that those who have "passed" a polygraph interview are an elite of unquestionably loyal employees with respect to whom security precautions may be relaxed is dangerous, especially in light of recent espionage cases in which foreign spies successfully "passed" CIA polygraph interviews.

(6) No adequate mechanism exists within the government for ensuring that information of counterintelligence and security value possessed by one intelligence agency is available to other intelligence agencies which would benefit from it.

(7) The potentially most damaging long-term development in classified information security practices is erosion of the principle that access to classified information requires not only the requisite clearances and special access approval, but also a need to know the information to perform official duties.

(8) Too many clearances are granted.

(9) Too much information is classified that would not reasonably cause damage to the national security.

(10) Superficial background investigations often do not discover alcohol, drugs, and financial problems.

(11) No focal point exists within the government for centralized storage, retrieval, and dissemination of background investigation information.

(12) Financial pressure, not ideology, constituted the primary motivation of many spies apprehended in the United States in recent years.

(13) In several recent espionage cases, intelligence agency employees satisfied security standards at the time of employment, but after employment decided to engage in espionage, and never were subject to routine security reinvestigation after employment.

(14) Former employees of intelligence agencies who had access to sensitive secrets may pose as potentially great a risk to security as current employees with such access.

(15) Other than the intelligence committees of the House and the Senate, the Congress has no personnel, physical, document and communications security programs which meet or exceed all applicable executive branch security standards.

(16) Dangerous laxity exists in the communications and computer security practices of many federal agencies.

The Committee's Recommendations

The Committee makes the following key recommendations:

(1) U.S. intelligence agencies should undertake a coordinated review of their hiring practices.

(2) The President should authorize an independent group of experts outside the intelligence community to examine thoroughly the damage to U.S. intelligence capabilities resulting from recent espionage cases and to urge needed adjustment of U.S. intelligence collection techniques.

(3) All U.S. intelligence agencies should be required to report as appropriate to the Director of the Federal Bureau of Investigation or the Director of Central Intelligence information they possess which raises a suspicion of possible espionage.

(4) U.S. intelligence agencies should institute a rigorous need-to-know policy to govern access to classified information and back that policy by disciplinary action against employees who breach that policy.

(5) The Director of Central Intelligence should consider establishing a system for dissemination of intelligence with minimal source identification, restricting full knowledge of sources only to those who absolutely need to know.

"That espionage efforts are highly productive for hostile foreign nations can be seen in the sometimes startling technological advances in Soviet weaponry."

(6) The executive branch and the Congress should work to standardize, expedite, and adequately fund the security clearance process. The Secretary of Defense, in consultation with the Director of Central Intelligence, should examine whether the Defense Investigative Service (DIS) can serve adequately the personnel security background investigation needs of the military departments and defense agencies and should consider whether such departments and agencies should undertake their own background investigations and whether they should contract with private firms for such investigations. The Congress should carefully examine the budget request for DIA [Defense Intelligence Agency] within the FY [fiscal year] 1988 Defense budget review process.

(7) Background investigations should focus more on the financial status of the subjects of the investigations.

(8) Periodic reinvestigation of personnel with access to sensitive compartmented information, i.e. the nation's most sensitive intelligence secrets, should be given priority equal to that of initial investigations.

(9) Legal and administrative mechanisms should be established to ensure that agencies which possess information of security relevance on an employee or applicant for employment of another agency share that information with that agency.

(10) The National Security Council, the Attorney

General, the Secretary of Defense, and the Director of Central Intelligence should review jointly executive branch policy with respect to former government personnel and personnel of government contractors who have access to sensitive compartmented information and consider changes, such as requiring exit interviews and a separation non-disclosure agreement, to deter post-employment unauthorized disclosures of classified information.

(11) The leadership of the House of Representatives should examine the feasibility of establishing uniform security procedures for House committees, offices and organizations which meet or exceed executive branch standards.

(12) The Federal Bureau of Investigation should establish a program of rewards for information leading to the arrest of individuals for espionage.

(13) Strict, rigidly applied communications and computer security practices should be established within the U.S. Government.

(14) The Attorney General, the Director of the Federal Bureau of Investigation and the Director of Central Intelligence should consider realigning some FBI surveillance resources to high priority intelligence targets. The Congress should carefully weigh the amount of resources requested for this purpose in the FY 1988 budget review process.

Recent Espionage Cases

From 1984 to 1986, twenty-seven U.S. citizens were charged with espionage. To date, all but one (Craig Smith) who have been brought to trial have been convicted. Among this number were naval officers John and Arthur Walker, John's son Michael and friend Jerry Whitworth, both sailors; naval intelligence analyst Jonathan Pollard; FBI agent Richard Miller; ex-NSA specialist Ronald Felton; CIA analyst Larry Wu Tai Chin; and CIA secretary Sharon Scranage. Never apprehended was fugitive ex-CIA officer Edward Howard, who is now in Moscow.

"Significant security breaches are not being taken seriously."

These examples of espionage did not occur in a vacuum. The Committee receives regular reporting from the intelligence community concerning the vigorous, well-financed and widespread efforts of the Soviet Union and its communist allies to steal U.S. national security information. The occasional arrest of diplomats, United Nations employees and foreign commercial representatives reveals only the tip of the iceberg of foreign espionage. That espionage efforts are highly productive for hostile foreign nations can be seen in the sometimes startling

technological advances in Soviet weaponry and in the compromise of formerly productive U.S. intelligence operations. . . .

Management Failure

Overall, the Committee perceives a serious management failure in the U.S. intelligence community. Major flaws exist in implementing existing security procedures, including the granting of too many security clearances, improper document handling, violations of the need-to-know principle, poor supervision of personnel with access to classified information and a lack of coordination between agencies on security matters, to name but a few shortcomings. Underlying all of these problems has been a lack of either urgency or top priority at departmental and lower levels with respect to needed security changes, despite the high priority given to counterintelligence issues over recent years by the White House and by the Congressional intelligence committees. Once the glare of public scrutiny leaves the problems of espionage and security, the Committee is concerned that the political will to advance security programs and maintain high levels of attention and necessary funding for their implementation will not be sustained. The very size of the U.S. national security community, its complexity and lack of unitary management and the historically lower priority assigned to security concerns have produced cynicism and failure to change in the past and could once again. . . .

The Committee has found a puzzling, almost nonchalant attitude toward recent espionage cases on the part of some senior U.S. intelligence officials. The Committee understands that "there will always be spies" but the attitude of some officials toward these cases raises concern that significant security breaches are not being taken seriously.

As an example, the Committee was struck by the manner in which Navy officials underplayed the disclosure of the Walker spy ring in closed session before the Committee while other government officials publicly and more accurately described them as extremely grave. Similarly, the Committee has had difficulty obtaining from CIA officials clear statements and judgments about the damage caused by the Howard case. While the long term damage caused by Howard's disclosures may be difficult to gauge, certain damage must be assumed. Yet CIA officials have avoided enumerating such matters to the Committee.

Grave Problems, Lackadaisical Attitudes

A further concern of the Committee pertains to intelligence community use of the polygraph. Two spies employed by CIA—Karl Koecher, a Czech agent, and Larry Wu Tai Chin, a Chinese agent—took polygraph tests while they were spying for these countries but were not disqualified. Despite this knowledge, CIA officials have stated to the Committee that "quality control" problems caused this failure of the polygraph. The CIA and other intelligence agencies have used the polygraph in the past to detect other attempted espionage, but the Committee is very concerned that the present community attitude is not sufficiently critical of its present dependence on polygraph results. The Committee believes that the intelligence community needs to place additional emphasis on other means, such as background investigations, of checking the loyalty and trustworthiness of its employees, contractors, and others involved in intelligence activities. The Committee is puzzled by the lack of commitment of necessary resources to make clearly indicated improvements in the background investigation process.

Members of the Walker family spy ring betrayed key U.S. submarine technology. The technology led to improvements in Soviet submarines sooner than expected. These notable improvements in Soviet capabilities apparently were not considered as indicators of espionage. This lack of openness to the potential for espionage, or the related phenomenon of institutional overconfidence in U.S. advanced technology weapons such as submarines, leads the Committee to recommend that the DCI give greater emphasis to the comprehensive review of information concerning hostile foreign power activities.

The Committee does not believe that the U.S. intelligence community can go ahead on a business-as-usual basis in the wake of these espionage disasters. . . .

Defectors

As the well publicized case of defector Vitaly Yurchenko demonstrates, the intelligence community has experienced difficulty in handling some defectors. In part this has resulted from the high expectations and inflexibility of defectors themselves. As difficult as handling defectors may be, it is also crucially important to the national security.

The Committee believes higher priority for the program and more compassion for defector's needs should be devoted to the defector handling process. Some improvements have been undertaken in the wake of the Yurchenko case. The Committee believes that even incremental improvements in these areas could be of enormous importance in the retention of key defectors and their disclosure of foreign espionage activities.

The discovery that the Walker-Whitworth espionage ring provided the Soviets with the ability to decode U.S. Naval communications dealt a serious blow to the national security.

The Committee has found appalling those communications security lapses that made the

wholesale theft of cryptographic materials by John Walker and Jerry Whitworth possible.

Further, senior U.S. Government officials often are careless about how they use car telephones. Sensitive matters also have been discussed on non-secure communications by senior Administration officials communicating with Air Force One. Apparently, Drug Enforcement Administration personnel in overseas posts frequently use open telephone lines to discuss anti-narcotics activity, in open disregard for vigorous and successful communications intercept efforts aimed at local, state and federal anti-narcotics agencies by international narcotics traffickers. The final go-ahead request for Navy aircraft to force down the Egyptian airliner carrying Archille Lauro terrorists was phoned in the open to Air Force One. HAM operators, and presumably interested foreign powers, regularly listen to Air Force One communications.

The Committee recommends the development of

The Committee recommends the development of strict, rigidly applied communications security practices within the U.S. Government if the U.S. is to successfully thwart the active, extensive and often successful electronic espionage conducted every day by the nation's adversaries. The Committee believes that this only will be possible if officials from the President on down make communications security a top priority.

The Committee also recommended that higher priority executive branch attention be given to computer security issues. Vulnerability in this crucial area, where so much of U.S. military and economic superiority is based, could have disastrous results for U.S. national security.

"Any of the weaknesses identified by the Committee, taken alone, would be of concern. What has emerged is a pattern that causes deep dismay about the way U.S. intelligence is managed."

The FBI is in the midst of a program to improve its counterintelligence capabilities and respond appropriately to the growing counterintelligence threat posed by the presence of foreign espionage agents in the United States. The Committee has fully supported this program and has from time to time augmented it. The Committee is concerned, however, that the pace of FBI personnel increases and other counterintelligence augmentations may require readjustment. In particular, the FBI's surveillance capabilities require improvement and expansion. Several recent espionage cases have pointed to a need for such improvement. While it is difficult to predict a direct correlation between increased counterintelligence capabilities and espionage convictions, throughout its review of recent espionage cases the Committee has been struck by the efforts undertaken by foreign intelligence services to evade FBI surveillance. This suggests that the FBI is effective, but that further improvement is helpful. An investment in better counterintelligence capabilities may be the most cost-effective method of preventing espionage. Clearly also, the statutorily required reduction of Soviet personnel in the United States has helped and will help to reduce the greatest foreign espionage threat to the United States. . . .

Any of the weaknesses identified by the Committee, taken alone, would be of concern. What has emerged is a pattern that causes deep dismay about the way U.S. intelligence is managed.

The Committee has also detected faulty hiring practices, poor management of probationary employees, thoughtless firing practices, lax security practices, inadequate interagency cooperation, even bungled surveillance of a prime espionage suspect.

A Litany of Disaster

That is a litany of disaster. It leads to concern about the possibility of other undisclosed security vulnerabilities and suggests that the top levels in the U.S. intelligence and the national security communities need to take more aggressive action to improve management regularly and review potential vulnerabilities constantly. Problems that are uncovered should be brought to the attention of appropriate elements of the Congress—with recommendations for statutory changes and new funding, if necessary—and should be promptly reviewed and acted upon.

The Permanent Select Committee on Intelligence investigates and makes recommendations to the House of Representatives on issues concerning the nation's intelligence policy and national security.

"Intelligence agencies . . . spent more time trying to score off each other, protecting their budgets, . . . and inventing new justifications for their existence, than in gathering intelligence."

Intelligence Activities Should Be Stopped

Phillip Knightley

The 1980s were boom years for intelligence agencies, especially the CIA. Although Jimmy Carter made intelligence reform part of his platform, although a bi-partisan Bill for an all-embracing charter for the CIA was introduced in the Senate in 1978, the American mood had changed entirely by the end of the 1970s. . . .

The main cause was a changed perception of the Soviet threat, heightened by the Soviet invasion of Afghanistan. But even before that, the CIA had [to] take steps to present the American public with a scenario of communism on the move against an increasingly ill-informed and defenceless United States. In Angola, for example, a team of CIA propaganda experts was employed to plant stories in the Western press highlighting Russian and Cuban aggression. Sometimes a propaganda officer got carried away. One planted a story that Unità forces had captured forty-two Russian advisers. When journalists from all over the world came flocking into Angola to see what would happen to the Russians, the Unità leader, Jonas Savimbi told them: 'What Russians? There aren't any Russians in this country.' But mostly they were successful. A story that Cuban soldiers who had raped some Angolan girls had subsequently been captured, tried and executed by their victims appeared widely in the Western press, complete with a photograph of the 'firing squad'. In 1985 John Stockwell, one of the CIA officers in charge of the propaganda exercise, admitted that the story was fiction and the photograph a fake.

The Growth of the CIA

Even the debacle in Iran—the Shah was overthrown early in 1979 just five months after a CIA report had said that there was no sign of any

revolution—was turned to the agency's advantage. In the last years of the 1970s there had been a 40 per cent reduction in the funding for the intelligence community and a 50 per cent cut in the work force. If you emasculate us, the CIA argued, then you cannot blame us if you are caught unprepared. If we got it wrong in Iran, then this was because we did not have the money or the men to do a proper job. The way to correct this is obvious: fund us properly; let us off the leash. This was exactly the line that Ronald Reagan made a major issue in the 1980 election: 'We will revitalise the nation's intelligence system.'

Reagan was as good as his word. As his administration moved from détente to confrontation with the Soviet Union, the intelligence community's role was broadened and strengthened. Its budget was increased: by 15 per cent in 1982, and a huge 25 per cent in 1983, not allowing for inflation, more generous even than the increases granted the Defence Department. By 1985 the CIA was spending at least $1,500 million a year, more than the entire budget of many a Third World country. It was also the fastest-growing major agency in the Federal government. . . .

The time-honoured work of the spy still goes on. . . . In many ways, little has changed in thirty years. George Young, a former deputy director general of [Britain's Secret Intelligence Service] SIS, recalled that in the 1950s it was 'a matter of the utmost importance' that the West should discover the thickness and strength of the armour on Soviet tanks. 'The only way of finding that out was to find somebody on the other side of the Iron Curtain.' And there, in the 1980s, was the CIA still trying to find out exactly the same information. The CIA station in New Delhi suborned four Indian service officers and plied them with questions about Soviet arms supplied to the Indian army. Among the questions was: 'Can you bore a hole in the armour

Phillip Knightley, *The Second Oldest Profession*. London: Andre Deutsch, Limited, 1986. Reprinted with permission.

of a Russian T-72 tank if we supply you with special instruments?' (The Indians replied that this was too risky.)

Finding Out About Their Rivals

And the traditional work of intelligence agencies also continues. For the most part, this is not, as the public which paid for them might naively believe, the gathering of timely information useful to decision-makers, but the gathering of information about other intelligence agencies. What the CIA and SIS would most like to know is what the KGB is up to, and vice versa. . . . This is why defections are such exciting events in the intelligence world and why agencies attach such importance to them. Defectors bring knowledge of the rival agency which enables the CIA, or SIS, or whoever to update their voluminous files about the rival's order of battle, the personal details of his officers, their postings and promotions, and the quirks and preferences which might, one day, make one of them a target in the defection game.

In between defections, intelligence officers spend a lot of their time in the 1980s, no matter where in the world they are posted, keeping an eye on officers from the opposition agency. Thus, in Iran, before students seized the American embassy in 1979, the CIA station spared no effort to track down every Russian in the country, find out whether he was KGB, and decide what he was doing. No private detail in the Russian's life was too mundane to note, sometimes inaccurately. When the station located a Soviet journalist, Levon Vartanyan, probably KGB, who had arrived in Tehran from Kabul, it asked CIA headquarters in Langley for any trace it had on him.

The Tehran CIA station request read: 'It is said Vartanyan's wife is or was a Kosygin mistress. The Vartamians [sic] apparently enjoy perks accruing to this kind of intimacy, dacha, etc. Seems likely Vartamian's [sic] colourful background may serve to identify him. Is he known to HQs?' Langley confirmed that Vartanyan was known to it, corrected the Tehran station's misspelling of the name, and put it straight about Mrs. Vartanyan: 'His wife was secretary (not mistress) of Kosygin.'

Deranged Five-Year-Olds

It has puzzled some observers of the intelligence world that most defectors seem to come from intelligence agencies themselves and not from other government departments. 'It is a strange commentary that members of these supposedly high security organisations should be most susceptible to subversion', wrote Herbert Scoville Jnr in *Foreign Affairs*. The answer, although few intelligence officers would admit it, is that intelligence officers have often more in common with officers from a rival agency than they have with their own employers.

The former CIA officer, John Stockwell, has described how a CIA case officer on a foreign posting is always under bureaucratic pressure to show that he is active: 'If you don't recruit agents, if you don't generate operations, your fitness reports are at best bland and you don't get promoted. If you do all this, then you get a reputation for being an operator, as they call it, and nice things begin to happen to you and you get the good posts.' Exactly the same pressure is on the KGB case officer, so rival officers tend to develop some sympathy with each other's professional problems and often reach unspoken agreement on certain rules of the game. Stockwell said: 'It is a lot like professional football. You knock heads on Sunday then on Monday you're getting drunk together. I played with KGB officers at a couple of my posts and went to lunch with them. It's like a five-year-old's game, but deranged five-year-olds.'

"You can't spend your life bribing people, seducing people into committing treason, betraying their own movements, . . . and come away a healthy, whole person."

By the mid-1980s none of the major agencies played the game so that the players themselves got hurt. The KGB no longer killed CIA officers, and vice versa. But there were other casualties. Stockwell recalled: 'I had an agent I had recruited picked up and shot. No trial, just bang and he was dead. He left behind a wife and six children. When I reviewed his file there wasn't one report, not one report in five years that we hadn't gotten from some overt source somewhere. There was nothing he had done that had saved the world from anything.' . . .

Unnecessary Tragedies

There are many instances of lives, careers and marriages ruined in the intelligence world. Greville Wynne, a simple patriot who believed he was helping his country in the Cold War, now cannot bear to live in Britain and says his espionage activities changed his life: 'When I came back [from a Soviet prison] I was rejected by my wife, my family, and my business associates. . . . My first wife knew me as a businessman and never forgave me for keeping the other side of my life a secret from her. . . . My relationship with my son, Andrew, ended with my marriage. I don't even know if I have grandchildren. . . . My life was totally changed by what I became involved in.'

Nikolai Khokhlov, a KGB officer on an assassination mission in West Germany in 1953 (his target was the leader of NTS, a Russian exile movement) had pangs of conscience and warned his victim. He then planned to return to Moscow and report that his mission had been a failure. But his victim told American military intelligence and it was decided to force Khokhlov into defecting. He recalled later: 'Without my knowing what was going on the Americans called a press conference and announced that I had defected. They publicly demanded that the Russians allow my wife and child to join me in the West. . . . My family disappeared immediately. I never heard another word from them.'

It is an interesting reflection on human character that these tragedies, and many others, were created by high-minded people, often of deep religious faith, who wanted to do good. There is, of course, an element of self-deception at work. Normal people develop, alter their views in the light of new information, change to new circumstances. An intelligence officer must remain absolutely fixed in the attitudes that made him decide on his career in the first place. The tiniest crack in his ideological motivation and he risks collapse.

An Immoral and Corrupting Job

He has strong support. Within the CIA and SIS there is no lack of high-minded discussion on the role of intelligence services in saving the world from communist aggression; and in the KGB no lack of emphasis on the officer's role as the sword and the shield in the fight against capitalist encirclement. But the officer will also pay a price. 'You can't spend your life bribing people, seducing people into committing treason, betraying their own movements, sometimes betraying their own families—and that's the nice-guy stuff—and come away a healthy, whole person whatever your rationales are', John Stockwell has said. 'You can't go through your entire career with a plausible denial to your own conscience.'

Some officers try to convince themselves that there is a moral justification for their work. Donald Maclean said that spying was as necessary and as disagreeable as cleaning out lavatories. Others argue that in an imperfect world it is the duty of a nation to survive and that any means justifies that end. Michael J. Barrett of the CIA has suggested that spies of *both sides* may be morally correct in what they do, and that in protecting the interests of their respective countries *both* can be acting honourably. Dick White, the former chief of SIS, has warned that spies can work only within the moral climate of the day, and that society will not for long tolerate its intelligence agencies going outside the moral climate. The Americans have also considered the dangers of excesses in the spy war. 'Finally there remains the ultimate moral and ethical question', says Roger Hilsman, of Columbia University, 'whether the means we use will eventually corrupt our values so as to change the nature of our society just as

fundamentally as if we were conquered.'

All the argument about the morality of espionage is superfluous if, in fact, spies are unnecessary. There is some case to be made for their use in wartime, although even here their record . . . is patchy. As David Kahn has pointed out, in only one of Creasy's *Fifteen Decisive Battles of the World: From Marathon to Waterloo* does the author ascribe victory to an intelligence coup, and the very many decisive battles fought since Creasy's book came out in 1851 yield few additional examples. But is there justification for expensive, virtually uncontrollable, intelligence agencies in peacetime?

We have seen how intelligence agencies have ensured that there is seldom failure in the secret world. Indeed, the agencies discourage discussion of success and failure, as such, arguing that in many situations it is impossible to distinguish one from the other. If there is intelligence of a surprise attack and the intended victim mobilizes in time, the aggressor, realizing that surprise has been lost, may cancel the operation. The successful prediction then appears to have been wrong.

"One wonders what the agencies did before the Red threat existed. The answer is: they invented one."

Other rationalizations are common. 'We have had great successes but we cannot reveal them; we do, after all, inhabit the secret world.' And, 'We could have offered the vital intelligence if only we had not been starved of funds. The failure was, therefore, not one of intelligence but of government lack of foresight.' Or, 'We may appear to have been wrong, but the failure was one of analysis, not of collection. See, here in our files is the correct information.' The CIA is usually well prepared to offer this last excuse: since the Iranian debacle it is now careful to arrange for a dissenting analysis which it can produce from its archives when its main analysis proves incorrect. And SIS has widened its recruiting to try to inject a 'nonestablishment' view into the service. In 1985 it recruited its first CND (Campaign for Nuclear Disarmament) member.

Cloaking Themselves in Secrecy

By removing themselves from the scrutiny which other governmental organizations undergo to ensure their efficiency, intelligence agencies have been able to proliferate unchecked for much of this century. Governments no longer know the real cost of their intelligence agencies, or how many people they employ. The agencies defy government control. George Young, a former deputy director general of SIS, has said that during his time in office some politicians did not know their job properly so, 'I was quite certain of my judgement to carry out the operations, and to tell them afterwards that's that'. The CIA showed in Nicaragua that it was prepared to act first and inform its oversight committees later.

The KGB, originally formed as a small defence group to counteract foreign sabotage and subversion in the chaos following the Bolshevik Revolution, grew to be a major force in Soviet government, producing from its ranks leaders of the nation, including one head of government.

So far, all efforts to check this growth, to rationalize the structure and purpose of intelligence agencies, seem to have resulted only in their further proliferation. The US Defence Intelligence Agency (DIA) was created in 1961 to unify all American military intelligence and to prevent the three service intelligence agencies from duplicating each other's activities. Logically, this should have led to a reduction in the size of the three agencies, and at first it did. But the agencies regenerated themselves and in less than ten years they were larger than they had been before the DIA had been created. The really explosive growth was in small countries which felt that they had to follow the major powers' lead. In six years, 1978-84, the budget for the Australian intelligence community increased by 270 per cent.

Inventing a Threat

How did they get away with it? The history of intelligence agencies has shown us that they justify their existence by promising to provide timely warning of a menace. In the Western world we have become so accustomed to this menace being the Soviet Union—and its intelligence arm, the KGB—that one wonders what the agencies did before the Red threat existed. The answer is: they invented one. . . . Before the First World War, William Le Queux, Erskine Childers and John Buchan acted out their fantasies in spy novels which used that most ancient of plots, the overcoming of the monster. But these pre-1914-18 spy writers projected their fantasies into the real world. Le Queux bore some direct responsibility for the creation of Britain's Secret Intelligence Service, from which all others flowed; Buchan became a recruiter of SIS spies. Both decided that the monster menacing Britain was Imperial Germany, a proposition enthusiastically supported by the intelligence services, who quickly realized that without a threat they were out of business.

When the monster was beheaded in 1918, SIS's future looked bleak. There was no need for the intrepid spy-hero in peacetime. Fortunately, an even more convincing monster was to hand. Imperial Germany had suffered from one major drawback for the part of out-and-out villain: it was a Christian country that bore too close a likeness to the hero to be portrayed as irremediably evil. But Bolshevik

Russia was, on its own admission, Godless, a murderer of princesses, and bent on world domination. Buchan quickly saw the trend. His *Huntingtower*, published in 1922, was the first anti-Bolshevik thriller; ever since, fictional KGB agents have continued to meet their match at the hands of Her Majesty's Secret Service or the CIA—except, that is, in Soviet fiction where it is the other way round.

Bolshevism proved a godsend to the intelligence agencies. It was here, there, and everywhere. It was as much a threat in peace as in war, and it was capable of corrupting the hero's own kith and kin. Therefore, it was not only necessary to discover the monster's secrets but to protect your own from the monster's disciples who could be, like the fifth man, always beside you. So intelligence agencies were able to insinuate themselves into politics, suggesting or inventing uses for their skills, until they were rewarded with constitutional acceptance, and became an institutionalized part of the government in virtually every modern nation. They have become a focus of power in our society, secret clubs for the elite and privileged, which demand—and are too often granted—the right to define reality for their fellow citizens.

Intelligence Agencies Need Each Other

Like the spies who work for them, these clubs have much in common. Each owes its survival to the existence of its fellows. What would the CIA and SIS do without a KGB, and vice versa? Each has helped create the state of tension in which all thrive. All feel threatened by detente. All have a direct interest in the continuation of the Cold War. 'The Russians are coming' is as potent a stimulus to intelligence power in the West in the mid-1980s as 'the Germans are coming' was in 1909. 'The capitalists surround us' gives power to the KGB in the 1980s, as it did to its forerunner, the Cheka, more than sixty years earlier.

"[Intelligence agencies] have become . . . secret clubs for the elite and privileged, which demand— and are too often granted—the right to define reality for their fellow citizens."

In this can be found a possible explanation for the spate of spy stories—defectors, double agents, espionage coups, mole scares which appear in the media the moment that there is a likelihood of a thaw in the Cold War. It is the intelligence agencies 'going public' in a way they would not contemplate at other times. All these stories are, in effect, controlled by the agencies themselves: if they did not provide the information, no one outside the secret world would know about it.

What I have looked for, as some evidence of this theory, has been a correlation between the number of published spy stories and the state of East-West relations. There were 2,258 stories about espionage in the *Washington Post* between 1977 and 1985. A month-by-month breakdown of these stories shows a distinct increase in their frequency when international events indicated an *improving* climate of relations with the Soviet Union.

> "Open, published information and that obtained through traditional diplomatic and other overt contacts, have proved . . . the most useful source of military, political and economic intelligence."

For example, there was a dramatic rise in the number of espionage stories as the Soviet Union and the United States moved towards the Geneva summit in November 1985. Obviously, it would be a mistake to place too much emphasis on an unscientific study like this. But we have seen how intelligence agencies are skilled at using the media to advance their cause when an outbreak of peace has threatened either their funding, or, in the case of OSS in 1945, their very existence. It is only reasonable to assume that in times of approaching detente the intelligence and security services of both sides feel the need to justify their bureaucratic existence by drawing attention to the monster.

Juggling Our Destinies

So in the mid-1980s we are faced with an intelligence community which has grown to a size and power which is unprecedented. It is so big and so expensive that we can only guess at its size and cost. But there is no doubt about its power. In the Soviet Union national leaders come from its ranks. In the United States its influence on presidential decisions is such that it is sometimes difficult to decide whether the President is running the CIA, or the CIA is running the President.

The intelligence community hates the government of the day, of whichever party. It juggles all our destinies in the name of protecting them. And it is able to do all this because of the secrecy with which it surrounds itself, a secrecy which corrodes a democratic society; it is no accident that as intelligence agencies have expanded, our civil liberties have contracted.

There might, just might, be some justification for the intelligence community if it did what it claimed to do: provide timely warnings of threats to national existence. But . . . this claim is exaggerated even in wartime and, in peacetime, intelligence agencies seem to have spent more time trying to score off each other, protecting their budgets and their establishments, and inventing new justifications for their existence, than in gathering intelligence.

Perhaps this is because—when not deep in their fantasy world—the intelligence community knows that open, published information, and that obtained through traditional diplomatic and other overt contacts, have proved this century by far the most useful source of military, political and economic intelligence for both sides. 'What role does [the spy] play?' said Harry Rositzke, once one himself. 'It's way down there.'

Journalist Phillip Knightley has been the editor for the Sunday Times *in London and has written several books on espionage.*

bibliography

The following bibliography of books, periodicals, and pamphlets is divided into chapter topics for the reader's convenience. The topics are in the same order as in the body of this *Opposing Viewpoints SOURCES*.

Interventionism, Case Study: Afghanistan

Alexandre Bennigsen — "Winning the War for Afghanistan," *National Review*, May 8, 1987.

Jean-Francois Deniau — "Two Hours After Midnight," *Encounter*, September/October 1986.

Jan Goodwin — *Caught in the Crossfire*. New York: E.P. Dutton, 1987.

The Heritage Foundation — "The Report that the U.N. Wants To Suppress: Soviet Atrocities in Afghanistan," *Backgrounder*, January 12, 1987. Available from The Heritage Foundation, 214 Massachusetts Ave. NE, Washington, DC 20002.

Anthony Hyman — "The Afghan Politics of Exile," *Third World Quarterly*, January 1987.

Craig M. Karp — "Afghanistan: Seven Years of Soviet Occupation," *Department of State Bulletin*, February 1987.

Criag M. Karp — "The War in Afghanistan," *Foreign Affairs*, Summer 1986.

Warren P. Mass — "Bleeding Afghanistan," *The New American*, December 8, 1986.

Harbart S. Okun — "Situation in Afghanistan," *Department of State Bulletin*, January 1987.

Ahmed Rashid — "Pakistanis Want an Afghan Peace," *The Nation*, January 31, 1987.

Jonathan Steele — "Moscow's Kabul Campaign," *Middle East Report*, July/August 1986.

Marin Stremecki — "The Road to Kabul," *The American Spectator*, April 1986.

Rone Tempest — "Kabul Copes Under Soviet Occupation," *Los Angeles Times*, May 27, 1987.

Paul Trottier — "Soviet Influence on Afghan Youth," *Department of State Bulletin*, March 1986.

Case Study: Nicaragua

Elliott Abrams — "Development of U.S.-Nicaragua Policy," *Current Policy* No. 915. Available from United States Department of State, Bureau of Public Affairs, Washington, DC.

Bruce Babbitt — "Nicaragua, the Last Domino," *The New York Times*, March 12, 1986.

George Bush — "Defending Freedom: Forty Years Hence," *Vital Speeches of the Day*, May 15, 1986.

Ernest Conine — "Gambling Big in Foreign Policy," *Los Angeles Times*, April 2, 1986.

Gregory Fossedal — "Sandinistas Getting Mixed Signals from All Directions: A U.S. Policy in Theory Only?" *The Washington Times*, June 16, 1987.

Bill Gertz — "Fear of Soviet Strategic Base in Nicaragua Nags at U.S.," *The Washington Times*, March 19, 1986.

Georgie Anne Geyer — "Sandinistas Getting Mixed Signals from All Directions: What Are the Soviets up To?" *The Washington Times*, June 16, 1987.

Adam Meyerson — "Ronald Reagan's Peace Offensive: Containing the Soviets Without Going to War," *Policy Review*, Fall 1986.

Douglas W. Payne — "With a Soviet Nod, Mexico Gushes Over Nicaragua," *The Wall Street Journal*, July 3, 1987.

Ellsworth Raymond — "USSR: Arms Merchant to the World," *American Legion Magazine*, February 1986.

Charlotte Saikowski — "The Superpowers and Central America," *The Christian Science Monitor*, March 19, 1986.

John K. Singlaub — "Contras: Our First Line of Defense," *Los Angeles Times*, February 25, 1986.

Lewis A. Tambs — "The Future Belongs to the Free: The Reagan Doctrine and Central America," *Vital Speeches of the Day*, April 1, 1987.

Case Study: Southern Africa

James Brooke — "Cuba's Strange Mission in Angola," *The New York Times Magazine*, February 1, 1987.

William F. Buckley Jr. — "Help Savimbi?" *National Review*, February 28, 1986.

Congressional Digest — "U.S. Policy Toward Angola: Pro & Con," April 1986.

Chester Crocker — "The U.S. and Angola," *Department of State Bulletin*, April 1986.

Colm Foy — "The Target of Pretoria," *AfricAsia*, November 1986. Available from *AfricAsia*, 13 rue d'Uzes, 775002, Paris, France.

Louis Freedberg — "Inside Namibia: Stirrings in a Forgotten Land," *The Nation*, June 21, 1986.

Peter Godwin — "Mozambican Misconceptions," *The Wall Street Journal*, May 21, 1987.

Smith Hempstone — "Namibia's Pursuit of Identity," *The Washington Times*, June 3, 1987.

Allen Isaacman — "An African War Ensnarls the U.S. Ultraright," *Los Angeles Times*, June 28, 1987.

Holger Jensen — "Mozambique: Winning the War Against All Odds," *Insight*, January 12, 1987. Available from 3600 New York Ave. NE, Washington, DC 20002.

Erik V. Kuehnelt-Leddihn — "Namibia! Namibia!" *National Review*, May 22, 1987.

Tim Lambon — "Our Man with the Freedom Fighters Inside Mozambique," *Conservative Digest*, July/August 1987.

Anthony Lewis — "How To Isolate America," *The New York Times*, May 19, 1987.

Michael Massing — "Upside Down in Angola," *The New Republic*, March 3, 1986.

John H. McManus — "African Policy Unraveled," *The New American*, May 25, 1987.

Andrew Meldrum — "At War with South Africa," *Africa Report*, January/February 1987.

William Minter — *King Solomon's Mines Revisited: Western Interests and the Burdened History of Southern Africa*. New York: Basic Books, 1986.

William Pascoe — "Victory in Sight for UNITA Rebels in Angola?" *Human Events*, February 28, 1987. Available from 422 First St. SE, Washington, DC 20003.

People's Daily World — "Andimba Toivo ja Toivo: Interview," April 9, 1987.

William J. Pomeroy — *Apartheid, Imperialism and African Freedom*. New York: International Publishers 1986.

Christine Root and David Wiley — "Angola, Savimbi, and Us," *Christianity and Crisis*, June 16, 1986.

Wayne S. Smith — "A Trap in Angola," *Foreign Policy*, Spring 1986.

Peter Worthington — "Can We Trust Savimbi?" *National Review*, May 9, 1986.

Negotiations

Edward B. Atkeson — "Soviet Military Theory: Relevant or Red Herring?" *Parameters*, Spring 1987.

Tom Bethell — "Old Debates, New Twists," *The American Spectator*, June 1987.

Zbigniew Brzezinski — *Game Plan*. New York: Atlantic Monthly Press, 1986.

Danny Collum — "Breaking the Power," *Sojourners*, February 1987.

Jonathan Dean — "Gorbachev's Arms Control Moves," *Bulletin of the Atomic Scientists*, June 1987.

Bob Dole — "Grappling with the Bear," *Policy Review*, Fall 1986.

Matthew Evangelista — "Exploiting the Soviet 'Threat' to Europe," *Bulletin of the Atomic Scientists*, January/February 1987.

Matthew Evangelista — "The New Soviet Approach to Security," *World Policy Journal*, Fall 1986.

John Greenwald — "Closing the Gap," *Time*, September 7, 1987.

Jim E. Hinds — "Quid pro Quo," *The National Interest*, Winter 1987.

Henry A. Kissinger — "Kissinger: How To Deal with Gorbachev," *Newsweek*, March 2, 1987.

Charles Krauthammer — "Reykjavik and the End of Days," *The New Republic*, November 17, 1986.

Michael MccGwire — "Why the Soviets Want Arms Control," *Technology Review*, February/March 1987.

The New Republic — "Recovering from Reykjavik," November 3, 1986.

James Reston — "The Nuclear Treaties," *The New York Times*, May 24, 1987.

Jane M. O. Sharp — "After Reykjavik: Arms Control and the Allies," *International Affairs*, Spring 1987.

Raimo Vayrynen — "Minimum Deterrence, Mutual Security," *Bulletin of the Atomic Scientists*, March 1987.

Mortimer B. Zuckerman — "Why This Summit Was a Success," *U.S. News & World Report*, October 27, 1986.

Espionage

Philip Agee — *On the Run*. Secaucus, NJ: Lyle Stuart, Inc., 1987.

William S. Armistead — "Soviet Spying and the State Department," *Conservative Digest*, July/August 1987.

Russell Baker — "The Thing Is Bugged," *The New York Times*, April 11, 1987.

Ralph Kinney Bennett — "Expelled! How We Ousted 80 Soviet Spies," *Reader's Digest*, January 1987.

Alexander Cockburn — "Uproar Exceeds the Damage in Embassy Spy Scandal," *The Wall Street Journal*, April 7, 1987.

William R. Corson and Robert T. Crowley — *The New KGB: Engine of Soviet Power*. New York: William Morrow & Co., 1985.

Robert T. Crowley — "Leaks in Our Moscow Embassy Are Nothing New," *The Wall Street Journal*, April 7, 1987.

Don Edwards — "How To Protect Our Secrets," *USA Today*, January 1986.

Anne Garrels — "My Days as a Reporter in Moscow: Under Eastern Eyes," *The New Republic*, September 29, 1986.

Kirk Kidwell — "Letting Our Guard Down," *The New American*, May 11, 1987.

Jeane Kirkpatrick — "Blame State Department, Marines and Lax Teaching of Values," *Los Angeles Times*, April 17, 1987.

Daniel Lazare — "Zakharov Case Has the Earmarks of a Sting," *In These Times*, October 1/7, 1986.

Bernard Livingston — "New Guidelines for U.S. Spying," *People's Daily World*, May 1, 1987.

Ye Maksimov — "From the Canons of the 'Cold War': Hostile Actions of US Special Services," *Pravda*, April 10, 1987. Available from Associated Publishers, 2233 University Ave., Room 225, St. Paul MN 55114.

The Progressive — "Of Spies and Spying," November 1986.

Jeffrey Richelson — *American Espionage and the Soviet Threat*. New York: William Morrow & Co., 1987.

William Safire — "Stop the Espionage Race," *The New York Times*, April 20, 1987.

Michael Satchell — "Why the Secrets Slip Out," *U.S. News & World Report*, June 1, 1987.

Ronald Steel	"The Case for a Daniloff Swap: Our Guy, Your Guy," *The New Republic*, October 6, 1986.
Viktor Suvorov	*Inside the Aquarium: The Making of a Top Soviet Spy.* New York: Macmillan, 1986.
Calvin Trillin	"Uncivil Liberties," *The Nation*, May 23, 1987.
William H. Webster	"The Intelligence Community," *Vital Speeches of the Day*, March 15, 1987.
Amy Wilentz	"The Marine Spy Scandal: 'It's a Biggie'" *Time*, April 6, 1987.
David Wise	"The Spy Who Got Away," *The New York Times Magazine*, November 2, 1986.
Priscilla Witt	"'Do You Want Any More Secret Documents Put in the Safe?' 'No, Ivan, That's All for Tonight,'" *The Washington Monthly*, April 1987.

index

cumulative index

This index is cumulative for viewpoints 101-150,
1986 and 1987 annuals.

US, 177
Nunn, Sam, 73, 77

October Revolution of 1917 (USSR), 44,
  45, 95, 97
Ortega, Daniel, 129
Orthodox Church, (USSR), 49-50
  and patriotism
    as coerced, 50, 52
    as genuine, 45
  history of, 43-44, 50-51
  structure of, 46
Ostrovsky, Nikolai, 13

Pakistan, 17, 18, 19, 20, 109, 113, 120
  and Soviet-Afghan war, 1, 3, 4, 16
Pardey, Derek, 172
Pascoe, William, 163
PDPA (People's Democratic Party of
Afghanistan), 1, 6, 16
  see also Afghanistan
Pearlstein, Mitchell B., 39
Peltier, Leonard, 28, 30
Perle, Richard, 194, 195-196
Powers, Thomas, 99

Radio Afghanistan, 17
Radio Free Europe, 64, 65, 68, 80
Radio Moscow, 29
Reagan, Ronald, 3, 139, 187
  administration of, 29, 31, 33, 62, 68, 69
  and human rights, 40, 61
  and US-Soviet relations, 72, 75, 76, 77,
    79, 80, 83-86, 87, 91, 99-100, 101, 103,
    104, 105
  doctrine of
    and Mozambique, 163, 167
    and Namibia, 158
  supports aid to UNITA, 147-149
Reilly, Robert R., 133
Reykjavik arms control conference, see
  arms control
Rose, Francois de, 183
Rostow, Eugene V., 181
Rupert, James, 15
Rozhkov, S., 57
Russell, Harold S., 64-65

Sakharov, Andrei, 28, 40, 61, 62, 66, 76,
  80
SALT II treaty, 72
  missile dismantling after, 193, 196
  Soviets violated, 189-191
    con, 193-196
  US compliance with, 190-191
Samizdat, 29, 63
Schifter, Richard, 32, 59, 66
Scowcroft, Brent, 184, 201
Selassie, Bereket, 173
Shcharansky, Anatoly, 62, 69
Shultz, George P., 197
Somerville, Keith, 151
South Africa
  and Angola, 147, 149, 151, 161
  and Mozambique, 163, 166, 169-172
  and Namibia, 156, 159-162

and Nkomati accord, 171
US policy toward, 171-172
Southern Africa, see Angola; Mozambique;
  Namibia
Soviet-Afghan relations, 1-26
  as coercive occupation, 1-4, 15-20
  as cooperative, 5-7, 9-14
Soviet-Afghan war
  and foreign press, 17-18
  and human rights, 18
  as propaganda tool for US, 4, 9-14
  as propaganda tool for USSR, 4, 17
  as revolution for freedom, 5-7, 9-14
  as Soviet invasion, 1-4, 15-20
  parallel to American Revolution, 11
  parallel to British-Afghan wars, 16
  peace
    how to achieve, 3-4
    US opposition to, 11-12
Soviet-American relations, see US-Soviet
  relations
Soviet Union
  and Afghan children, 2-3, 6, 16, 21-26
  and Afghanistan, 1-26, 92, 93
    and Islam
      repression of, 16-17
      Sovietization of, 21-22
    cooperation of, 5-7
    military role in, 2, 12, 18
    resources of, 3, 11
    Soviet assistance to, 5, 10, 11
    Sovietization of, 2-3
  and anti-Semitism, 54
    as unfounded, 36
  and arms control, 27, 32, 59, 95-97
    as supporting, 85, 95-98
  and China, 73
  and human rights
    as deteriotating, 62
    definitions of, 27
      as specious, 27-28
    violations of, 2, 51, 63-66, 67-69
      US accusations of, 28-30
  and Poland, 93
  and religion, 26, 49, 50, 52, 53, 54, 55
    Orthodox Church, 49-50
      and patriotism
        as coerced, 50, 52
        as genuine, 45
      history of, 43-44, 50-51
      structure of, 46
    restrictions on, 49-50, 51-52
  and religious freedom, 43-47
    as non-existent, 49-55
    Constitutional guarantee of, 44, 45-46,
      47
  and Third World socialism, 152-153,
    164, 172-173
  and treaty violations, 99
    as commonplace, 68-69
  anti-US propaganda, 30
  arms control linkage, 181, 183, 184-185,
    198
  as desiring peace, 83-86
  as expansionist, 1-2, 80, 89, 93
    and goal of world domination, 72

and military aid to Third World, 93
economy of
  as flaccid, 92-94, 103
  glasnost in, 203-204, 208
  global expansion of, 133, 144
  nature of, 79-81, 92-93
    as open, 43, 95
    as repressive, 80
    as untrustworthy, 79-81
  supports terrorists, 156, 215
  threatens US sea lanes, 135, 140-141
spying
  and arms control, 209-212, 227
  growth of CIA, 223, 226, 227
  history of, 213-214, 226
  intelligence agencies and
    Congressional role in, 214-216, 217,
      221
    hiring practices of, 218-219, 221
  in US embassy
    is exaggerated, 209-211
    is immoral, 224-225
    is necessary, 213, 216
  Marine scandal, 205, 207, 209-211
  promotes Cold War, 226-227
  should be eliminated, 223-227
  Soviet, 21, 105
    description of, 205-208
    is exaggerated, 209-212, 223
    is rampant, 205-208, 219
    threatens democratic government,
      225-227
  US
    and counterintelligence, 217, 220
    and Soviet defectors, 220, 224
    and Third World terrorism, 215, 223
    is effective, 213-216
    is inadequate, 207, 217-221
  Walker ring, 206-207, 219, 220
  Zakharov/Daniloff case, 209
Stalin, Joseph, 50, 51, 53, 62, 81, 91
Stockwell, John, 223, 224, 225
Strategic Defense Initiative (SDI), 81, 93
  95, 101, 104, 105
  and Reykjavik conference, 177, 190, 202
  as defensive, 88
  dangers of, 85-86
  hinders arms control, 175, 176
  need for, 198
  threat of, 96
  violates ABM treaty, 177-178
Streiff, Gerard, 35
Sussman, Leonard R., 63
Szajkowski, Bogdan, 153

Thomas, Lloyd, 170
Thornton, Charles, 114-115

UN (United Nations, 19
  and Afghanistan, 1-2, 3
  Human Rights Commission, 68
UNITA, see Angola
Universal Declaration of Human Rights,
  67-68
US
  and Afghanistan